Life in America

The Colonial and Revolutionary Era

Handbook to
Life in America

Volume I

The Colonial and Revolutionary Era
Beginnings to 1783

Rodney P. Carlisle
GENERAL EDITOR

Facts On File
An imprint of Infobase Publishing

Handbook to Life in America: The Colonial and Revolutionary Era, Beginnings to 1783

Facts On File, Inc.
An Imprint of Infobase Publishing
132 West 31st Street
New York, NY 10001

Library of Congress Cataloging-in-Publication Data

Handbooks to life in America / Rodney P. Carlisle, general editor.
v. cm.
Includes bibliographical references and index.
Contents: v. 1. The colonial and revolutionary era, beginnings to 1783—v. 2. The early national period and expansion, 1783 to 1859—v. 3. The Civil War and Reconstruction, 1860 to 1876—v. 4. The Gilded Age, 1870 to 1900—v. 5. The age of reform, 1890 to1920—v. 6. The roaring twenties, 1920 to 1929—v. 7. The Great Depression and World War II, 1929 to 1949—v. 8. Postwar America, 1950 to 1969—v. 9. Contemporary America, 1970 to present.
ISBN 978-0-8160-7785-4 (set : hc : alk. paper) — ISBN 978-0-8160-7174-6 (v. 1 : hc : alk. paper) — ISBN 978-0-8160-7175-3 (v. 2 : hc : alk. paper) — ISBN 978-0-8160-7176-0 (v. 3 : hc : alk. paper) — ISBN 978-0-8160-7177-7 (v. 4 : hc : alk. paper) — ISBN 978-0-8160-7178-4 (v. 5 : hc : alk. paper) — ISBN 978-0-8160-7179-1 (v. 6 : hc : alk. paper) — ISBN 978-0-8160-7180-7 (v. 7 : hc : alk. paper) — ISBN 978-0-8160-7181-4 (v. 8 : hc : alk. paper) — ISBN 978-0-8160-7182-1 (v. 9 : hc : alk. paper) 1. United States—Civilization—Juvenile literature. 2. United States—History—Juvenile literature. 3. National characteristics, American—Juvenile literature. I. Carlisle, Rodney P.
E169.1.H2644 2008
973—dc22 2008012630

Facts On File books are available at special discounts when purchased in bulk quantities for businesses, associations, institutions, or sales promotions. Please call our Special Sales Department in New York at (212) 967-8800 or (800) 322-8755.

You can find Facts On File on the World Wide Web at http://www.factsonfile.com

Printed in the United States of America

Bang GB 10 9 8 7 6 5 4 3 2

This book is printed on acid-free paper.

CONTENTS

The Colonial and Revolutionary Era

PREFACE

"I always consider the settlement of America
with reverence and wonder,
as the opening of a grand scene..."
— John Adams

THE FLAVOR OF daily life in previous eras is usually only vaguely conveyed by examining the documents of state and the politics of the era. What people ate, how they spent their time, what entertainment they enjoyed, and how they related to one another in family, church, and employment, constituted the actual life of people, rather than the distant affairs of state. While governance, diplomacy, war, and to an extent, the intellectual life of every era tends to be well-documented, the way people lived is sometimes difficult to tease out from the surviving paper records and literary productions of the past.

For this reason in recent decades, cultural and social historians have turned to other types of *physical* documentation, such as illustrations, surviving artifacts, tools, furnishings, utensils, and structures. Statistical information can shed light on other aspects of life. Through examination of these and other kinds of evidence, a wholly different set of questions can be asked and tentatively answered.

This series of handbooks look at the questions of daily life from the perspective of social and cultural history, going well beyond the affairs of government to examine the fabric and texture of what people in the American past experienced in their homes and their families, in their workplaces and schools. Their places of worship, the ways they moved from place to place, the nature of law and order and military service all varied from period to period. As science and technology advanced, the American contributions to those fields became greater and contributed to a different feel of life. Some of this story may be familiar, as historians have for generations commented on the disparity between rural and city life, on the impact of technologies such as the cotton gin, the railroad and the steamboat, and on life on the advancing frontier. However in recent decades, historians have turned to different sources. In an approach called Nearby History, academic historians have increasingly worked with the hosts of professionals who operate local historical societies, with the keepers of historic homes, and with the custodians of local records to pull together a deeper understanding of local life. Housed in thousands of small and large museums and preserved homes across America, rich collections of furniture, utensils, farm implements, tools, and other artifacts tell a very different story than that found in the letters and journals of legislators, governors, presidents, and statesmen.

FRESH DISCOVERIES

Another approach to the fabric of daily life first flourished in Europe, through which historians plowed through local customs and tax records, birth and death records, marriage records, and other numerical data, learning a great deal about the actual fabric of daily life through a statistical approach. Aided by the advent of computer methods of storing and studying such data, historians have developed fresh discoveries about such basic questions as health, diet, life-expectancy, family patterns, and gender values in past eras. Combined with a fresh look at the relationship between men and women, and at the values of masculinity and femininity in past eras, recent social history has provided a whole new window on the past.

By dividing American history into nine periods, we have sought to provide views of this newly enriched understanding of the actual daily life of ordinary people. Some of the patterns developed in early eras persisted into later eras. And of course, many physical traces of the past remain, in the form of buildings, seaports, roads and canals, artifacts, divisions of real estate, and later structures such as railroads, airports, dams, and superhighways. For these reasons, our own physical environment is made up of overlapping layers inherited from the past, sometimes deeply buried, and at other times, lightly papered over with the trappings of the present. Knowing more about the many layers from different periods of American history makes every trip through an American city or suburb or rural place a much richer experience, as the visitor sees not only the present, but the accumulated heritage of the past, silently providing echoes of history.

Thus in our modern era, as we move among the shadowy remnants of a distant past, we may be unconsciously receiving silent messages that tell us: this building is what a home should look like; this stone wall constitutes the definition of a piece of farmland; this street is where a town begins and ends. The sources of our present lie not only in the actions of politicians, generals, princes and potentates, but in the patterns of life, child-rearing, education, religion, work, and play, lived out by ordinary people.

VOLUME I: COLONIAL AMERICA

In colonial America, life tended to be far more comfortable for the elite than for those with less power, wealth, and prestige. As the colonies developed, the wealthy merchants of the north, the large landholders of the middle colonies, and the planters of the southern colonies were able to surround themselves with increasing comfort and opulence. However, for the small farmer, artisan, shopkeeper, and tradesman, daily life was much more harsh, a story told through furnishings, houses, tools, clothing, and other artifacts. For those at the bottom of the social structure, the servants, slaves, seamen, and the poorest yeoman and tenant farmers, bare subsistence was the norm.

Elements of physical surroundings taken for granted, such as the layout of kitchens, the design of homes, the fencing of land, and the placement of common places such as churches, town squares, market places, and waterfront districts, all carried social and cultural implications. Each was the result of a cultural pattern and each imposed and sought to perpetuate that pattern, often to survive for decades and even centuries. In the colonial period, housing, diet, family life, and recreation all varied by class, and evolved through the era.

Severe mortality rates affected family structure in ways very unfamiliar in the modern era, as frequently widowed women in the early period had increased chances to improve their social status by remarriage. Family size, death rates, and availability of potential husbands and wives all varied from time to time and place to place. The status of women, children, and servants within the home was affected not only by religion and custom, but was frequently structured by legal constraints as well.

Inherited wealth in the form of land, buildings, and goods helped fuel the spread between social classes. Available unsettled land somewhat mitigated the growing class disparities for some, although in each freshly-settled region, a new elite would quickly emerge to exert dominance, influence, and political authority. Thus, underneath the emerging and pleasant myth of an egalitarian society lay a stern reality of wealth and poverty, power and weakness, comfort and suffering.

Roads from city to city were laid out, but were often impassable due to weather conditions, and where possible, travelers chose water routes by sail from city to city or up and down rivers and estuaries. Even in dry weather, it was difficult to travel more than 50 miles a day by road, and frequent inns and taverns dotted the inland countryside by the time of the American Revolution. All of the technology and techniques involved in such transport systems left a rich material legacy of ships, wagons, and waystations.

Some of the original country roads that linked 18th century cities became the routes followed by 20th and 21st century highways. The many ports that still shelter ships on the eastern seaboard of the United States can trace their origins to 17th and 18th century decisions about tide, weather, and refuge from the peril of the seas.

Through the 160 years of American colonial life, the settlers and their descendents fought literally dozens of major wars and minor engagements with Native Americans, the different European imperial powers, and each other. As the technology of warfare advanced, soldiers faced the horrors of conflict with weapons that by modern standards seem clumsy, inaccurate, dangerous to those who used them, and sometimes only moderately effective against the enemy. Yet such weapons systems imposed their own disciplines and techniques, requiring that militias and regular armies learn to fire hand-held weapons in unison to have maximum effect, and that the troops learn to assemble, march, and confront the enemy with discipline and order. The American way of war began to emerge, in which it was taken for granted that a war would be fought to a victory that included a defined defeat of the enemy. Further, the colonists learned the techniques that the weaker side in conflict have always preferred, that is, ambush, surprise, hit-and-run, and other methods that modern analysts define as asymmetric warfare. Those methods and lessons would prove valuable during the American Revolution.

FUTURE AMERICAN CULTURE

In areas of life taken for granted in more recent eras, such as science and technology, and health and medicine, colonial America was only a minor province of the Western civilization that flourished in the 17th and 18th centuries in Europe. Aside from a few colleges for the training of ministers and lawyers, and some academies for the preparation of youth for those colleges, there was little in the way of formal educational structure. For that reason, the formal high culture was correctly viewed from the more sophisticated European perspective as quite primitive. Yet among the increasing population of the colonies, some unique arts, crafts, and techniques, and the beginnings of a different social style, with a sense of equality and opportunity, began to emerge. By the mid-18th century, the hints of a future American culture could be discerned. A talented few men and women stood out as intellectual and creative leaders, showing the promise of a future rich contribution of Americans to the arts and sciences of the world community. Yet life remained difficult and, by European standards, quite rustic and provincial.

Each chapter of this work is devoted to a different cluster of aspects of life in colonial America, from the first settlements at Jamestown through the period of the American Revolution. The first chapter, as an introduction, reviews the political and governmental structures that evolved, and offers a summary of that framework. The rest of the volume is devoted to exploring the details of daily life, through the customs and culture, and the physical constructed environment that shaped and reflected that life. While a few elements of life were constant throughout the colonies, such as basic methods of heating homes through combustion of wood or making certain tools and implements, lifestyles varied greatly with region and religion, as well as social class.

There was great variation over time as well. The earliest period, when settlers first arrived, tended to be fraught with more hazards of disease, starvation, and conflict with Native Americans. The first period saw difficult struggles to build settlements and select and grow suitable crops. Within decades, however, numerous varied patterns of life emerged, ranging from the plantation systems of the southern colonies, through the thriving commercial waterfront cities of Philadelphia, New York, and Boston, and the spreading frontier of agricultural settlement. As the population increased, so did the differentiation of employment, with specialists in dozens of different crafts and various types of merchants. Even in farm life, great variation emerged rapidly, depending on crop, climate, region, and labor arrangements.

For all of these reasons, the complexity of daily life in the colonial period often defies generalization. Rather, the style of life varied with each period, in each region, in each social class, with gender and age, and also, with each separate niche in the economy. This Handbook to Life in America is intended to convey a sense of that rich tapestry of the life of people and to offer insights developed by modern researchers into the reasons for the variations.

RODNEY CARLISLE
GENERAL EDITOR

CHAPTER 1

Introduction

"The great mass of the people were zealous in the cause of America."
— John Adams

ALTHOUGH IT MIGHT seem so today, a British colony rising on the eastern shores of North America and developing into an independent, democratic nation was by no means inevitable. Had things gone just a bit differently, North America might well have become a Spanish possession much like Latin America, and today be called *los estados unidos Americas,* or perhaps *los estados unidos Florida,* the name early Spanish explorers gave to the dimly understood territory around the Gulf of Mexico, when they first encountered it in the early 1500s.

The British were relative latecomers to colonization in the New World. They were far too absorbed in defending themselves against their enemies across the English Channel and in their internal religious and political wrangling to waste too many resources on speculative adventures in an unknown land. The appeal for colonization began to grow in the 1580s, as relative peace and stability allowed people to think about new possibilities and opportunities in distant lands. After a lull in the 1590s, the drive for exploration picked up once again, particularly after the defeat of the Spanish Armada and a peace treaty with Spain in 1604 allowed British-flagged ships to ply the oceans more freely.

New economic realities also were at play in the final years of the 16th century. The merchant class was growing in power. Some were intrigued by tales of gold and other precious metals littering the ground of the New World, just waiting to be collected. Cooler heads saw more promising—though less dazzling—sources of income. Profitable commodities like sugar and cocoa were beginning to flow out of the Caribbean, leaving some businessmen to wonder what other types of riches might flow out of the Atlantic coast. Fish, fur, and virgin timber might turn out to be as worthwhile as gold and silver over time.

The rise of the joint-stock company, in which private investors could pool their financial resources in exchange for a cut of future profits, made colonization more appealing to the Crown, releasing it from the need to bear the full cost of expeditions. And there were other benefits for government as well. Overpopulation and unemployment were becoming real problems in the British Isles at the beginning of the 17th century. A satellite colony 3,000 miles across the Atlantic could become a convenient way to relieve that pressure, particularly when it came to the relocation of dissidents and undesirables. To that end, the London Company and the Plymouth Company were granted royal charters in 1606, and each given a portion of the coastline to call their own.

Early attempts to establish permanent settlements on the coast were disastrous. The most notable failure was the colony of Roanoke, established in the Carolinas in 1587, where over 100 men, women, and children vanished into an unknown fate between 1588 and the arrival of a supply ship in 1590. In all, there were close to 30 colonization attempts between the 1580s and the establishment of Jamestown in 1607.

JAMESTOWN

Jamestown also seemed destined for early failure. The group of 105 that embarked from England in December 1606 included 35 "gentlemen," 40 soldiers, a doctor, a minister, and a handful of artisans. In short, they were mostly adventurers, looking for excitement and hoping to make a quick fortune before returning home. They were ill-equipped for the situation that presented itself when they reached the Chesapeake Bay.

After a harrowing four-month crossing, the three ships of the Virginia Company arrived at the mouth of the James River in late April 1607. They selected a site about 50 miles up the river as protection against attack from the sea. At first, things seemed to go well. The company had set up a governing council before the group left Britain, and they directed the clearing of land and the construction of a small fort.

Problems quickly developed. The most serious was disease—dysentery and typhoid flourished in unsanitary conditions, followed by new fevers and viruses indigenous to the region. Fresh water and food supplies were tenuous. The "gentlemen" of the group refused to perform manual labor, and relationships between different factions soon bordered on mutinous. Relationships with local native tribes veered between cautious partnership and open war.

On several occasions the whole enterprise teetered on the brink of ruin. In the winter of 1609, supply ships from Britain were delayed by storms. Food supplies failed, with many settlers perishing from malnutrition, and others pushed to the point of cannibalism. Known as "the starving time," only 60 of 214 settlers survived to see the spring. Those that did survive were ready to leave when the supply ships arrived in June 1610. Only the arrival of new settlers and a new governor kept the colony from collapse.

To the disappointment of all, gold and diamonds were not abundantly scattered on the ground around Jamestown. At first, it seemed that the colony would never be able to find its economic footing. However, in 1612 settler John Rolfe experimented with some tobacco seeds he had imported from the West Indies, and found that it flourished. In 1614 he sent a shipment of about 2,600 pounds

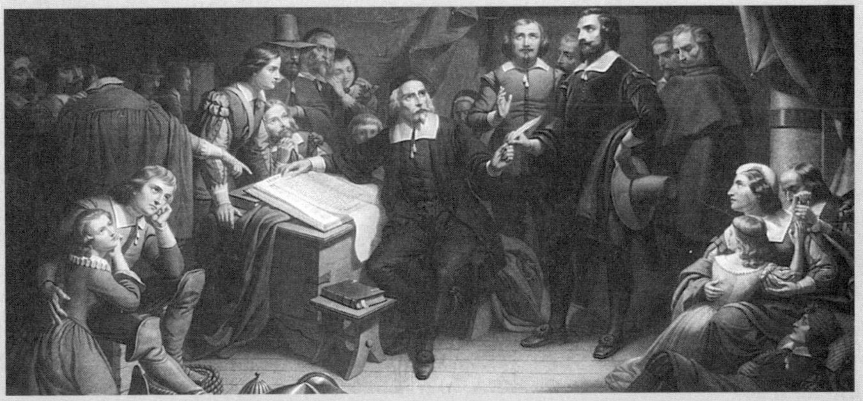

An engraving from a painting by T.H. Matteson of the Pilgrims signing the Mayflower Compact aboard the Mayflower, *on November 11, 1620.*

The Mayflower Compact

The first governing document of the Massachusetts Bay Colony and the earliest statement of self-rule in the British colonies, the Mayflower Compact was signed aboard the *Mayflower* as she sat at anchor off Cape Cod on November 11, 1620:

Haveing undertaken, for ye glorie of god, and advancemente of ye Christian faith and honour of our king & countrie, a voyage to plant ye first colonie in ye Northerne parts of Virginia, doe by these presents solemnly & mutualy in ye presence of God, and one of another, covenant & combine our selves togeather into a civill body politick, for our better ordering & preservation & furtherance of ye ends aforesaid; and by vertue hearof to enacte, constitute, and frame such just & equall lawes, ordinances, Acts, constitutions, & offices, from time to time, as shall be thought most meete & convenient for ye generall good of ye Colonie, unto which we promise all due submission and obedience.

Eyewitness: Starving Time in Virginia

In May 1607, 105 colonists from the Virginia Company disembarked from three ships at Jamestown, Virginia. Among the leaders of the company was Captain John Smith, a soldier who would become the historian of the group through his *Generall Historie of Virginia*. The excerpt below details the suffering the colonists faced upon landing and the struggle to survive and build a new colony. Their survival depended on the help of Native Americans.

1607. Being thus left to our fortunes, it fortuned that within ten days scarce ten among us could either go or well stand, such extreme weakness and sickness oppressed us. And thereat none need marvel if they consider the cause and reason, which was this.

While the ships stayed, our allowance was somewhat bettered by a daily proportion of biscuits, which the sailors would pilfer to sell, give, or exchange with us for money, sassafras, furs, or love. But when they departed, there remained neither tavern, beer, house, nor place of relief, but the common kettle. Had we been as free from all sins as gluttony and drunkenness, we might have been canonized for saints; but our president [Wingfield] would never have been admitted for engrossing to his private [use] oatmeal, sack, aquavitae, beef, eggs, or what not, but the kettle; that indeed he allowed equally to be distributed, and that was half a pint of wheat, and as much barley boiled with water for a many a day, and this having fried some twenty-six weeks in the ship's hold, contained as many worms as grains; so that we might truly call it rather so much bran than corn, our drink was water, our lodgings castles in the air.

But now was all our provision spent, the sturgeon gone, all helps abandoned, each hour expecting the fury of the savages; when God the Patron of all good endeavors in that desperate extremity so changed the hearts of the savages that they brought such plenty of their fruits and provision as no man wanted.

to London. By 1617 the colony was exporting over 20,000 pounds per year and could not begin to meet demand. Tobacco would be the staple crop of Virginia into the 19th century.

Although the population rarely exceeded a couple thousand people, settlement expanded outside of Jamestown by the late 1610s. A series of governors established codes of conduct for those living within the colony, laws that forced all to participate fully in the work, and live up to a strict moral code. Perhaps to ease the severity of these laws, in 1619 the company decided to form an assembly comprised of the governor and his council and two "burgesses" elected by the residents of each parish. This assembly met for the first time on July 30, 1619. Few events had as much lasting impact on

American history, for here the tradition of representative government in the new land was established. Jamestown had one more trauma to endure. After a period of tranquility, local native tribes became restive as British settlement reached 2,000 to 3,000 people. On March 22, 1622, they launched a sneak attack against the colony, killing about 350 men, women, and children before the settlers could mount a counterattack. Reprisals went on for months.

The massacre had several major consequences. The settlers took years to recover from the losses to property. Word of the attack dimmed the enthusiasm of many potential settlers back in Britain. It also proved to be the killing blow to the Virginia Company, which lost its charter in 1624. In 1625, the Crown took command, and Virginia became a royal colony.

SLAVES AND SERVANTS

Representative government was not the only thing established in the early years of the Virginia Colony. In 1619, a Dutch ship dropped anchor off Jamestown and asked to trade some of their property for food. In exchange for "victuals," the Dutch presented the governor with about 20 African slaves. Within a few days, they were at work in the fields, tending tobacco plants.

These anonymous men and women were the forerunners of the hundreds of thousands of Africans who would be brought to America in the following two centuries. At the time, it may have seemed like a stroke of good luck. The British had no laws regarding the keeping of slaves; legally they may have been free as soon as they stepped off the Dutch ship. The African population of Virginia

Interior of an original servant cabin at Boone Hill Plantation in South Carolina. Servants would receive room and board in exchange for labor under their contract or indenture.

A Currier & Ives lithograph depicting the landing of the Pilgrims at Plymouth on December 11, 1620. Pilgrims can be seen paddling to shore from the Mayflower *in the background.*

stayed quite small for many years. In 1634 Africans numbered less than 200, while the white population was nearing 10,000. Several Africans became landowners, and several are believed to have intermarried with white settlers.

Labor in the early colonies was dominated not by slaves, but indentured servants. The practice of indenture was well-established in Britain, which had often faced shortages in the agricultural labor force. A person wanting to build a new life in America would essentially sell himself or herself to a ship's captain, who would then transport the person at no cost and negotiate a contract with a buyer once they reached port, in exchange for a fee. The contract, or indenture, usually lasted for a period of four to seven years, during which time the servant would receive room and board in exchange for labor. At the end of the contract period the servant usually received "freedom dues," a piece of land and tools, or sometimes a lump sum payment, allowing the servant to set up his own farm. The system was rife with opportunities for abuse. Servants were not technically slaves, but they did not have basic rights. They had little recourse in cases of verbal, physical, or sexual abuse. They could be physically punished for disobedience. Terms of the contract could be renegotiated at the master's will. Like all colonists, servants risked death from infectious disease and injury. At certain points in colonial history, up to 75 percent of the population was held under some sort of service contract. While in the south it was eventually superseded by slavery, the practice lasted until the early 19th century.

A CITY ON A HILL

While Virginia was struggling to establish its permanent survival, nearly 700 miles to the north a very different group of people were staking their claim on the Massachusetts Bay.

For the Pilgrims, Massachusetts was the end of a much longer journey. They were a dissident group outside the Church of England, and they had left their homes in Scrooby, Yorkshire around 1609 for the greater religious freedom of Leyden, Holland. They had been somewhat successful there, but were at heart rural people, never happy with urban life, and they feared their children would grow up more Dutch than English. In early 1620 they decided to apply for a patent to set up a colony in America. With the help of some British merchants, they set up a joint-stock company, promising seven years of service and a split of any profits derived from their settlement. The group of 101 set out aboard the *Mayflower* in September 1620 and arrived at Cape Cod in November. Buffeted by heavy storms, they decided not to continue to their intended destination in Virginia, and by Christmas 1620 were hard at work building a fort in what they would call Plimoth.

The story of the Pilgrims has become one of the seminal events in colonial history, but their time on the historical stage was short. By 1628, a charter had been granted to the Massachusetts Bay Company, which opened the region to widespread settlement by Puritans, a group wishing for a more rigorously Protestant Church of England. About 900 Puritan colonists arrived with leader John Winthrop in 1630 and established a settlement at Salem. Between 1630 and 1640 an estimated 21,000 people crossed the Atlantic, most of them Puritans bound for Massachusetts.

POPULATION GROWTH

The Great Migration, as it is sometimes called, was very different from the experience of those coming to Virginia. Most of the migrants heading toward the Chesapeake Bay were young males; there were very few female immigrants and very few families. By comparison, most of those headed toward New England came as families. Sex ratios were generally balanced. Combined with a healthier climate, this allowed the northern population to grow at a much faster rate than in the south.

New England was also governed by different principles than the south. Like the Virginians, the Puritans were members of the Church of England, but felt the church had lost too much of its purity in trying to placate the Catholics. Most Puritans who embarked for America were followers of the doctrine of the theologian John Calvin. The five main tenants of Calvinism were (1) the total depravity of man means that sin is a part of human life and man is powerless to stop it; (2) predestination, or unconditional election, means that God saves only a few, and at his own discretion; (3) limited atonement means that Jesus died not for all but for a select few; (4) irresistible grace means that

Colonial Economies

The Revolution was driven in part by the tremendous economic expansion enjoyed by the American colonies in thc 75 years before the war began. Driven by population growth and a long period of high agricultural output, the American economy grew at three to four times the rate of the British economy, and residents of British North America had a higher standard of living than those back in their mother country.

There was no national economy before the 1780s. Each colony had its own dealings with British and foreign markets. Economic historians split the colonies into three loosely-connected groups with different roles in the colonial economy.

The colonies along the Chesapeake Bay, collectively known as the Upper South, were plantation economies that relied mainly on tobacco exports. Over 75 percent of their crops went to Britain.

The colonies of the Lower South, including the Carolinas and Georgia, were also plantation economies, although they had different staple crops. Their chief exports were indigo, rice, and naval stores such as timber. Almost 65 percent of their output went to Britain, and another 20 percent to the British West Indies. Once in Britain, most of these crops were re-exported to Continental Europe.

Rice in a winnowing basket, one of the chief exports of the colonies.

New England had the most independent colonial economy and was least dependent on shifts in the British market. Unlike the Upper and Lower South, New England did not have a staple crop. While they did export corn and grain, their real power was in their fishing and shipping industries. Over half of their exports went to the British West Indies, with another 25 percent going directly to southern Europe.

if God chose to save someone, they have no power to resist; (5) "preserverence of the saints" means that those chosen by God cannot lose their salvation. Calvinists believed that they could live by these principles more easily in America, and their society and laws were designed to help them do that.

John Winthrop gave a speech in 1630, probably just before his departure for New England. "For we must consider that we shall be as a city upon a hill. The eyes of all people are upon us. So that if we shall deal falsely with our God in this work we have undertaken ... we shall be made a story and a by-word throughout the world. We shall open the mouths of enemies to speak evil of the ways of God...We shall shame the faces of many of God's worthy servants, and cause their prayers to be turned into curses upon us til we be consumed out of the good land whither we are going ... ." The concept of America as "a city upon a hill," as a chosen land ordained by God, run on the word of God, has been an underlying theme in American history for more than 375 years.

DISTINCT CHARACTERISTICS

With the core colonies established, colonial America entered a phase of growth and consolidation that lasted for the next 150 years. During these years the population began to develop the distinct characteristics that would allow it to grow into an independent nation by the end of the 18th Century.

The burgeoning population spread out from Massachusetts and Virginia, creating the new colonies of Rhode Island (1636), Connecticut (1636), New Hampshire (1623), Delaware (1638), New York (1624), New Jersey (1623), Maryland (1633), Pennsylvania (1682), North Carolina (1653), South Carolina (1663), and Georgia (1732). Many of these were "proprietary colonies," established by individuals who had been given huge land grants by the British Crown, rather than the type of joint-stock companies that had founded Massachusetts and Virginia. The rights of the proprietors were not absolute; depending on the grant, the Crown retained certain rights, including that of taxation.

Maryland and Pennsylvania are good examples of the types of colonies that arose from the proprietary system. On June 20, 1632, King Charles I granted Cecil Calvert, the 2nd Baron Baltimore, the right to 12 million acres just to the north of Virginia. Baltimore was a Catholic convert, very rare among the aristocracy of the time. While there was a good level of religious toleration and most of the population of Maryland remained Protestant, Calvert and his family assured that the upper class that dominated the colony's social structure was primarily Catholic. Lord Baltimore was in complete control of his domain; settlers swore allegiance to him, not to the King.

PENN'S WOODS

By comparison, on March 4, 1681, King Charles II granted William Penn a huge tract of land west of the Delaware River in lieu of a £16,000 debt the Crown owed to Penn's father. Penn turned his colony, which he called *Pennsylvania*, meaning "Penn's Woods," into a haven for his fellow Quakers. It also soon became the focal point for German immigrants looking to begin a new life in a region supportive of their various reformed religions.

Even the proprietary colonies were eventually transformed into royal colonies, with only tiny Rhode Island and Connecticut managing to briefly hold on to their old charters. Tightening royal control had several underlying causes, but mostly came down to the desire of the Crown to use the colonies for maximum profit. The colonies proved rich in raw material—timber, wool, furs, minerals—and the growing colonial population was willing to buy finished products from British suppliers, often for top prices. This economic arrangement suited the Crown very well.

In the early 1660s Charles II issued the Navigation Acts, essentially trying to strangle the nascent economy of the American colonies by ruling that nothing could be carried out of colonial ports on foreign-flagged ships; colonial crops could not be shipped to foreign ports; and no finished products could be shipped to America without first passing through English ports for inspection and taxation. The Navigation Acts were not well enforced by the British authorities, and clandestine trade between the colonies and non-British sources flourished.

By the first quarter of the 18th century the colonies had reached a point of maturity. With immigration at a low level, colonial society was somewhat homogenous, with most of the 1.3 million residents who were not Native American consisting of those of English descent. There were some exceptions: the Dutch in New York, the Germans in the Mid-Atlantic States, and the approximately 250,000 African slaves at work from New England to Georgia.

EDUCATION

American education had its roots in New England and the Puritan ethos. The Puritans believed that one must be able to read and understand scripture to have a chance of salvation. This led to the establishment of a system of common schools designed to teach children basic literacy and arithmetic, and laid the foundation for compulsory education in America. In 1642 the first education law was passed by the colony of Massachusetts, stating that it was the duty of parents or masters to make sure their children or apprentices were able to read and write. This was bolstered in 1647 by a law that all towns with 50 or more inhabitants must hire a schoolmaster.

"Dame" schools were an early innovation. These were small private schools, usually taught by women out of their homes in return for a small fee. Children learned by rote, reciting off small "hornbooks," a wooden paddle with printed sheet of paper protected by a transparent sheet of cow horn. The paper usually contained the letters of the alphabet, a basic vocabulary, and the Lord's Prayer. Religion was never far away from education in this era. The quality of dame schools varied greatly, and they were eventually supplanted by common schools run by formal schoolmasters or mistresses, and supported by community dollars.

In the south neither the rural geography nor social custom favored the development of primary schools. The children of the elite might have private tutors and their sons might go off to college. A lucky few in the middle classes could sometimes be taught by literate parents or relatives. But those in the lower classes, or locked into slavery, had no virtually access to education. Literacy rates would remain low in the south until the late 19th century.

Access to education was not evenly divided through the population; it varied depending on location, social status, gender, and race. Few American youths advanced beyond their village primary school. What we would now recognize

Colonial Wars

The Revolutionary War was hardly the first time the guns rang out on the North American continent. During 170 years of British settlement in America, there were numerous armed conflicts between settlers and Native Americans, between the British and French, and minor rebellions between different groups of colonists or the royal colonial governments.

The Pequot War (1636–37). As the number of British colonists rose in Massachusetts Bay, the local Pequot Indians became more aggressive, finally prompting royal governor John Endicott to raise a force to confront them. The colonists won the fight in a battle near present-day New Haven, Connecticut, killing nearly 500 Pequot men, women, and children.

King Philip's War (1675–76). Forty years of relative peace in the Massachusetts Bay Colony following the Pequot War came to an end in 1636 with the rise of Metacom, called King Philip by the British, as the leader of the Wampanoag Confederacy. The colonists were eventually victorious, but King Philip's War was perhaps the bloodiest of the colonial wars, with 600 colonists and 3,000 Indians killed during the conflict and numerous towns and settlements destroyed.

Bacon's Rebellion (1676). Tensions between Virginia colonists living on the frontier and the landed elite along the James River led to open conflict between followers of young Nathaniel Bacon and the royal government of Sir William Berkeley.

Culpeper's Rebellion (1677–79). Like Bacon's Rebellion two years earlier, this was a popular uprising against the royal governor's attempts to enforce the British Navigation Acts, this time in the Albemarle region of present-day North Carolina.

King William's War (1689–97). The first of the French and Indian Wars, this conflict was mostly fought in Europe. However, French troops working with Indian allies did launch a series of raids on the New York and Canadian frontiers. In February 1690 a party of 200 attacked the small settlement at Schenectady, New York, killing 60 and capturing 27.

Queen Anne's War (1703–13). Another of the French and Indian Wars, Queen Anne's War allowed the British to destroy Spanish dominance in Florida and drive the French out of the Acadia region of Nova Scotia.

The War of Jenkins' Ear (1739–42). Also known as King George's War, this conflict affected mainly the southern colonies.

The French and Indian War (1754–63). The final in the series of geopolitical wars affecting both Europe and the American colonies, this nine-year conflict ended with the British conquest of Spanish Florida and all French-held territories east of the Mississippi River.

as secondary schools were established in urban areas like Boston, Philadelphia, and Charleston to prepare young men to enter the colleges that were being established throughout the region. Harvard opened in 1636, just 16 years after colonists first reached New England's shores. It was followed by the College of William and Mary in Virginia in 1693, St. John's College in Maryland in 1696, Yale in Connecticut in 1701, the College of New Jersey (later Princeton) in 1746, King's College (later Columbia) in New York in 1754, and the College of Philadelphia (now the University of Pennsylvania) in 1755.

COMMUNICATION

The first printing press arrived in the colonies in 1638. The first North American newspaper rolled off the presses in September 1690, only to be promptly shut down by the royal government. In 1704 a Boston postmaster inaugurated the *News-Letter,* which managed to survive government scrutiny to become the first newspaper to publish more than a single issue. The establishment of a postal system within the colonies helped speed the flow of news, and within a couple of decades most colonies had at least one newspaper. Book publishing remained moribund; most books tended to come from England or continental Europe, and at a prohibitively high cost for the common person. In 1731 a group lead by Benjamin Franklin opened the Library Company of Philadelphia, where people could read and enjoy a collection of books for an annual subscription. By 1760 there were at least 20 subscription libraries all across the colonies.

The grave marker for the victims of the Boston Massacre on March 5, 1770.

Despite improved communications, many colonies remained isolated and suspicious of one another. Border disputes, religious and social differences, or a simple lack of contact all played a role in colonial isolationism. But colonists had many common bonds and shared beliefs that would ultimately outweigh their differences.

CONFLICT WITH FRANCE

A common enemy helped cement the colonial mindset in the mid-18th century. During their first century in America, English settlers had been remarkably sanguine about the French presence on the continent. By the start of the 18th century the French had solidified control of Canada, the Great Lakes region, and the Mississippi River Valley as far south as the port of New Orleans, itself a French city. Prior to the late 1680s the only colonists seemingly concerned about the French were New Yorkers on the frontier.

The fall of the Stuart monarchy and the ascension of William III in 1689 changed this attitude. Unlike the Stuarts, William was determined to challenge French power in Europe and abroad. The two countries embarked on a string of wars over the next century or more, with fighting taking up a full 60 years. The American colonists were inevitably drawn into these conflicts, known collectively as the French and Indians Wars.

On July 8, 1776, the Liberty Bell rang out in Philadelphia, calling citizens to the first public reading of the Declaration of Independence.

Fighting between the factions was often brutal, but in the end, the British were victorious. In a peace treaty signed at Paris in 1763, France ceded their North American lands except for two tiny islands off the coast of Newfoundland. Future American military leaders like George Washington had gotten to test their skills in battle. Indian resistance had been put down in the process of the fighting against the Indians' French allies, and as a result the trans-Appalachian west was now open to the burgeoning colonial population.

CONFLICT WITH BRITAIN

In over 160 years of colonial living, the British American populace had developed some bedrock political principles: the right to representative government, freedom of speech, freedom of the press, and the right to trial by jury. These principles were basically the freedoms and privileges of Englishmen. Yet by the mid-1760s many colonists were feeling that they were no longer receiving their due as Englishmen. Instead they were confronted with a mother country that seemed determined to steal their rights and bleed them dry with taxes, not to mention dictatorial laws enforced by a standing army.

The fight against the French, however sweet the victory, had cost the British dearly. The British national debt had doubled by the Peace of Paris in 1763. To drive up tax revenues from the colonies, the British began to enforce the old Navigation Acts, as well as the Sugar and Molasses Act of 1733. To this was added the Stamp Act of 1765—a tax on the official government stamps needed

General George Washington and other officers of the Continental Army arriving in New York amid a jubilant crowd on November 25, 1783.

to conduct all types of business and law within the colonies. The Stamp Act was so universally hated that agitators managed to get it repealed a year later. However, this was followed by the even more hated Townshend Acts of 1767, which levied a tax on almost all items imported into the colonies.

Tensions between British soldiers and locals in Boston had been high since the violent protests against the Stamp Acts years earlier. On March 5, 1770 these tensions led to bloodshed. The so-called Boston Massacre began when locals began heckling the "lobsterbacks," as they call the red-coated soldiers. The jittery soldiers ended up firing at the mob, killing five and wounding several others. As the story of the massacre spread through the colonies, it helped to further galvanize colonial resistance to British imperial rule.

At the same time the king had decided to abandon the Townshend taxes, keeping only the tax on tea. Colonists responded with a boycott. On December 16, 1773, a group of prominent Bostonians decided to make a stronger statement. Dressed as Indians, they boarded a ship in Boston Harbor, and proceeded to toss 90,000 pounds of expensive tea into the water—an event later dubbed the Boston Tea Party.

Outraged, the British sent even more soldiers and tried to exert even more control over their rebellious subjects. In 1774 Parliament passed the "Intolerable Acts," a series of acts designed to punish Boston for the £10,000 of destroyed tea. The port of Boston was closed. The governor was given the right to move trials out of the colony if they felt a fair trial in Massachusetts was impossible. The Quartering Act allowed British soldiers to take over any uninhabited building they desired for housing.

INDEPENDENCE CATCHES FIRE

On the day the acts went into effect, the Virginia House of Burgesses announced a day of prayer and fasting in solidarity. This earned them a rebuke from their royal governor for sympathizing with the Massachusetts "rebels." Leaders in Virginia then suggested a general convention of the colonies to discuss the crisis. The idea quickly caught fire, and the first Continental Congress assembled in Philadelphia in September 1774. Among the attendees were John and Samuel Adams, Stephen Hopkins of Rhode Island, Patrick Henry of Virginia, and Roger Sherman of Connecticut. They constructed a petition to the king, asking for a redress of grievances for the 13 separate Acts of Parliament that they believed violated their rights under British law.

They were still awaiting the king's response when war broke out in Massachusetts. On April 19, 1775 local militia confronted British troops on the village green in the small town of Lexington. Eight militiamen were killed in the melee, but at the end of the day, the British were forced back to Boston, trapped by some 16,000 militia assembled from the surrounding countryside. The fighting would go on for the next six years, and peace would not come until the Treaty of Paris was signed in 1783. In the intervening years, America declared its independence from England, and took its place on the world stage as a democratic nation.

HEATHER MICHON

Further Readings

Booth, Sally S. *Seeds of Anger: Revolts in America, 1607–1771.* Winter Park, FL: Hastings House Daytrips Publishers, 1977.

Breen, T.H. and Timothy Hall. *Colonial America in an Atlantic World: A Story of Creative Interaction.* New York: Longman, 2003.

Butler, Jon. *Becoming America: The Revolution Before 1776.* Cambridge, MA: Harvard University Press, 2001.

Faragher, John M., ed. *The Encyclopedia of Colonial and Revolutionary America.* Cambridge, MA: Da Capo Press, 1996.

Henretta, James A. and Gregory H. Nobles. *Evolution and Revolution: American Society, 1600–1820*. New York: Houghton Mifflin, 1987.
Hoffer, Peter C. *The Brave New World: A History of Early America*. Baltimore, MD: Johns Hopkins University Press, 2007.
Schechter, Stephen L., ed. *Roots of the Republic: American Founding Documents Interpreted*. Lanham, MD: Rowman & Littlefield, 1990.
Taylor, Alan. *American Colonies*. New York: Penguin, 2002.
Thomas, Peter D.G. *Revolution in America: Britain and the Colonies, 1763–1776*. Cardiff: University of Wales Press, 1992.

CHAPTER 2

Family and Daily Life

"A man who strikes his wife shall be fined 10 pounds. A woman who strikes her husband shall be punished as the law directs."

— Connecticut Blue Laws

THE DAILY LIFE of the colonial American family centered around the home, a home that could be large or small, permanent or semi-permanent. Dwellings could be seen as stepping-stones to better houses or as the culmination of a particular family's search for status in the New World. Often, this search heralded the growth of dependent members of these households. Their daily domestic lives became increasingly geared toward industrious work that could provide extra funds for the household's patriarchal head, the man of the house. The work of dependent householders enabled the purchase of more goods for these homes. Rooms were increasingly filled with objects that were emblems of male dominance over dependent women, children, and even enslaved persons. Thus, under the colonial system of coverture, goods could not be truly owned or inherited by married women. In the American colonial south, enslavement within the home increasingly replaced an earlier system of indentured servitude. This change exerted an ever more defined racial boundary between the parlor and the outside world.

Some historians assume that colonial American family life provided a crucial element of stability in the New World. The instability of the frontier environment could be kept out of domestic space on a day-to-day basis. Although social hierarchies were formed within these homes along the lines of age, sex, and status, there was implied accepted agreement within the family about their position. Order was more important than equality within the home when a relatively unknown outside environment threatened its very foundations. Other historians, however, locate conflicts within the family during the colonial period. They challenge the notion that such internal hierarchical differences were tacitly accepted by the household members. They argue that household power structures were often designed to replicate the exertion of power by elite males on a wider political level. This chapter notes both of these interpretations, and sets them against the daily experience of the various inhabitants of colonial American homes. The domestic environment could provide a venue for certain hierarchies and power structures to be challenged, or modified. This was a part of daily life in colonial America. The relative strength of weakness of "household government" could act as a microcosm for the wider social and political developments in colonial America, however conservative or revolutionary they were.

The first few years of settlement for a New England family in the 17th century would often take place in an intermediate, semi-permanent dwelling akin to a barn or homestead. Such dwellings were rarely built on foundations, and were instead built on a crude form of wooden scaffolding that often simply consisted of timber posts nailed into holes in the earth. This would be covered with a relatively thin colonial clapboard structure. On plantations in 17th century Virginia and its surrounding colonies, one-story timber frames were often known in slightly exaggerated terms as "manner houses." In these structures,

A restoration of a typical colonial kitchen in a museum at Old Stone House Village, New Jersey. The kitchen was a source of home heating as well as a place for the family to congregate.

three-part English-style plans were most often utilized, so that the home was the center of both domestic and farm labor. There were often through-passages, in which indentured servants and enslaved African Americans were to move from one side of the home to the other without entering its familial environment. This enabled them to move to dairy and work sheds where only their social peers would reside, as well as kitchen areas where there would be far greater social mixing. Indeed, it was in the kitchens that indentured servants, temporary agricultural workers, and members of the family who lived in the home's more genteel quarters would most often mix on a day-to-day basis.

Archaeological evidence, as well as remaining house plans, demonstrate that as generations went by, and the 17th century turned to the 18th, social intermixing within the home decreased significantly. It is no coincidence that this change took place as enslaved labor replaced white indentured servitude as the dominant form of work around homes in plantation colonies in the south, and working apprenticeships encompassed a far younger and wider population in the north. Thus, through-passages often led straight to places of work, rather than also leading to kitchens and communal mess areas. Increasingly, passages within the home were completely closed off. Work sheds often disappeared by the 1730s, and were replaced by separate slave quarters and kitchens. Evidence for the changing use of space in colonial homes therefore demonstrates wider social and demographic changes that surrounded them. For smaller homesteads in Maryland and Virginia, the unpredictable tobacco economy combined with a relatively high death rate to prevent their inhabitants from moving to more permanent dwellings, in the manner of later generations of New England farmers and traders.

HOUSEHOLD DEATHS

This impermanence of these dwellings demonstrates a stark fact: the early colonial period witnessed households in which daily life was often made difficult by the recent or imminent death of one of their members. Historians paint a picture of 17th century Virginia households dominated by the threat or experience of mortality. Most children in the region during the 17th century grew up without both parents. There were between seven and nine children in families, with or without two parents, during the 18th century in Virginia, over a third of whom would die before they reached adulthood.

The number of offspring living under one roof during the 18th century in New England was roughly the same, although fewer died before adulthood, resulting in larger families. Many colonial Chesapeake women did not experience the level of familial stability and consensus regarding domestic power relations that some might argue characterized southern plantation life. Demography in 17th and early 18th century Virginia and Maryland, for example, suggests that many white women experienced fluid and abnormal forms of family life. Some women married twice in their lives, as the ratio of living men to women remained unequal. If white women could survive "seasoning" and indentured servitude, then this demographic fact meant that they could potentially experience greater opportunities for social advancement by marrying above their rank. This was the case because they were able to choose between men desperate to create a familial home after their own servitude had ended. Yet owing to the scarcity of women in the region, and the continuing problem of malnutrition and disease, marriages could be rare, and short lived affairs. Historians Lois Carr and Lorena Walsh traced

Good Wives and Nasty Wenches

Historians have pointed to a class-based distinction that differentiated "good wives" from "nasty wenches" in 17th-century Virginia, and point to the growing role of race in this distinction by the 18th century. Day-to-day family life changed as a result. More white women moved into a domestic sphere ever more separate from the public workplaces that surrounded these homes.

There came about a racial opposition in which women of English descent embodied the privileges and virtues of womanhood, while women of African descent shouldered the burden of its inherently evil, sexual lust in the same manner that indentured white women were seen in the previous century. Virginia law was changed in 1662 in order to modify a received common law tradition that legally identified children through their fathers.

In these times, children were born free so long as their mother was white. This was an important distinction, because the majority of interracial offspring were the products of white men and African women. A legal mechanism had been put in place whereby enslaved status could be born into, and perpetuated, thanks to the nature of birth patterns in plantation states such as Virginia.

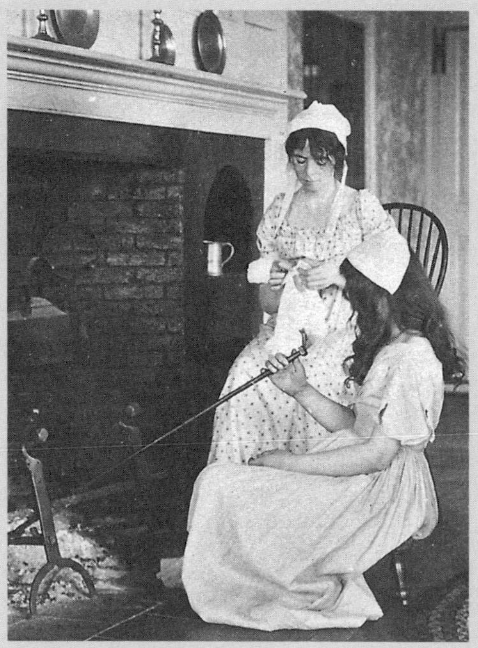

Young women interpreters depict a fireside scene in colonial America, where white women began to move into a domestic role.

the domestic lives of several generations of Chesapeake women during the colonial period, and concluded that as the sex ratio balanced out in the 18th century, women in the domestic sphere lost some of the opportunities for upward mobility and independent property accumulation afforded to them by their position of scarcity in previous generations. Thus after the early challenge to male household leadership caused by demography in colonies such as Maryland and Virginia, family historians such as Carole Shammas argue that "household government most likely expanded over the colonial period." Within the home, this may have decreased the level of self-control enjoyed by women and children regarding their work patterns.

In cases where the majority of children survived childhood, this added very different tensions to domestic familial life. In New England, for example, fathers often carried out agonized battles over the necessary division of the family estate among all their surviving sons, while daughters received dowries. The kind of compromises made over the division of family land often became too hard for ensuing generations. This was the case because daily life on these allotted plots of land was made less productive by their diminishing size in relation to their number of inhabitants. Many sources demonstrate the increasing movement of sons away from the daily familial environment within which their parents and grandparents had grown up.

DOMESTIC CONFLICT

These movements were linked to the increasing pressure for inherited land in colonies such as New England, which led to domestic conflicts. First- and second-generation settlers sometimes held onto land without passing out portions of it to their sons, or to their daughters in the form of a marriage dowry. An increasing proportion of their offspring therefore left the familial environment in search of their own plot of land. Historian Philip Greven carried out a case study on daily home life in colonial Andover, Massachusetts, which supports this link between domestic conflict and the search for land among new generations. Many colonial Andovans held onto their land until old age, refusing to sacrifice even a square foot to their married sons living on or near the same land, for as long as they possibly could.

Tellingly, this allowed these fathers to maintain their patriarchy for as long as possible, by exerting it over offspring denied the land that could otherwise have given them the necessary autonomy to establish their own patriarchal identities. This domestic internal tension could only diminish when first- and second-generation settlers in areas such as Andover had run out of enough land to satisfy the exponential growth of their offspring. This was obvious to younger generations long before their second-generation parents died. As a result offspring often moved into frontier and backcountry communities, seeking earlier domestic autonomy from their fathers. Sources and legal rulings from 18th-century America suggest that parents increasingly sought to influence the choice of bride or groom, at the same time that they wanted this choice to be made at a later point in life, thus delaying the independence and adulthood of these offspring. This caused tensions on a daily basis, and may have influenced a move toward the frontier on the part of these children.

AFRICAN-AMERICAN FAMILIES

The daily life for enslaved African-American families during the colonial period was even more ruptured than in the white environment because of the legal ambiguity regarding the very possibility for a family life among this population. Given the fact that marriage between enslaved persons was not legally recognized, parental control over offspring from these unions was at times non-existent. This meant that daily life for these communities often took place on plantations which separated the various constituents of African-American families. Young children often accompanied their mothers in both the domestic and working plantation environment on an average day. Because of wet nursing, they often remained by their mothers' side until age two.

Some fathers remained on plantations with their families, but many were sent to other plantations without any relatives present. It was not uncommon for children to be sent away to different plantations as well. Even if a master had made an effort to keep an enslaved family together, his death would often bring to an end the luck that had kept their family together. Estates were often divided up between different people who made different claims on the various items of "property" that were contained in these plantations. Different members of enslaved families were often separated among these different claimants of their individual lives.

An analysis of colonial American domestic life that emphasizes a willing consensus among household members, therefore, does not give a completely accurate picture of the power relations that took place within the home, and around it. As well as failing to account for the experience of enslaved and indentured persons, such a view of family consensus does not take into account the imposition of coverture (see below) upon colonial wives, and the mechanisms through which dependency could be maintained against their will. As well as wives, children, enslaved persons, and servants within the home were considered people "under household government" whose legal and political standing was only viewed in relation to the male head of household, who was able to vote, and register full property ownership, as well as administer physical punishment.

Unmarried adult women were known as "femmes soles" under the common law tradition established throughout the colonies during the 17th and 18th centuries. This status allowed them to own property, register for home ownership in certain circumstances, and appear in court under their own name and jurisdiction. Married women, on the other hand, were deemed to be "femmes coverts" (hence, the term *coverture*). This meant that all her property and previous personal wealth were held in her husband's name.

By the 1730s separate slave quarters and kitchens emerged. These well-built slave cabins were better than most, accounting for their survival into the modern era.

The legal system of coverture therefore reinforced existing systems of patriarchal control within the family.

Women in Puritan New England families lived under a system in which English Common Law property qualifications were tightened even further than in the Old World. Puritan New England, did, however, change certain parts of the Common Law practice so as to allow women to divorce, which at least gave them greater legal support if they wished to leave the system of coverture imposed by marriage. A married woman's control over her property within the domestic sphere was dependent on the existence of chancery courts within a particular colony. These regulated and enforced trust estates, which were the trusts under which wives owned property separately from their husbands. Massachusetts, Connecticut, and Pennsylvania all abolished such courts during the colonial period, thereby diminishing a married woman's ability to own property within the domestic sphere. On the other hand, South Carolina, Maryland, Virginia, and New York all preserved these chancery courts during the colonial period. This, to an extent, regulated the system of coverture in women's domestic lives, as their independence through legally separate property ownership could be maintained over time.

An increasing daily working role for dependents—such as women—may still have caused some anxiety for men. A man's patriarchal control within the home often rested on his ability to work to fund his "household government." Such an anxiety is demonstrated by European settlers' views of Native American family life, which allowed them to project their own anxieties regarding changing gender roles onto non-European families. That is, European settlers in colonial America often responded to perceived differences in Native American family life when it came to the differing domestic roles of men and women. The European perceptions of just what was "revolting" about Native American daily family life tells much about how these Europeans perceived the role of patriarchy within their own daily domestic lives.

For example the 17th-century English settler, William Wood, pointed out the strange nature of Algonquian gender roles within their homes in southern New England. Women were more "laborious than their lazie husbands." Similarly, the late 18th century Moravian missionary David Zeisberger was startled that "in the management of household affairs the husband leaves everything to his wife." Similar criticisms of Native American family structures were made in southern colonies during the 17th and 18th centuries, often pointing to the heavy labor carried out by women within households on a day-to-day basis. Of course, as many historians point out, this European view of Native American domestic work patterns was often based on misconceptions, such as the categorization of male fishing and hunting as leisure activities, as opposed to hard female domestic labor.

Nonetheless, in these criticisms of Native American customs, there was an underlying European anxiety regarding the exertion of patriarchy within the home. Consensual or not, daily life in colonial homes turned on the relations between various dependents and a male head. The mother-centered Native

An accused witch proclaims her innocence in a print by George Walker. Many women accused of witchcraft were engaged in commerce and property accumulation.

American society encountered by Europeans seemed to threaten this patriarchal model, which was felt at its most base, domestic level. This explains the male fear over power and property being inherited through the female line. "Household government" meant that the male leader of that government drew from powers that were expressed more widely by the state, such as coverture. Any threat to the inheritance patterns that were inherent in coverture—as demonstrated by the alternative matrilineal system in Native-American homes—would directly threaten patriarchal control of their respective households.

HERESY AND WITCHCRAFT

Witchcraft accusations and heresy trials involving women during the 17th and even 18th centuries are also a sign of public (male) power asserting its influence and disapproval over women who did not assume the role of good wives or mothers who were prevented from full legal status by coverture. A woman like Anne Hutchinson could cause such a stir in 17th-century New England by advocating a different approach to divine grace to that taught by male heads of families and church congregations, precisely because her religious beliefs were seen as symptomatic of her failure to live within an orthodox familial environment on a day-to-day basis.

It is no coincidence that middle aged and/or unmarried women were most likely to be accused of witchcraft, given the perception that their social lives did not conform to received norms of family life. In fact, many women accused of witchcraft were engaged in commerce and property accumulation; or as widows, had failed to transfer assets to their offspring according to accepted inheritance patterns.

Accusations of female heresy demonstrate that stability within domestic environments was not as consensual as some historians would have it. Instability from without (accusations and legal penalties) could often result from instability or unorthodoxy within family homes (women not abiding by the norms of proper motherhood under coverture). As historian Carol Karlsen has demonstrated, women without sons or brothers to inherit familial wealth ruptured the orderly transmission of property from one generation of males to another that coverture sought to cement within the home.

SOCIAL DISTINCTIONS

Up until the early 18th century, the nature of family life had governed social distinctions between different white women. Those who were unable to marry owing to their indentured servitude could often be classed as promiscuous or somehow unfeminine. This label came about because their daily work patterns prevented their marriage. Their singlehood was the same as the working men who surrounded them in farms and workshops that clustered around elite homeowners. It also made them supposedly more sexually available to these men on a daily basis. However the shift to a system of enslaved African

Reverend John Williams

Some historians suggest that Puritan New England's culture embedded a natural form of hierarchical rule within the family home. This made it so sturdy an institution that it was able to serve several social purposes, without ever witnessing an abusive form of patriarchal control. When the home was the setting for vocational and religious instruction, education, business development, and penal correction, a system of child abuse and male dominance could not characterize familial life, according to historian John Demos.

The story of the family of the Reverend John Williams neatly demonstrates this particular interpretation of daily family life during the colonial period. Williams's Deerfield, Massachusetts, home was attacked during Queen Anne's war by French-backed Native Americans. Williams witnessed the captivity of his family members, and the loss of a daughter. Yet there is not much evidence that he lamented these events in terms of his own loss of patriarchal control.

Several members of Williams's family, including his wife, were killed, while others were taken into captivity. Most of the latter were returned to neutral French forces, apart from his daughter Eunice. She was adopted by a group of Catholic natives, and despite her father's cries for her to return home, she married one of the Native American men. For Demos, a man like Williams was filled with love, rather than rage, and lamented the loss of loved ones, rather than any loss of control over dependents within the familial home.

This would seem, therefore, to support the claim that stable family environments experienced destabilization from without, rather than instability from within as a result of any internal resentment of patriarchal control. Williams lamented the loss of his daughter, rather than resenting the challenge to his patriarchal control of her movements.

rather than indentured white labor in colonies such as Virginia by the end of the 17th century increasingly allowed white women within southern domestic spheres to utilize a racial definition of their feminine virtue. Where slavery replaced indentured servitude, heavy work became associated with African women. White women could define themselves against this vision, and gain a sense of entitlement otherwise denied to them by the system of coverture that constrained their daily actions within the home.

In colonial America, English Common Law was not the primary code of power that impacted their familial lives. Roman-Dutch law, which descended from the Justinian Code, was present in New Netherland until Britain's conquest of the area in 1674. This could have potentially given greater freedom to women within the home than the English system of coverture ever could. Married women in New Netherland, for example, had the same right to accumulate property in their own name that men enjoyed. Historians have therefore argued that the move away from this Dutch legal system diminished female freedom within married homes.

It is true that in contrast to the Dutch system in which the rights of dependents within the home could be upheld in public courts, power increasingly ended with the male head of household. Yet it is also true that the phenomenon of fathers appointing male guardians for their offspring (as opposed to living mothers) in their wills significantly diminished by the 1730s. Widows with dependent children therefore had comparatively more power in this respect. In this way, the move from Dutch to English law led to a mixed experience for dependent women within families in terms of the enhancement or diminishment of their own freedoms.

FASHIONABLE FURNITURE

Greater consumption of goods in the 18th century could also strengthen a family's patriarchal relations. Although parlors in both northern and southern colonies were increasingly used by householders and their visitors, the furniture that appeared in them often served several purposes on an average day: eating, sleeping, storage, and even business management. This meant that fashionable furniture often took a back seat to cheaper, more dual-purpose fittings, well into the 18th century. As less necessary, and even more luxurious goods were purchased to fill the home, they rarely introduced purely new tastes or influences. Rather, the extra funds that enabled their purchase were used to acquire fine linen, furniture, or decorative objects whose

Furniture was durable, rather than fashionable well into the 18th century, such as this infant cradle above. An exception would be made for the patriarchal head of the household, and would often include special seating, left.

Typical early household equipment included candle racks and spinning wheels, which created not only the necessary goods for the home, but at times surplus goods that could be sold.

domestic style and patterns could reinforce existing social ranks and identities. These could include special seating for the patriarchal head of household, or cupboards/table-boards to store his special crockery.

Consumption patterns within colonial homes did vary over time. Records such as probate inventories and floor plans detailing the use of domestic space demonstrate the changing socioeconomic stature of these homes' inhabitants. Newly arrived homesteaders from England in colonies such as Massachusetts and even Virginia often consciously denied themselves even moderate domestic consumption patterns that they had maintained in the Old World. This would enable them to concentrate their resources on income generation, mostly in the form of land, labor, and animal husbandry. For the middling sort in colonial America, the consumption of marketed goods within the home grew significantly in the mid-18th century. Cheaper consumer goods could transform one social rank into another, because their styles often imitated more expensive products.

FOODSTUFFS, GOODS, AND SERVICES

Even if these purchases did allow lower ranks to imitate supposedly higher social figures, and gain a sense of self-direction in so doing, more members of the household than ever were engaged in more constant and market-driven work. This work was carried out in order to create a small economic surplus that could enable the purchase (rather than subsistence production) of foodstuffs, goods, and services, all of which could be increased with greater industry. As a result, in mid-18th-century Virginia, children as young as eight years old were apprenticed to work, while in Massachusetts during the same period, children in poor homes were apprenticed at the soonest possible moment. This could be as early as three years old, and younger in some cases, if the child in question had finished his or her period of nursing.

CHILDREN'S DAILY LIVES

The majority of children's daily working lives were spent on farms during the colonial period, with an element of self-support in terms of labor coming as early as five years old. In both the north and south, apprenticeships for children became rather similar to a form of indentured servitude. On an average day, supposedly apprenticed children in rural families often simply took the role as workhand, without any skills being learned on the job. It is true that poor relief mechanisms in the New England colonies allowed more families to stay together, rather than sending children to work on other farms or estates as servants. Nonetheless, hard domestic servitude still governed daily life for many larger families for whom poor relief was simply not enough.

Where apprenticeships were served by children in order to gain specific skills—particularly in less rural areas—they often left their family homes and spent their daily life in the domestic environment of their masters. Offspring from the same family would often serve in the same master's house. Masters could maintain as much, if not more, control over the marriage of their servants, than the servants' parents. Marriage without consent could often result in extra time being added to an indenture contract, for example.

As a result of ever younger apprentices and an ever-expanding base of hard working family members, by around 1770, a quarter of the household budget in many American colonies was spent on goods imported into the particular colony. This paved the way, and even created the necessary capital, to implement more industrial systems into production toward the end of the 18th century.

OBEDIENCE TOWARD PARENTS

In Puritan New England, well into the 18th century Puritan theology maintained a relatively harsh disciplinary environment in the home, and contributed to this focus on children's daily work discipline. Puritan theology intersected with daily child rearing habits and work patterns. If children were deemed to be the natural inheritors of Original Sin, then they were justifiably inflicted with the repression, and suppression of their daily movements and desires.

The Puritan religious focus on the need for consent for proper religious membership combined with a heightened focus on the Fifth Commandment in the Old Testament, which related to the obedience toward parents. This meant that within the home, children were often separated from parents whose ability to maintain control over them was not constant. This applied particularly to fathers within the home.

Yet historians have increasingly focused on the material culture of childhood within colonial American homes, and the extent to which evidence for the development of such a culture might be seen as a sign of the diminishment of parental discipline, or at least, a parental indulgence of childish sentiment and frivolity within the home. For example, instances of swaddling, which involved the neck being placed in a rigid support mechanism, were abandoned by the end of the 18th century. This demonstrated a decreased wish to control the physical movements of children within the home. Inventory records demonstrate that children's toys became more widely used by the end of the 18th century.

Paintings created at the beginning and end of the 18th century, obviously confined to wealthier homes, demonstrate more distinctively separate children's clothing, as well as tentative signs for separate children's spaces within larger homes. Historian Philip Greven has shown that particularly in southern households, a more moderate religious culture could sometimes indulge childish values, such as the wish for play and recreation, within the home.

In fact, daily family life in New England during the 17th and early 18th centuries revolved around what Edmund Morgan has termed Puritan tribalism. This came to undercut the supposed religious homogeneity of the region. A Puritan dilemma took place within New England communities that were made up of family units whose members could side with family, rather than community leaders. The supposed decline of communal Puritan religious control in the 18th century thus partially related to the role of day-to-day family life.

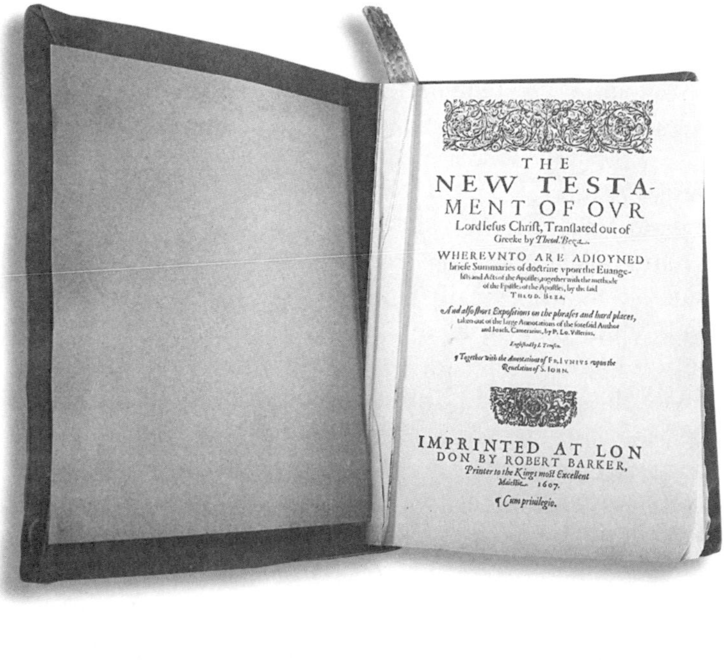

William Penn's Bible: Born into an Anglican family, Penn converted to the Quaker faith at age 22 and his colony became a haven for other members of the Society of Friends, or Quakers.

Family hierarchies and dependencies remained during the colonial period, with any threats to this domestic stability coming from without (communal rather than family leadership). Puritan tribalism manifested itself primarily from within the family unit. Puritan family love promoted a primary duty to family dependents, and allowed compromises against received communal religious orthodoxy. The power of love within Puritan families meant that, for Edmund Morgan, "theology became the handmaid of genealogy," leading to a certain decline in institutional religious orthodoxy.

DIVINE INCLINATION

Quaker families in colonies such as Pennsylvania were even more moderate in their daily child rearing practices. As a result of a shared theology that emphasized that children were born with an "inner light" from Christ, they were deemed naturally good, guided by this innate divine inclination. Quaker parents were therefore less likely to punish children harshly, or to assume that certain actions and relations between parent and offspring were somehow indulgent or frivolous. For the heads of Quaker families, Original Sin was not deemed to have been directly transmitted to children at birth. Rather, the outside world represented human corruption, and it was the job of the family unit to protect and rear a child so as to be immune to its problems.

A stable consensus within the family needed to be maintained so that outside influences could not corrupt the "inner light" of children yet to experience this outward corruption. This allowed greater leeway for daily engagement between parents and children, as well as greater autonomy for children themselves to learn and play among themselves. External forces often caused the conflicts that Quaker children increasingly experienced with their parents.

For example, a theological emphasis on marriage within the Quaker community, or "meeting," caused a good deal of day-to-day problems for those families who were not wealthy enough to be able to give their offspring large marriage gifts. This meant that the children within such family units were less marriageable, as they would not be able to offer a strong economic basis for their union with a member of another Quaker family. In this way, any tensions between offspring who married out, and parents who lamented this fact without understanding the social difficulties that caused it, resulted from outside influences. Children were forced to marry out by a clash between family theological doctrine and external socioeconomic expectations.

Historians link the internal experience of the family with the developing political culture in the colonial north and south. New England's family-based migration pattern, for example, influenced the formation of daily town meetings that were modeled on the home. Even though they were most often led by male figureheads, women (and even children) could still take part in their discussions. On the other hand, Virginia's high proportion of men and indentured servants meant that the hierarchical model of a nuclear family could not completely influence the colony's developing political culture. Instead, political meetings were partly modeled on the exertion of power outside of the family unit.

Daily life, daily dependencies, and daily allegiances within the family environment had a wide impact on the development of colonial America's social, economic, and political culture.

GIDEON MAILER

Further Readings

Brown, Kathleen. *Good Wives, Nasty Wenches, and Anxious Patriarchs: Gender, Race, and Power in Colonial Virginia.* Chapel Hill: University of North Carolina Press, 1996.

Carr, Lois, and Lorena Walsh. "The Planter's Wife: The Experience of White Women in 17th-century Maryland," *William and Mary Quarterly* (v.34, 1974).

Demos, John. *A Little Commonwealth: Family Life in Plymouth Colony.* New York: Oxford University Press, 1970.

Demos, John. *The Unredeemed Captive: A Family Story from Early America.* New York: Alfred A. Knopf, 1994.

De Vries, Jan. "Between Purchasing Power and the World of Goods: Understanding the Household Economy in Early Modern Europe." In John Brewer and Roy Porter, eds. *Consumption and the World of Goods.* London and New York: Routledge, 1993.

Greven, Philip. *Four Generations: Population, Land, and Family in Colonial Andover, Massachusetts.* Ithaca, NY: Cornell University Press, 1970.

Karlsen, Carol. *The Devil in the Shape of a Woman: Witchcraft in Colonial New England.* New York: W.W. Norton, 1987.

Levy, Barry. *Quakers and the American Family: British Settlement in the Delaware Valley.* New York and Oxford: Oxford University Press, 1988.

Morgan, Edmund. *The Puritan Family: Religion and Domestic Relations in 17th-Century New England.* New York: Harper and Row, 1966.

Narret, David. *Inheritance and Family Life in Colonial New York City.* Ithaca, NY: Cornell University Press, 1992.

Norton, Mary Beth. *Founding Mothers and Fathers: Gendered Power and the Forming of American Society.* New York: Alfred A. Knopf, 1996.

CHAPTER 3

Material Culture

"Culture requires in the first place
a certain balance of material and spiritual values."
— Johan Huizinga

MATERIAL CULTURE INCLUDES the common objects and artifacts people use as they live their everyday existence. An overview of colonial homes, furnishings, and colonial styles of dress reveals several patterns of colonial material life. Early colonists faced the problems of improvising and adjusting with scarce resources in a new environment. Later colonial households became accustomed to the environment and thus became more settled. America also began developing an elite with the wealth to obtain not only practical goods, but luxurious items as well. Everyday objects reflect these trends through their growing abundance and sophistication as time passed. The material culture of the American colonies also reflects their dependence on British manufactured goods.

Most material possessions of colonial Americans were kept in the home. The colonial home was the centerpiece of family life just as the family was the centerpiece of colonial society. Thus homes and furnishings are key components to an understanding of colonial American material culture. Most daily activities, including meal preparation, dining, sleeping, childrearing, prayer, schooling, entertainment, medical care, and the production of goods, took place in early colonial homes. The household served a variety of functions, and its space and contents were thus marked by flexibility of use and crowded conditions.

The Study of Material Culture

Material culture is an interdisciplinary field that combines such disparate areas of study as history, historical archaeology, cultural geography, art history, architecture, the decorative arts, science, and technology. Historians interested in material culture examine everyday artifacts and objects in order to gain a more complete picture of the daily routine of life for average citizens in a particular place and time. In addition material culture seeks to understand how people view those artifacts and their place in the world. Material culture can also reveal how a society or culture changes over time.

The study of material culture is important because the written historical record tends to emphasize the activities and worldviews of the literate, elite members of society. Average citizens are often underrepresented. Material objects available for recovery and analysis include houses and their furnishings, pottery, weapons, clothing, grave markers, and objects of art. Historians even glean information and items from trash dumps. Historians supplement the recovered artifacts themselves with information from personal diaries, land deeds, and court records such as probate records, among others.

COLONIAL HOUSES

During the initial years of colonial settlement, houses were simply small, rustic structures designed to provide immediate shelter from the elements of a wilderness environment. Styles of architecture and construction methods were adapted to the new environment from the typical manor houses and family cottages of England. They were built with available materials, including tree branches, cloth, mud, and woven rushes. Historians rely on documentary evidence and excavated foundations for information for this time period, as those few remaining early colonial structures tend to be the sturdier dwellings of wealthier colonists. Most colonial houses were examples of vernacular architecture, made without the use of formal plans, usually by their owners, rather than trained architects.

Early 17th century homes usually consisted of one large room in which all daily activities took place. Early colonists often referred to this room as the "hall." A few larger early homes had two separate rooms instead of just one. They were communal spaces that afforded little to no individual privacy, as typically large colonial families sought to amicably share the small houses that were the centers of colonial family life. Early American colonial homes took a variety of forms, as their builders experimented with local materials and tried to determine which forms were best suited to their new environments. The log cabins that many people traditionally associate with wilderness and life on the frontier were not very common in the colonies in the 17th century, although Swedes and Finns settling along the Delaware River in what became New Jersey, did import the log style of construction.

Most early New England homes were constructed with timber frames and clapboard siding, as the colonists found an abundance of wood in the New World. Early Plymouth Colony dwellings were largely constructed with wattle and daub. The shortage of lime in the area, essential for mortar, made the use of stones or bricks impractical. They often filled cracks in the walls with clay to keep out the winter wind. Roofs were either thatch or wood shingled. A central chimney provided the opening for the smoke of the fireplaces that were essential for both heat and light. Floors were either bare or sanded wood and were sometimes covered with reeds. Windows were covered with oiled linen, as glass was unavailable and unaffordable for all but the wealthiest colonists. These small dwellings were usually crowded, damp, cold, and smoky.

In the southern colonies, early homes were usually wood frame or brick farmhouses with roofs made of rushes. Brick was much more common in the southern colonies than in the New England region due to the abundance of the lime necessary to make mortar. Windows and doors were simply openings covered with wooden shutters in these warmer climates, as glass was also rare and expensive in the south. Both mid-Atlantic and southern homes featured end-chimney designs to help diffuse the fireplace's heat. This was especially important in the hot summer months.

As the colonies gradually grew and the communities became more permanent in nature, both houses and public dwellings became larger and better built. Architecture became another form through which wealthy colonists

A recreation of a Puritan hearthstone. Floors were either bare or sanded wood and their small dwellings were usually crowded, damp, cold, and smoky.

A Currier & Ives lithograph titled "The Old Plantation Home." This romanticized depiction of happy slaves was far from reality, but it does capture the distinction between owner and slave dwellings.

could express their social status, and houses became more elaborate, sometimes through a period of additions over time. More two-story homes began to appear. Larger houses added outbuildings that served as kitchens, dairies, storehouses, or stables. Room uses became more specialized, and the addition of bedrooms created more individualized living spaces and privacy within colonial households. Many colonists began referring to their parlors as "best rooms" where they displayed their most cherished possessions and met on ceremonial or solemn occasions. Architectural forms became less variable as colonists found the few key styles most suited to their environments and then added small regional variations to these basic designs. Blacksmiths produced ornamental knockers and railings for colonial homes.

Small New England cottages featured one multipurpose room and a steeply pitched roof. They were designed to best withstand the harsh New England winters through features such as facing south for warmth from the winter sun, low ceilings to preserve heat, and central chimney and fireplace locations to help diffuse heat throughout the house. Attics or lofts were sometimes added as sleeping quarters for children or servants. Unlike the southern colonies, the New England region featured a large number of middle class homes. Two popular house types were the "saltbox" house and the Cape cottage, which came in half, three-quarter, or full sizes. The "saltbox" featured two rooms, one on either side of a narrow hallway. Common additions included a lean-to, which could serve as storage space, sleeping quarters, or a kitchen. Some homeowners dug underground cellars to hold vegetables or other goods.

In the southern colonies, most houses were either small farmhouses, or large plantation residences. Only a small number of middle-class dwellings existed. Southern colonial houses were designed to maintain coolness in a hot, humid climate and to attract cool breezes during the summer months. As slavery became a widespread and legalized institution, larger plantations developed separate slave quarters. Summer kitchens located away from the main property became common throughout the south and helped keep

Georgian Architecture in the American Colonies

Georgian architecture became popular in Great Britain in the early 18th century and was later popularized in its American colonies, where it would also commonly be known as Federal style architecture. Historians credit renowned architect Inigo Jones for introducing the style in Britain. Georgian architecture is noted for its classical basis in ancient Greece and Rome and its strict, mathematical adherence to rigid symmetry of design elements. Proportion and balance are hallmarks of the Georgian style. Like other British architectural styles carried to the colonies, it would be adapted to American conditions. A growing availability of architectural books and manuals and trained architects made its American introduction possible. The growth of a colonial elite with the money to afford such homes and buildings was also a key component. It would remain popular in America until roughly the mid-19th century.

Colonial Georgian buildings included both public buildings and private residences. They first began to appear in urban areas such as southern capitals and northern seaports, and gradually spread into rural areas. Colonial Georgian homes most often featured red brick walls with white window trimmings and cornices. There were two evenly spaced windows on either side of a central paneled doorway with a portico and a second-floor window centered above the door. Inside there were two rooms on either side of a central hallway. Northern Georgian houses were usually wooden while those in the south were usually brick. Some colonial houses simply added Georgian features or façades and as a result were not exactly symmetrical. The first colonial Georgian building, known through engravings and contemporary descriptions, is the Foster-Hutchinson House of Boston, Massachusetts. Other well-known examples include the Hammond-Harwood House in Annapolis, Maryland, and the College of William and Mary in Williamsburg, Virginia.

The Georgian style Pennsbury Manor is a reconstruction of William Penn's 17th-century plantation on the Delaware River.

homes cool. By the 18th century the wealthiest plantation owners could afford to maintain separate residences in northern cities such as Newport, Rhode Island or in coastal cities, such as Charleston, South Carolina, where they escaped during the hottest months.

More formal, academic architectural styles appeared in the colonies as the number of available architectural books and manuals and the number of trained architects grew. There were also more wealthy colonists with the means, desire, and connections needed for the creation of sophisticated mansions. By the 18th century Georgian architecture would migrate from Britain to its American colonies. Georgian style became popular among wealthy colonists for both their homes and their public buildings. Regional colonial architects adapted the main Georgian style to suit regional tastes and environments. The main colonial sites of Georgian style buildings were the key New England seaports like Boston and important government southern colonial towns like Williamsburg, Virginia. The Georgian style slowly filtered from the urban areas into rural America.

HOUSEHOLD FURNISHINGS

The colonial period of early American furniture lasted from the beginning of settlement to the late 18th century. Early colonial families initially made their own crude furniture, which was solid and heavy. Carpentry tools, such as saws, axes, and nails, could be found in many early colonial homes. Early seating included mostly stools and benches. There were few chairs in this period, and those households that did have chairs usually had only one. It was usually reserved for the head of the household. Storage chests were essential items, as most colonial houses did not have closets and were often crowded with both people and possessions. Chests also provided additional seating. Mattresses on the floor provided early sleeping quarters, with bedsteads slowly becoming more common. Many were joined to the wall and folded up out of the way or trundle beds that slid under the main bed to save room in tight quarters. Chamber pots were stored underneath or nearby. Early tables were simple wooden planks set on trestles.

A niddy noddy, a tool used to measure yarn and keep it from tangling.

Furniture gradually became more comfortable and more decorative. By the 18th century wealthier colonists imported furniture from Europe. An American furniture industry also emerged in major urban areas such as Philadelphia. Colonial furniture makers found an abundance of native maple, cherry, oak, walnut, and other wood for materials. Popular colonial period styles

In colonial households, barrels like these were often used to bring water from the well to the kitchen. Other household items included butter churns, warming pans, and pewter mugs.

included Jacobean (Stuart), Queen Anne (Early Georgian), William and Mary, Windsor, and Chippendale furniture. Popular federal period styles that began appearing at the end of the colonial period in the 1780s included Hepplewhite and Sheraton.

Colonial home life often revolved around the hearth, so colonial homes featured large chimneys and fireplaces. Wrought iron fireplace tools, such as andirons, shovels, tongs, and bellows, would be located nearby for easy access. Many colonial men kept a pipe and a pipe box filled with tobacco on the mantel. A broom also usually stood at the ready. Fireplaces provided essential heat and light, as well as places to cook and relax. Some fireplaces had an oven built into the rear. Cookware was conveniently located nearby. Colonial cookware, such as pots and kettles, were heavy and made of iron and other metals. Colonial cooks also used skimmers (known as scummers), dripping pans, trivets, and gridirons. Ladles were popular serving utensils. Colonial households also had a cheese press, a butter churn, and a mortar and pestle for grinding corn and other grains. Barrels served as important means of storage for certain types of food and beverages. Most colonial households also possessed fishing tackle, as well as guns and knives that were essential for defense.

Most colonial households used their pottery and tableware primarily during mealtimes. Like other household furnishings, a family's pottery reflected their social status. Most pottery in the 17th century was of simple design and local manufacture. Depending on availability, financial means, and other factors, pottery was earthenware, wooden, pewter, stoneware, or porcelain. Earthenware was usually undecorated and purely utilitarian. This was especially true among groups like the Puritans, who disliked excess ornamentation. Other

Paul Revere: Colonial Silversmith

In addition to his role in the Patriot movement leading up to the American Revolution and his famous "midnight ride" through the Massachusetts countryside warning of the approach of British soldiers, Paul Revere was also a well-known colonial silversmith. Paul Revere was born in 1735, although the exact date and location are uncertain. His father was a silversmith, and Revere began his career at a young age as an apprentice in his father's business.

Revere served in the French and Indian War after his father's death in 1754, but later returned to the family business. He opened his own shop, and eventually trained his own apprentices, and supervised journeymen in his employment. He oversaw every aspect of the shop, from pounding out the hot silver to its design and engraving. His business became well-established with a good reputation. The maker's mark with which he engraved all his pieces was his assurance of their quality.

Revere's shop made flatware and tableware, including popular tea sets; personal items, such as jewelry, buckles, and buttons; and surgical instruments and dental plates. He also repaired and engraved items. In addition to silver, Revere sometimes worked in brass and gold, but never worked in pewter. Revere also engraved metals for printing portraits, sheet music, advertisements, currency, as well as political cartoons. One of his most famous engravings is of the 1770 Boston Massacre. One of his most famous silver pieces, the Liberty Bowl, is frequently reproduced through pieces known as Revere Bowls. The original Liberty Bowl is housed in Boston's Museum of Fine Arts. In later years, he expanded his business interests to include a hardware store, a foundry, and a copper rolling mill, while his son took over the daily management of the silver shop. Paul Revere died in 1818.

A portrait of silversmith Paul Revere by John Singleton Copley.

common pottery types included creamware, delftware, and pearlware. Plates were uncommon until the later colonial period.

Many early serving dishes and glasses were communal. Small wooden trays known as trenchers, often used communally to hold food, were common in the early colonial period. Colonists drank from tankards, beakers, cups, and bowls most commonly made of leather, pewter, pottery, wood, or silver. Like the serving dishes, beverage containers were also communal, passed from person to person during the course of the meal. Utensils were also made of pewter and wood. Knives and spoons were common, but forks would not appear until the late colonial period. Early knives had pointed edges to spear food in the absence of forks. The late introduction of the fork to America from Europe led many to comment on the distinctive American use of the knife, fork, and spoon as compared to the European way.

During the late 17th and 18th centuries the colonists began switching to individual place settings and more complete services. Tableware also became more decorative. China and glassware, initially rare and unaffordable to all but the wealthiest families, gradually become more common. Better production techniques, lower prices, and regular trade with England made a wide variety of pottery more affordable as well. American silversmiths like Paul Revere also began selling silverware to a growing market. Wealthy tables also featured silver salt cellars. By the mid-18th century imported English pottery and complete tea services were popular among the urban elite and middle classes.

LINENS AND QUILTING BEES

Linens for the table and bed ranged from nonexistent to extensive, based on a family's means. Tablecloths and napkins were common, as were bed sheets, pillow cases (called pillow "beers"), blankets, and coverlets. Average households used mattresses known as flock beds, which were stuffed with readily available materials such as rags or wool scraps. The wealthy could afford feather beds and bed curtains. Most households had warming pans near the fire that heated cold beds on winter nights. Colonial women held quilting bees and sewing circles, where they created woven or patchwork quilts and samplers featuring letters, pictures of flora and fauna, biblical quotations, or popular verses.

Farm implements were often stored inside the house during the early colonial period, and outside as barns became more common. Early farm implements were of simple design and often handmade from wood. Most families possessed a few basic tools, as most colonial Americans lived a rural existence and farmed their land. Harrows with wooden teeth crushed dirt clods, scythes or sickles cut grain, and flails beat grain. Other common tools included hoes, spades, rakes, and pitchforks. Plows were inefficient and much less common, even in the later colonial period. Sowing the fields was mostly done by hand. The basic and often inefficient tools and methods made farming a tedious process. Carts pulled by oxen provided simple transportation. Many families also had saddles, harnesses, and other accessories needed for the care and riding of horses, a common means of transportation.

Colonial households also had a variety of other products necessary for daily life and entertainment. Many families made their own candles and soap, and owned molds to aid in their manufacture. Some households, especially of the wealthy or middle class, featured small family libraries made up of books imported from London or bought from one of a rising number of colonial booksellers. In a society in which literacy was not common or widespread, nearly every home had a Bible. Inventories and probate records show that even illiterate households had small book collections, perhaps as status symbols. Most households also had one or two musical instruments, including the popular dulcimer and fiddle. Childhood toys ranged from homemade cornhusk and rag dolls and carved wooden toys for the poor, to imported store-bought fine toys for the wealthy. Popular games included jumping rope, playing marbles, and rolling barrel hoops with a stick.

COLONIAL DRESS

Initially most colonists chose their clothing based on availability and suitability to the environment, and these characteristics continued to be key factors for the lower and working classes throughout the colonial era. Early colonial clothing was made heavy and durable, and was often passed down through the generations as either hand-me-downs or family heirlooms. Some colonial families made their own homespun clothing, as imported or store-bought clothing was unavailable or unaffordable. Making homespun clothing was a difficult and time-consuming process. Common materials included wool, leather, and linen. Cotton was both rare and expensive. For making thread and weaving cloth, some colonial homes had spinning wheels and handlooms, as well as buttons, thread, and other sewing supplies.

All but the poorest colonists had a wide range of clothing items that they wore in various combinations. Colonial dress was often tied to the wearer's social standing, especially as the colonial period advanced. Public opinion, and in some colonies legal restrictions, ensured that colonial clothing reflected the wearer's social class and status. For some groups, such as the Puritans and the Quakers, clothing also reflected religious beliefs. For example, Puritans did

Children were dressed as miniature adults, reflecting the colonial attitude toward childhood.

not wear any jewelry, including wedding rings, and shunned excessive trim, ruffs, or skirt widths. Clothing also followed gender-specific customs, such as preventing women from appearing in society with their heads uncovered. Everyday clothing was often made colorful through the use of vegetable dyes, even among the Pilgrims and Puritans who are stereotypically pictured in somber black- and-white clothing.

A woman in colonial dress poses in a photograph taken in 1911.

Colonial women traditionally wore gowns that consisted of a skirt, a bodice, and separate sleeves. These were supplemented with underskirts, petticoats, chemises, and aprons worn in various combinations. The traditional women's undergarment was a loose-fitting linen smock. Stockings, leather shoes, handkerchiefs, neck kerchiefs, and linen caps (called "coifs") completed the daily outfit. Women usually wore their hair bunched on the back of the head. Colonial men traditionally wore a suit that consisted of a doublet (or a jerkin or waistcoat), a cloak, and knee breeches. This basic male wardrobe varied only by material, color, and price. The traditional men's undergarment was a linen shirt. Stockings, leather laced boots, and caps completed the daily outfit. Babies wore a linen smock, while toddlers wore a long robe. By the ages of six to eight, children appeared as miniature adults, reflecting the colonial attitude toward childhood. Servants and slaves wore much simpler styles of dress made of poor quality materials.

Upper-class dress became more formal and sophisticated by the 18th century, as the colonies became more settled and an American elite began to develop. Dress became a key element in their desire to set themselves apart from the average colonists. Women wore dresses with wide skirts and tall hairstyles. They often wore long gloves and masks to shelter themselves from the sun, and muffs to protect their hands, as white skin and smooth hands became status symbols. Men wore embroidered coats, knee britches, ruffled shirts, and stockings with garters. Their shoes featured large silver buckles. They began to powder their hair and pull it back. Powdered wigs became commonplace later. Common fabrics included silks, satins, velvets, and damasks in bright colors with lace trims. Even the lower and middle classes had so-called "best clothes" that were frequently of the same style as everyday wear, but of finer fabrics. Black was the most common color for "best clothes."

The changing material culture of the colonial period revealed both a growing general leveling of well being among all but the poorest Americans, and a growing divide between the wealthy and poorer classes. Dress, like other aspects of material culture, had increasingly come to reflect one's wealth and social status. Houses became larger and their furnishings more diverse as the colonial period advanced. Material goods became not just status symbols, but important forms of investment in an era where there was little currency in circulation. Changes in material culture also demonstrated the increasing American obsession with imported English goods and styles in the period leading up to the American Revolution. London became the key arbiter of American fashions in material goods. Material culture would play a symbolic role in the American Revolution, as many patriotic colonists boycotted English products as a form of political statement.

Marcella Trevino

Further Readings

Carson, Cary, Ronald Hoffman, and Peter J. Albert. *Of Consuming Interests: The Style of Life in the 18th Century*. Charlottesville: University Press of Virginia, 1994.

Deetz, James. *In Small Things Forgotten: The Archaeology of Early American Life*. New York: Anchor Books, 1996.

Hawke, David Freeman. *Everyday Life in Early America*. New York: Harper and Row, 1988.

Hume, Ivor Noel. *A Guide to Artifacts of Colonial America*. Philadelphia: University of Pennsylvania Press, 2001.

Polk, William K. *The Birth of America: From Before Columbus to the Revolution*. New York: HarperCollins, 2006.

Reich, Jerome R. *Colonial America*. Upper Saddle River, NJ: Prentice Hall, 1998. Schlereth, Thomas J. *Artifacts and the American Past*. Nashville, TN: American Association for State and Local History, 1980.

Schlereth, Thomas J. *Cultural History and Material Culture: Everyday Life, Landscapes, Museums*. Charlottesville: University Press of Virginia, 1992.

St. George, Robert Blair, ed. *Material Life in America, 1600–1860*. Boston, MA: Northeastern University Press, 1988.

Taylor, Dale. *Everyday Life in Colonial America from 1607–1783*. Cincinnati, OH: F&W Publications, 2002.

Thompson, Eleanor. *The American Home: Material Culture, Domestic Space, and Family Life*. Hanover, NH: University Press of New England, 1998.

Weitzman, David. *Underfoot: An Everyday Guide to Exploring the American Past*. New York: Scribner, 1976.

Wolf, Stephanie G. *As Various As Their Land: The Everyday Lives of 18th-Century Americans*. New York: HarperCollins, 1994.

CHAPTER 4

Social Attitudes

"The class of citizens who provide at once their own food and their own raiment, may be viewed as the most truly independent and happy."
— James Madison

COLONIAL AMERICAN SOCIETY can be characterized by a series of contradictions. Colonial Americans viewed community and family as social organisms, the overall health of which was more important than that of its individual components. And yet this belief was coupled with the ideal of the self-made man. The belief in a social hierarchy would give rise to a natural colonial aristocracy at the same time that the equally cherished belief in social mobility ensured that social levels remained fluid throughout the colonial period. Colonial Americans would seek to maintain their European cultural heritage, while also seeking to adapt to a new environment. American colonists came from mixed origins, but came to share a number of homogenous beliefs. This blend of old and new traditions would find its ultimate expression in the period leading up to the American Revolution, as Americans began to see themselves as a separate and unique society, rather than a frontier extension of the society they had left behind in England.

SOCIAL CLASSES

The colonial social structure was hierarchical at its core, but individuals in the colonies enjoyed a much greater degree of social mobility than was possible in England. Despite this mobility, public opinion expected colonists to know their place in the social order and to act accordingly. Social structure and social attitudes toward class were yet another way in which the colonists tried to recreate their British and European heritage. Even the original 1607 Jamestown settlers in Virginia included gentlemen who felt the hard work necessary for survival was beneath their social station. Distinct levels of society existed from the beginning of the colonial period, and a distinctive American elite would develop by the late 17th and early 18th centuries.

A person's place in society was usually related to their occupation and financial situation and was usually displayed through their houses, dress, and material possessions. Outward material signs of social status became increasingly common, as houses became larger and more commercial goods became available for a wider audience. One's social rank and gender also determined such things as where one sat in church, the severity and type of punishment one faced for crimes, and one's access to education. Social position even determined a gentlemen's class standing at Harvard College. Social forms of address were an important arbiter of one's standing, as well. Colonials addressed the upper classes as esquire and madam, next were gentleman and lady, followed by mister and mistress, and goodman and goodwife. Those at the lowest levels were addressed by no title at all.

Those at the top level of colonial society included the large landowners, wealthy merchants, governors, and other royal officials. America did not have hereditary nobility that Europe had for centuries. Many colonial Americans believed that there were natural born leaders, such as first-born sons, or those born to wealthy families. A natural colonial American aristocracy had begun to appear by the late 17th century. Social superiority was expected to extend into all aspects of life, including politics, education, manners, and dress. A colony's economic, social, and political elite tended to include the same membership, even if this membership was often fluid. The middle and lower classes were expected to show deference to their social superiors.

The bases of wealth for the developing American aristocracy included land ownership and the mercantile trade. Land ownership was a mark of social status from the earliest colonial times. A colonial merchant aristocracy took longer to develop in America, but gradually began to appear by the late 17th century in key ports such as Boston, Balti-

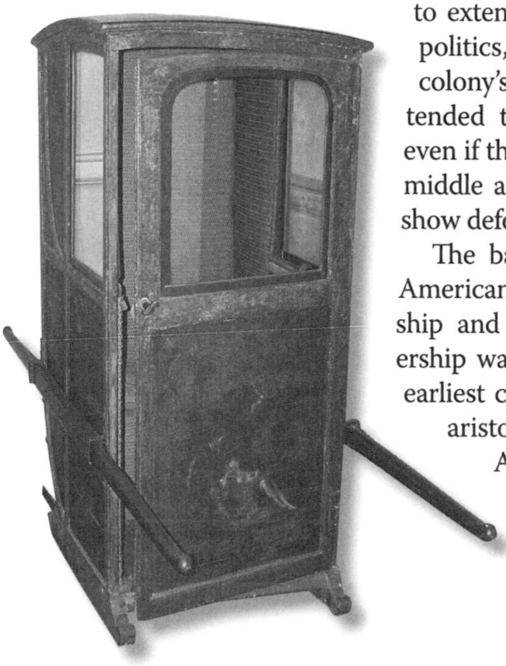

A sedan chair was used to transport members of the top level of society.

Deference to the Elite

Deference was a vital component in the maintenance of the hierarchy that dominated colonial American society, as early colonists sought to recreate their British social heritage in the New World. The lower and middle classes were expected to defer to the wealthy elite. Wives were expected to defer to their husbands, and children were expected to defer to their parents and other elders. The family was the basic unit of colonial society and such deference preserved order and harmony in the home, especially in the early colonial period when houses tended to be small, one-roomed, and cramped. Slaves and servants were expected to defer to their owners and to anyone else above their station. Natives and African slaves were expected to acknowledge European cultural superiority.

Colonial leaders viewed deference not just as their natural right, but also as critical to the maintenance of social harmony and their place on the social ladder. The force of public opinion and legal regulations, such as those that forbade anyone but the elite from wearing fine items of clothing, reinforced the engrained belief in deference as the natural right of one's social superiors. Religious leaders also used public opinion and the legal system to maintain their authority. Some colonies had state-sponsored religions, such as the Puritans in Massachusetts Bay, and the Anglican Church in Virginia. Both ingrained and legally sanctioned deference helped the elite maintain their place in a fluid, mobile society.

more, and Charleston. The leading merchants built their power by establishing control over the primary colonial trade routes. They also served as the major importers of desired British manufactured goods.

The major economic routes to the upper class often combined with political forces. Colonial governors had the patronage power to appoint lower government officials, which assured them of loyal followers. Colonial elites viewed political offices as another method of gaining and holding onto social status. Political influence could also affect one's ability to gain land and trading contracts with key British merchants and companies. In a time when church and state often mixed, religion was another means of achieving elite status. For example, the Puritans believed that God rewarded the elect in this world as well as the next, and viewed economic well-being as a sign of God's favor.

Land ownership was one of the most important bases of social status in America throughout the colonial period. Land was a source of money and prestige, and large landholders dominated politics in most colonies. Large colonial landholders included the Penn family of Pennsylvania, the Calvert family of Maryland, Earl Granville of North Carolina, and Lord Fairfax of Virginia.

The main value of land was in its resale, since tenant farming never became widespread in America. Most colonists, even indentured servants, aspired to own their own land. Land speculation and sales became a popular enterprise. Those landholders who sought to establish a system of tenancy on a large scale, particularly those in the originally Dutch colonies of New York and New Jersey, often met with violent resistance.

In the 18th-century south landownership was coupled with the ownership of slaves, another key source of wealth once the system of slavery became legalized. The majority of white southerners could not afford the slave labor necessary for the operation of a large plantation; therefore greater disparity between the rich and the poor existed in the southern colonies. Those that could imitated the European landed aristocracy in terms of dress and housing styles, but differing circumstances meant that they managed their everyday lives much differently. They were not leisured landlords whose tenants ran the daily operations on their small parcels of allotted land. Instead the southern plantation ran as a single unit and the owner oversaw management of the land, crop, and labor. Their gracious style of living built up debts to local merchants, and their reliance on commercial crop prices rather than land rents made their wealth and social status vulnerable.

The middle-class level of colonial society included smaller businessmen and professionals, such as skilled artisans and shopkeepers, and small but independent farmers. Self-employed artisans and workmen in small family businesses formed a large part of the population of colonial towns by the end of the 17th century. This group included doctors and lawyers, whose careers would not begin to professionalize and acquire a higher status until the 18th century. In

A late 18th-century engraving depicts William Penn conferring with a group of settlers and Native Americans. The result was the founding of Pennsylvania in 1681.

the early colonial years many Americans viewed lawyers with great suspicion, and some colonies legally prevented them from practicing. Most of the early colonists in this group came from Britain's working-class population of farm laborers and industrial workers looking for land and opportunities in the New World.

This lithograph of a Native American holding a scalp perpetuated images of savagery among indigenous peoples.

The lower levels of colonial society included landless laborers, unskilled workers, sailors, and indentured servants. Many of the colonists who came as indentured servants to pay for passage to the New World received "freedom dues" of money, clothing, or land and began careers as independent farmers, moving up the social ladder into the middle class. Colonial towns had small numbers of day laborers, who had no steady employment and were hired for various temporary jobs. Colonial Americans were often suspicious of outsiders and wary of change. New immigrants found their place in colonial society marked by their status upon arrival, as well as by what part of the world they had formerly called home. Many entered the colonies as indentured servants near the bottom of the social ladder, but with full expectations of moving upward once they had finished serving their periods of indenture. Free blacks and slaves were at the bottom of the social ladder.

Many colonists were encountering both Africans and natives for the first time, and viewed them as lesser beings who were expected to acknowledge the superiority of European culture. The treatment of natives and African slaves would increasingly deteriorate as the colonial period lengthened. Growing population pressures and westward expansion fueled conflicts with the Native Americans, and white fears of slave rebellions and uprisings grew when slavery became a widespread and legalized institution. There is little direct historical evidence for how African slaves and Native Americans viewed colonial society and their roles in it. Both groups had to adapt and transform their cultures in order to survive.

The British colonists did not freely intermingle with the natives they encountered in the New World and held sometimes-contradictory views of them. On the one hand, natives fit the ideal of the noble savage living in close and harmonious communion with nature. On the other hand, they were also categorized as the brutal savage, particularly as colonial population growth fueled rising land conflicts that often erupted into war. The colonists viewed the European diseases that decimated the native populations as a sign of their own superiority in God's eyes. Colonial-native relations were generally characterized by hostility, although there were exceptions, such as the policies of Roger Williams in Rhode Island and the Quakers in Pennsylvania. Intermarriage and religious conversion was much rarer in the British colonies than in those of the French and Spanish colonies.

Phillis Wheatley, the first published African-American poet, is shown composing a verse.

Slavery provided the answer to the southern labor problem, but also raised a number of social issues, which changed social relations among whites themselves as well as between the races. The wealthy that could afford large numbers of slaves could run large plantations, but most white southerners owned small farms that they worked themselves, sometimes alongside a few slaves. Social distinctions among southern whites became deeper, preventing a large middle class from developing. There were levels of social stratification within slavery as well, such as those slaves who worked as servants, cooks, and nannies in the plantation house versus those that labored as field hands.

Racial attitudes also impacted one's legal treatment in the colonies. White indentured servants were legally protected from the worst forms of abuse and could sue their masters, but most Africans, even those who were indentured servants rather than slaves, could not. The growing proportion of the southern population made up of slaves soon further restricted their legal rights through the development of increasingly stringent laws known as slave codes. These codes regulated their movements and called for harsh, often brutal, punishment of offenses. The colonists were openly distrusting of free blacks as well as slaves, and laws also restricted their freedoms. Laws also regulated the interaction of the races. For instance, many colonies had laws forbidding racial intermarriage, or miscegenation.

SOCIAL MOBILITY

A number of inherent weaknesses would prevent the American colonies from developing a true hereditary aristocracy. One of the greatest challenges to the development and maintenance of a colonial American elite was the unusual geographical and social mobility available in the New World as compared to the European society the early colonists had left behind. Although social mobility tended to weaken in the 18th century as the population grew and the frontier became more distant, the social classes remained fluid throughout the colonial era. The elite were not a distant group that seemed unattainable and aloof. In fact, all but the largest and wealthiest plantation owners and shopkeepers worked side by side with their employees. The alienation of owners and employees would not develop until the later Industrial Revolution of the 19th century. Thus Americans commonly held the belief that anyone could rise to a higher social class through the ownership of wealth or property. Visiting Europeans frequently commented on this aspect of American society.

The lack of a hereditary aristocracy reinforced this belief. The American elite was an often-unstable group with a fluid membership. There were no inherited political offices such as the British Parliament's House of Lords, and no inherited titles with which a colonial gentleman could distinguish himself. Political leaders faced an ever-present competition from both royal officials sent by the British government and local men in lower offices. Most colonies extended voting rights to the majority of adult white male property owners. Elite status was often based solely on wealth, which often fluctuated as economic conditions varied. Colonial bankruptcies were common. Only gradually did the elite begin to set themselves apart through material goods, dress styles, and education as colonial society stabilized. The colonial elite also did not form one cohesive class. As opposed to European aristocrats, American elites tended to focus on

William Penn's bedroom at Pennsbury Manor. Colonial society stabilized and the elite began to set themselves apart through material goods, style of dress, and education.

their individual and local goals, rather than working for the greater good of the class as a whole.

The overall high level of economic well-being in the colonies also hindered the development of a colonial elite on par with that of the European aristocracy. Although America experienced a growing gap between the rich and the poor throughout the colonial period, both groups improved their economic status on the whole. The rich simply improved at a greater pace. The colonial

Bacon's Rebellion

The events leading up to Bacon's Rebellion began as death rates declined, gender ratios became more balanced, and life became more settled in the Chesapeake region by the mid-17th century.

Virginia planters migrated to the western backcountry known as the Piedmont region seeking land that was becoming increasingly scarce in the colony's eastern Tidewater region. A new western elite began to emerge that demanded more of a voice in the colony's government, as well as help with the problem of increased resistance from natives, many of whom had earlier been pushed out of the older eastern areas. These goals conflicted with those of the established eastern elite under Governor William Berkeley. Wealthy western planter Nathaniel Bacon soon emerged as a leading spokesmen for his region.

He led a series of raids against natives in the Virginia and Maryland backcountry in open defiance of the governor. His western supporters soon elected Nathaniel Bacon to the Virginia House of Burgesses. Once Bacon arrived in the capital of Jamestown, he pushed to open up the availability of political offices and demanded native policies that were more aligned to western interests. He also sought to become commander of the colony's military, which the House of Burgesses granted over Governor Berkeley's objections.

An 18th-century engraving of Nathaniel Bacon by T. Chambars after a painting by Seipse.

Soon, the conflict between Berkeley and Bacon flared into a civil war. Bacon's followers seized control of Jamestown and published a "Manifesto and Declaration of the People." Berkeley fled Jamestown, which was burned in September 1676. Bacon's Rebellion fell apart, however, when Bacon died suddenly of dysentery shortly thereafter. Governor Berkeley regained control and had 37 of Bacon's followers hanged.

elite frequently complained that the middle and lower classes were not showing the proper deference through their dress and attitudes. They felt that skilled workers, for example, were demanding higher wages than they were due. Also as material goods became more varied, available, and affordable, the middle and lower classes could copy trends that appeared first among the urban elite and the wealthy.

EXPANDING FRONTIER

Yet another deterrence hindering the emergence of an American aristocracy was the continual draw of available land on the frontiers of colonial society. According to this Frontier Thesis, as falling death rates in the southern colonies increased population pressure, and the dividing of New England farms among children created land shortages in the original settled areas of the colonies, new lands along the expanding frontier continually beckoned. The possibility of starting over and gaining access to material wealth in the form of land was the constant promise of American society. Class distinctions were thought less obvious in the frontier areas of the colonies. The great number of American farmers who owned their own land, rather than rented or worked for a larger landowner, limited elite authority. Colonial leaders had to appease those in the middle social ranks who could move to the frontier and start over if they did not find their needs met or their place in the economic, social, or political system to be satisfactory. However, for many in the middle and lower social ranks, particularly slaves, women, servants, and urban dwellers, the availability of undeveloped land made no difference whatsoever. Thus the idea that the frontier provided a social-leveling force and a force for democratization of values must be tempered with a realization that the impact of the frontier was limited to those who could take advantage of it.

Furthermore, westward migration resulted in the rise of a new western elite in many colonies, and growing instances of conflict between the established, older eastern elite and their newer, western counterparts. Late 17th- and 18th-century America would thus experience a rash of western rebellions against more established eastern authority, led by a new elite, rather than by an empowered middle class. Colonial governments had difficulty controlling the distant frontiers, where the goals and interests of the growing western elite often conflicted with their own. Growing tensions between the expanding colonial settlements and nearby natives along the frontier would also drive these east/west conflicts. One of the earliest and most well-known examples was Bacon's Rebellion in 1670s Virginia. Others included the Paxton Boys in Pennsylvania in 1763 and the Regulator Movement in North Carolina and South Carolina in the late 1760s.

All of these conditions meant that colonial leaders were constantly vulnerable to criticisms and threats to their authority. Thus they often instituted harsh penalties against those who openly criticized the government or the British

Crown. Many colonies went so far as to pass laws forbidding the lower and middle classes to wear such items of fine clothing that were traditional marks of elite status. Colonial leaders also sought to utilize public opinion against such practices in an effort to maintain the social order.

AMERICAN ATTITUDES TOWARD THE BRITISH EMPIRE

The American colonists realized that they existed as provincials on the edges of the British Empire. Throughout most of the colonial period, the colonists sought to recreate British housing, dress, politics, social life, and culture as best as possible in their new environment. By the mid-18th century, however, Americans would also have a growing sense of themselves as something more than merely transplanted British citizens. They began to see themselves as unique in character and culture, a fact that visiting Europeans increasingly commented upon in their writings. Americans were a blend of the traditions and heritage they had carried with them to the New World, and the new ideas that had arisen as a result of their interaction with a new environment.

Americans viewed themselves as a simple, unsophisticated people uncorrupted by the decadent aspects of European culture. Their unprecedented social mobility gave rise to their belief in the ideal of the self-made man. Both Americans and Europeans pointed to the colonial printer, philosopher, and statesman Benjamin Franklin as a well-known exemplar of the self-made ideal because of his humble background and his emphasis on hard work and frugal living. During the same period that many Americans were beginning to recognize the unique features of their character, they began deliberately copying British material culture and society in a process that historians such as T.H. Breen have termed Anglicization. This process was especially prominent in material life as increased consumerism and demands for British manufactured goods swept the colonies, beginning among the wealthy in the large urban ports, and filtering into rural areas.

The process of Anglicization would be halted by the growing imperial crisis leading up to the American Revolution. The crisis began in 1763 with the end of the French and Indian War, when the British Empire began to tighten its control on the colonies and pass a series of Navigation Acts, touching off mass protests and the Patriot movement. The crisis would have a profound effect on Americans' views of themselves in the context of the British Empire, as well as their views of themselves as a distinct culture.

The American Revolution helped Americans further develop their growing sense of possessing a common nationality. Revolutionary ideals, including freedom, equality, a constitutional form of government, and the pursuit of happiness, became common goals enshrined in the American social fabric. J. Hector St. John de Crevecoeur's 1782 *Letters from an American Farmer* was one of the first books to seek to explain what exactly comprised the new American character, a forerunner of such well-known 19th-century works as Alexis de

Benjamin Franklin and the Image of America

An 18th-century print shows Benjamin Franklin, with an electrical device to his right, and lightning striking a building at left.

Benjamin Franklin was one of 18th-century America's most celebrated figures, both at home and abroad. Franklin was born one of 20 children in Boston, Massachusetts on January 17, 1706, to the candle maker Josiah Franklin and his wife Abiah Folger. His formal schooling lasted only two years, but he continued his personal education throughout his life.

He was initially apprenticed in the shop of his brother James, a printer, but was not allowed to write for the newspaper. He then ran away from home at 17 years old and would later run several prosperous printing businesses of his own, including the *Pennsylvania Gazette*, before retiring at age 42 to pursue politics and other interests. He lived in a commonlaw marriage with Deborah Read, whose first husband had never legally divorced her. He had an illegitimate son named William, in addition to two children with his common-law wife, named Francis and Sarah.

Franklin became well-known for both his newspaper articles and his other writings, through which he advocated his personal and political beliefs. He created *Poor Richard's Almanac*, published annually between 1732 and 1757. The almanac introduced a number of common sayings into the American language, including "a penny saved is a penny earned" and "early to bed, early to rise, makes a man, healthy, wealthy, and wise." His *Autobiography* also exhorted Americans to follow the ideals of industry, morality, and frugality to achieve success. Franklin was also interested in science and was a member of the prestigious Royal Society. He wrote books on his scientific experiments and discoveries, including the 1751 *Experiments and Observations on Electricity*. His inventions include the Franklin stove, bifocal lenses, and the lightning rod.

Franklin was a renowned statesman with a lengthy political career and a prominent role in the American Revolutionary movement. He served in the Pennsylvania Assembly beginning in 1751 and represented Pennsylvania in Great Britain in 1757. He was a member of the Second Continental Congress that produced the Declaration of Independence in 1776. He also represented American interests in France in that same year, helping to secure French aid for the coming war with Britain. Franklin was also present at the negotiations that produced the 1783 Treaty of Paris, which ended the American Revolution. Franklin's long and distinguished American career came to an end upon his death on April 17, 1790. He was 84 years old.

Tocqueville's *Democracy in America*. Through the form of a fictional American farmer named James, he commented on developing American beliefs such as the work ethic, individual responsibility, and anti-intellectualism. He also put forth the small farmer as the key American character, an idea upon which later Americans such as Thomas Jefferson would expand.

MARCELLA TREVINO

Further Readings

Axtell, James. *The Invasion Within: The Contest of Cultures in Colonial North America*. New York: Oxford University Press, 1985.

Breen, T.H. "An Empire of Goods: The Anglicization of Colonial America, 1690–1776." *Colonial America: Essays in Politics and Social Development*. Stanley N. Katz, John M. Murrin, and Douglas Greenberg, eds. New York: McGraw-Hill, 1993.

Carson, Cary, Ronald Hoffman, and Peter J. Albert. *Of Consuming Interests: The Style of Life in the 18th Century*. Charlottesville: University Press of Virginia, 1994.

Hawke, David Freeman. *Everyday Life in Early America*. New York: Harper and Row, 1988.

Jordan, Winthrop D. *White Over Black: American Attitudes Toward the Negro, 1550–1812*. Chapel Hill: University of North Carolina Press, 1968.

Maier, Pauline. *From Resistance to Revolution: Colonial Radicals and the Development of American Opposition to Britain, 1765–1776*. New York: Alfred A. Knopf, 1972.

Polk, William K. *The Birth of America: From Before Columbus to the Revolution*. New York: HarperCollins, 2006.

Reich, Jerome R. *Colonial America*. Upper Saddle River, NJ: Prentice Hall, 1998.

Taylor, Dale. *Everyday Life in Colonial America from 1607–1783*. Cincinnati, OH: F&W Publications, 2002.

Tunis, Edwin. *Colonial Living*. Baltimore, MD: Johns Hopkins University Press, 1999.

Wolf, Stephanie G. *As Various As Their Land: The Everyday Lives of 18th Century Americans*. New York: HarperCollins, 1994.

CHAPTER 5

Cities and Urban Life

"They have purchased the island of Manhattes from the Indians for the value of 60 guilders..."
— Notification of the Purchase of Manhattan by the Dutch, November 5, 1626

THE INITIAL AMERICAN cities were established in the first two North American colonies, which were founded for vastly different reasons. Jamestown was established in 1607 in what would become Virginia by Englishmen seeking adventure and gold. The colony was almost wiped out from a combination of greed and harsh circumstances, never managing to reach the stature of latter settlements. Thirteen years after Jamestown was settled, a group of Protestant immigrants founded the Massachusetts Bay Colony to escape the restrictions of the Church of England within their home country. Many other immigrants who came to the New World in search of religious freedom, such as the Quakers who founded Philadelphia, were essential contributors to the founding of the cities that became population and trade centers.

By 1690 the most populous American cities were Boston (7,000), Philadelphia (4,000), New York (3,900), Newport (2,600), and Charleston (1,100). Within a century, Philadelphia and New York had passed the 25,000 mark, and Boston, Charleston, and Baltimore reported populations of over 10,000. Other significant cities of the late 17th century included Salem, Newport, Providence, Marblehead, Middletown, Portsmouth, New Haven, Savannah, Hartford, Lancaster, Richmond, Albany, New Bedford, Norfolk, Alexandria, and Annapolis. As the colonies prepared to take on the mother country to assert what they

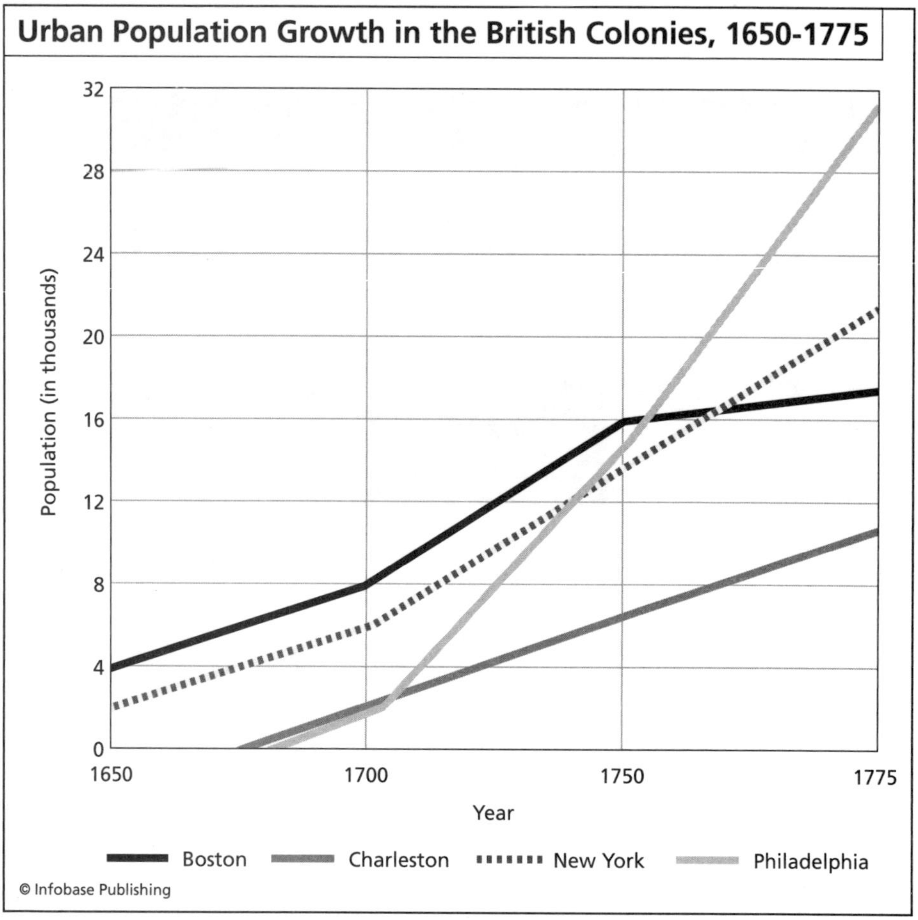

believed were their inherent rights as Englishmen, approximately 95 percent of the American population lived in rural areas.

Because of their locations on major waterways, Boston, Newport, New York, Philadelphia, and Charleston emerged as leading colonial trade centers. Forward-thinking city and business leaders developed an early interest in keeping their cities safe, economically successful, and competitive. They understood the importance of handling problems inherent in city life, developing policies for dealing with crime and poverty, and establishing public services designed to protect health and property.

The physical structure of American cities was often similar, containing public buildings such as churches and schools, gathering places such as taverns, and private homes ranging from the simple to the magnificent. Because England was the standard by which many colonists measured themselves, early American cities were often British in design and layout. However, daily life was different for Americans because class structures were less well defined, and people of all classes felt free to express opinions on political and social issues, both at informal gatherings and in public meetings.

City planning surfaced early in the American colonies, influenced not only by England, but by other countries that had settled in America. St. Augustine, Florida, for instance, mirrored the Spanish influence, just as New Orleans, Louisiana, reflected its French heritage. Within geographic regions, Philadelphia, Charleston, Savannah, and New Haven became focal points for the physical and economic development of their respective colonies. The English influence was particularly strong in cities such as Williamsburg, the first capital of Virginia. However, city planning in America would not come into its own until after the Revolutionary War.

EARLY CITIES

In comparison to English counterparts, early American cities were small. Even though economic interests dominated all others, there was surprisingly little competition among cities. Perhaps this was because local economies were based almost entirely on the natural resources specific to certain regions. In the northeast, lumber and livestock dominated, while tobacco and rice were produced in warmer southern cities. Without English-type trade guilds or restrictive city charters, American cities had a good deal of autonomy, which was at times limited by English representatives who governed American colonies according to their own whims.

In a failed attempt to discover the elusive Northwest Passage, Henry Hudson, a British captain working for the Dutch government, reached the river that later bore his name in 1609. Recognizing the significance of the region's vast resources, the Dutch established New Amsterdam in 1624. The English laid claim to the city in 1664, changing the name to New York and setting up a more formal system of city government. By 1680 the population of New York had climbed to 3,000, and trade was flourishing in New York City, where

A view of houses in Albany, New York, from the late 18th century. Albany was one of seven major colonial North American cities, and was a leading center for trade and commerce.

Other Early Colonial Cities

SANTA FE, NEW MEXICO. In 1540, Francisco Vasquez de Coronado, the governor of Spain's New Galicia, arrived in what became the New Mexico Territory in search of the mythical riches rumored to be hidden in the Seven Cities of Cibola, with orders to claim the land's resources for Spain. Instead of untold riches, Coronado found only Pueblo Indians who had occupied the land since the 11th century. In 1598 Juan de Onate was appointed governor and captain-general of a permanent Spanish settlement. The following year, he moved the capital to nearby Santa Fe, which became a trade center, linking Mexico City with its northern neighbors. In 1680 the Peublo Indians revolted, killing 400 settlers, driving others out of the area, and destroying most of Santa Fe. It was not until 1692 that don Diego de Vargas reclaimed the area for Spain. Seventy of the original adobe structures remain in historic Santa Fe.

ST. AUGUSTINE, FLORIDA. St. Augustine is the oldest permanent European settlement in the Americas. While searching for the fabled Fountain of Youth, Spanish explorer Ponce de Leon sighted the land he named Florida, "Land of Flowers," on Easter Day 1513. Attempts to settle the area failed until 1564 when the French managed to establish a settlement on the St. John's River. The Spanish responded by appointing Don Pedro Menendez de Aviles as governor and sending him to explore the territory. He arrived at Seloy, a Timucuan Indian village, on August 28, 1565, and renamed the site St. Augustine. Menendez evicted the French and began settling the area for Spain. Englishman Sir Francis Drake attacked and burned St. Augustine in 1586, and pirates such as John Davis plundered the town. After the Carolinas and Georgia were settled, the Spanish increased efforts to protect St. Augustine. In 1763 the British gained control of Florida, using the territory as a base of southern operations during the American Revolution. The United States bought Florida in 1821.

NEW ORLEANS, LOUISIANA. Located 20 feet below sea level and bordered by both the Mississippi River and Lake Pontchartrain, New Orleans is known as the "city that should never have been." Geography has been a problem since the area was selected as a means of providing a more direct route from Baton Rouge to the Gulf of Mexico in 1699. French founders recognized that the area had geographical, military, and commercial advantages. Jean Baptiste Le Moyne de Bienville founded a city there in 1718, naming it after Phillip II, the Duke of Orleans, and established it as the capital of French Louisiana. Once levees were erected to control encroaching waterways and swamps, New Orleans grew quickly, becoming a major trading and cultural center. New Orleans was planned by French engineer Adrien de Pauger along 18th-century European lines, with a central square surrounded by churches, walls, and towers. Over time, the French were forced to battle both Britain and Spain to maintain control of the city. President Thomas Jefferson obtained New Orleans in 1803 as part of the Louisiana Purchase.

growth was a natural response to the city's protected harbor, which provided easy access to the rest of the state.

Representative of many New England towns, Albany, New York, was chartered in 1686. Although founded to enhance the fur trade, Albany soon developed into the economic and political center of the state. The 120 buildings of early Albany included a city hall, Dutch Reformed and Lutheran churches, and a British fort. City buildings were surrounded by a wooden stockade that ensured the safety of city residents. Between 1697 and 1790, Albany's population grew from 714 to 3,498. Indicative of the city's growing culture base, *The Albany Gazette* printed its first edition in 1771.

Some scholars insist that the Puritans, who were responsible for founding many early American cities, were hostile to the idea of vast urban areas, opting for rural-style designs. Some New England cities, including Plymouth, Cambridge, New Haven, and Hartford, were modeled after Old Testament towns, which were laid out with nine smaller squares as opposed to the traditional central town square.

Typical of many early cities that required farmers to live within cities, William Penn organized Philadelphia as a network of farming communities to maintain a rural atmosphere and keep political and economic power in the hands of the landed gentry. Penn pledged 10 Philadelphia acres to anyone who would purchase 500 acres elsewhere in Pennsylvania.

Many modern suburban areas began as isolated farmland that grew into small farming cities. When urban decay set in during the mid-19th century, many wealthy Americans fled to surrounding rural areas, swelling populations. Development in such areas was highly dependent on access to water resources for domestic and farm use. The products that farmers grew were necessary to provide basics for their own families, and for townspeople who provided essential services to the entire area, such as physicians, ministers, store owners, and blacksmiths. As New England towns became overcrowded, city leaders developed policies that

Wood: The City Material

Colonials used a lot of wood for building, sawed from local timberyards. At a typical colonial timberyard, the customer would have a variety of products, variable by region, from a single plank to a full log. Sizes would be reasonably standard. Like a modern lumberyard, products would be displayed outside under some sort of protective cover. Wood would be stacked in marked piles or on end, allowing the buyer to inspect and approve before buying. The air would smell of wood, sawdust, sweat, and alcohol. Not too far away would be a saw pit, possibly manned by slaves in the south and freemen in the north.

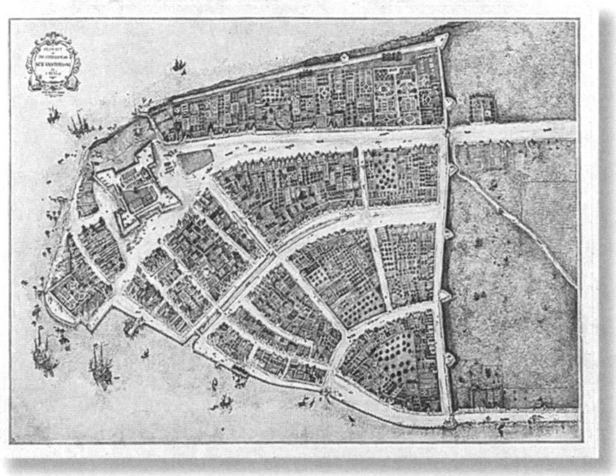

Above, Philadelphia's Elfreth Alley, dating from 1702. The 32 houses are privately owned and occupied, making it one of the oldest continuously inhabited residential streets in America.

At left, a map showing the residences and structures of the walled city known as New Amsterdam in 1660, now the southern tip of Manhattan in New York City. Wall Street, now in lower Manhattan, runs along the site of the original wall shown in the plan.

sought to keep out transients and undesirables and encouraged outward migration. in order to promote economic and social stability.

COMMERCIAL CITIES

Eighty percent of the American population during the colonial and revolutionary eras was located in coastal areas. Newport, Boston, Philadelphia, Charleston, and New York developed into the major port cities, with New London, Wilmington, Norfolk, and Savannah serving as satellite ports. Colonial merchants exploited Britain's trading dominance to amass huge fortunes from world trade. Within each port city, a cadre of support services developed, providing a wide range of employment opportunities and offering adventure to those brave enough to set sail for distant lands with American-grown products and return with items from around the world. Because none of the prominent trading groups were able to meet English demands directly, colonial traders became involved in a triangular trading route in which Americans used the profits from such products as tobacco to buy sugar and molasses from the Caribbean Islands. New England distillers used the sugar and molasses to produce rum for Britain, which English ship owners used to purchase African slaves to sell to the American colonies, particularly to the agrarian south.

Geography played a major part in fostering the autonomy and growth of early American cities. Along the Hudson River Valley, one of the first commercial American cities eventually developed into modern-day New York City, which became the financial center of the United States. The growth of port cities such as New York was less limited than that of inland New England towns, which tended to develop as tightly knit communities.

Populations of port cities were generally heterogeneous, comprised of different classes, ethnicities, races, and religious backgrounds. Dependent on the safety of seagoing vessels and the stability of production and markets, port city economies could change quickly. Easy accessibility by water made port towns more vulnerable to attack by outside forces. For instance, during King George's War (1744–48), Boston became a city in mourning, with widows outnumbering married women seven to three. Many families were left with no means of financial support. Boston city leaders responded by establishing almshouses. Philadelphia, on the other hand, managed to avoid

The capital of South Carolina, Charleston was the only significant southern seaport. The city was fortified with walls for protection against enemies, and used a grid pattern for its streets.

A Man Full of Trouble Tavern is the only surviving pre-revolutionary tavern in Philadelphia. Taverns, or public houses, were the center of social, business, and political activity in cities.

much of the devastation of the war, and costs for public relief remained minimal. As populations increased throughout the American colonies, all major cities were forced to provide some form of public relief. By the 18th century, Philadelphia and New York had also built almshouses to house colonials who were poor, disabled, physically or mentally ill, young, or elderly, as well as for prostitutes, vagrants, and other "undesirables."

In the deep south, South Carolina developed into the richest city in the colonies, claiming nine of America's 10 wealthiest men as residents. In Governor James Glen's official reports of 1750, he estimated that 80 percent of the population was able to afford the necessities of life. Although South Carolina's people included the middle and working classes, economic and social power remained in the hands of the other 20 percent who were classified as affluent. Over half of the colony's population was composed of African slaves who were instrumental in producing the rice and indigo that fueled South Carolina's economy.

Charleston, the capital of South Carolina, was a cultural mecca for many southerners in colonial times. Class lines were fluid but well defined, with elites composed of aristocrats; successful doctors, lawyers, and merchants; and wealthy landowners. Both social and economic links were strong among Charlestonian elites, enforced by generations of intermarriages and business dealings. The second layer of Charleston society was made up of artisans, including silversmiths, bricklayers, and craftsmen, who provided essential services to the city. Shop owners and less successful professionals such as physicians and lawyers were also classified as middle-class, but success sometimes propelled them into the ranks of the elite. The working-class was composed of sailors, day laborers, journeymen, and apprentices. Slaves, who sometimes comprised as much as 80 percent of the colony's population, were divided into artisans, house servants, and field hands, with assigned privileges equivalent to individual ranks.

Charleston's influence stretched outside of South Carolina's borders, in large part because the city was the only major seaport in the South. Charlestonian merchants established trading routes with those in other American colonies as well as with the merchants of England, the West Indies, and Portugal. During

Colonial Cities and the Birth of Insurance

The establishment of an insurance industry in the American colonies was essential because it affected the ways in which cities were laid out and protected the lives and health of colonists. In 1721 insurance agent John Copson opened the first colonial insurance office near Penn's Landing in Philadelphia. Although his specialty was selling marine insurance, Copson, who developed an expertise for self-promotion, extended his interests to pubs, newspapers, and coffee and tea houses. He enticed buyers and sellers of insurance into building roads, wharves, and harbors and making trade more stable. By 1758 the London Coffee House had become the center of the insurance industry in Philadelphia, employing 150 underwriters in 15 separate offices.

In 1724 notary Joseph Marion opened a more traditional marine insurance office in Boston. This office was the first full-service operation in the colonies, allowing buyers and sellers of insurance to meet in a business-like atmosphere. Marion was more low-keyed than Copson, and he refused to push underwriters toward insuring vessels when they did not wish to do so.

Fire insurance was not sold in America until the mid-18th century because it required a greater commitment of capital than insuring voyages for relatively short periods. Mutual companies in which policy holders became investors were created to deal with the low-capital problem. Charleston's Friendly Society, established in 1775, failed due to lack of capital. By the middle of the 18th century, insurance was well established in America, although a shortage of capital continued to be a widespread problem. Many colonial Americans turned to better-financed London companies such as Lloyd's Coffee House to meet their insurance needs. It was not until the 1790s when Secretary of the Treasurer Alexander Hamilton succeeded in reforming the banking industry that America's insurance industry became a stable enterprise.

The London Coffee House served as the early focus of Philadelphia's political and commercial life and was its insurance center by 1758.

the latter colonial period, Charleston was ranked with Boston, New York, Philadelphia, and Newport as the most important American seaports. Built along European lines, Charleston was walled to offer protection from hostile natives and would-be invaders from around the world. The streets were laid out in grids. Commercial warehouses, stores, and other port-related enterprises were located along the banks of the Cooper River. Elsewhere on the peninsula, state and public buildings were interspersed with homes and businesses.

The wealthiest Charlestonians lived on plantations or in large city houses, and wore clothing imported from England. Housing for the middle-class was generally cramped, and many store owners lived over their shops. The middle-class made their own clothing. Housing and clothing for slaves was dependent on individual standing and on the whims of plantation owners. Like most cities of the time, animals ran loose throughout the streets, and sanitation was primitive. The lack of a local police force meant that Charleston's streets were unsafe after dark, and wealthy Charlestonians ventured out at their own risk.

Charleston's strong sense of culture produced the most sophisticated theater anywhere in the American colonies, and one of the first lending libraries. The city's three newspapers were distributed throughout the Carolinas, Georgia, and western Florida. Other entertainments focused on horse races, coffee houses, and taverns. By the late 18th century, the similarities in America's port cities began to decline as New York gained in prominence. New York's geographical advantages were considerable, consisting of a deep-water harbor that was navigable throughout the year, the Hudson River, easy access to inland areas, and a central location. New York's prosperity drew the wealthy and the adventurous, and its port was filled with people and goods. By this time, the colonists had begun to develop a political sense of themselves as Americans with strong loyalties to individual colonies. Yet, European tastes were still in evidence in architecture, clothing designs, and cultural tastes. The Dutch influence gave way in New York as European-style entertainments flourished, offering New Yorkers their choice of clubs, concerts, balls, and theaters. The shores of the Hudson were dotted with magnificent homes, some of which may still be viewed in the Hudson River Historic District.

CLASS STRUCTURE

In general class structure in the American colonies was much different than in England. While there were some who classified themselves as aristocrats, the majority of the population in the northern colonies was made up of individuals who worked hard to make lives better for themselves and their families. These hard-working Americans included farmers, merchants, fishermen, artisans, and craftsmen.

A large number of immigrants had come to the colonies to seek their fortunes because English inheritance laws left all family property in the hands of older brothers. Many from working-class backgrounds came to America as

"Gezicht op Nieuw York" by Johannes Vingboons (1664). An early picture of New Amsterdam made in the year when it became the British territory of New York.

indentured servants; some worked as seamen to pay for passage. American immigrants were of various races, ethnicities, and religions. In the northern and middle colonies, the majority of immigrants were of European ancestry, while residents of African and Native American descent tended to be shunted to the fringes of society.

Because Quakers were generally against slavery, there were initially few slaves in Philadelphia. Menial jobs were performed for the most part by indentured servants who worked from four to seven years to buy their freedom while learning a trade or skill. Throughout the 1730s and 1740s large numbers of indentured servants came from Scotland, Ireland, and Germany. Some Africans and Native Americans also hired themselves out as indentured servants. The majority of female indentured servants worked as domestic servants. Farmers contracted for seasonal labor to meet the demands of the growing season. Immigrants in search of steady jobs found them in tanneries, mills, inns, and foundries.

While Europe struggled to hold onto their colonies during the Seven Years' War (1564–70), the supply of immigrants and slaves temporarily dried up, driving up prices and wages. After the war, immigration resumed, but the price of slaves remained high. Many Americans saw apprenticeships as having a strong advantage over slavery and indenture. Apprentices were usually white, and they ranged from young men learning to become lawyers or physicians by working with respected members of their professions, to butchers, blacksmiths, and printers.

In most cities of the colonial period, political leaders understood their roles as regulators of economic and social activities and protectors of the general welfare. They accomplished these goals by exercising considerable control over who resided in individual colonies. Boston was less restrictive than some areas and granted all property owners the right of participating in town meetings. However, in much of the Massachusetts Bay Colony, citizenship was reserved for "freemen" who were viewed as upstanding men interested in leading moral lives and promoting the community good.

In some cities, freemanships were sold to bring in revenue and establish control over the trading process. Other city revenues were raised by charging stallholders fees for selling agricultural products on market day. Trading rules were strictly controlled, and violators were fined, sometimes losing the right to participate in city markets. Several cities exercised the right to confiscate the merchandise of nonfreemen violators. In Boston, farmers sold their products door-to-door rather than at a general market. By the 19th century most cities had relaxed municipal control, allowing free trade to develop.

As was true in Charleston and other southern cities, elites in northern and middle colonies tended to have strong links to other elites. Yet America's urban elites did not cluster in a narrow range of occupations as they often did in Europe. Family ties and religion exercised strong influences on American class lines; yet those lines were more loosely drawn, without a single religion dominating others as with the Church of England. At the same time populations expanded, encompassing a wider range of cultures. As Enlightenment thought took hold in America, a new understanding developed concerning political and economic rights, which Thomas Jefferson defined in the Declaration of Independence as the right "to pursue happiness." After natural rights were identified, religious and civic powers began to decline.

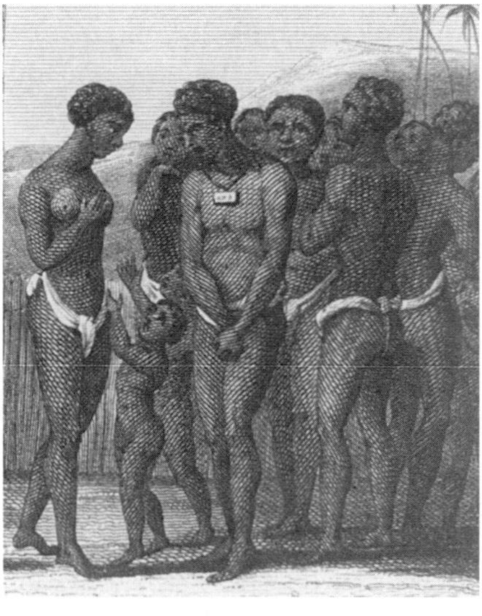

A print titled "Slaves exposed for sale." By 1800 there were already 16,000 Africans living in New England, most of them slaves.

As a center of trade and communication, New York had attracted immigrants from all cultures and religions since its days as Dutch New Amsterdam. One of the religious immigrant groups that played a major role in settling New York was the Jewish people who had arrived in New Amsterdam in 1654. Other Jews had arrived even earlier, reaching Sir Walter Raleigh's Lost Colony of Roanoke in 1597. A group of Jewish immigrants came to

Jamestown, Virginia, on the second ship that touched land in 1608. In less than a century 250 Jews had settled in Jamestown. In New Amsterdam, Jews contributed to the economy as traders, merchants, and landowners. However they were forced to worship in private homes after the Dutch refused their request to build a synagogue for worship. In 1730, the first temple was finally erected on Mill Street.

Jewish immigrants first arrived in Philadelphia around 1710, but it was not until 1735 that Nathan Levy, a merchant and ship owner, built the first Jewish cemetery in Pennsylvania on land purchased for that purpose. Jewish immigrants faced fewer barriers in Rhode Island cities than in many others. The first settlers arrived in Newport from Barbados, establishing the Congregation Jeshuat Israel in 1702. A permanent temple was built in Newport in 1763. Jews, like other immigrants, were welcomed in the South, and Charleston's first temple was built in 1797.

In New England and the middle colonies, Native-American women were sometimes used as house servants. In this capacity, they were given responsibility for such domestic chores as sewing, baking, washing clothes, and dairying. In southern states, Native Americans were used to meet the labor shortage and often worked in fields alongside African slaves. Outside the south, a class of urban slaves developed, but this slavery never became integral to the economy as African slavery did in the agrarian south. The urban slavery of Native Americans petered out during the American Revolution.

URBAN SLAVES

Urban slaves were trained as coopers, carpenters, weavers, wheelwrights, and butchers. The south also had urban slaves, but they were less common than in other parts of the American colonies. In 1743 the city government of Charleston passed a law banning Native and African slaves from skilled trades in order to attract white immigrants to the colony.

Most colonial cities used Native American and African slaves for backbreaking manual labor, such as building fortifications. New York passed an ordinance in the early 1690s that mandated slave participation in erecting fortifications, and in 1638 Hartford classified slaves along with cattle as necessary elements in providing public services.

By 1700 1,000 African slaves were residing in New England; and over the next century, that number grew to 16,000. Many had come to the area as children and by colonial times made up a significant percent of urban slave populations. In South Kingston, Rhode Island, 30 percent of the population was slaves; and slaves made up nine percent of New London's residents. On the eve of the American Revolution New York's urban slave population was second only to Charleston's. Throughout the colonies, urban slaves worked at varied tasks that ranged from shipbuilding and trade to teaching music and gardening. One urban slave even worked as a dog catcher.

Starting in 1750, whenever elections were held, urban slaves celebrated their own "'Lection Day" with much frivolity, selecting their own governors and kings. Whole days in which slaves were allowed to enjoy themselves away from their owners were rare. Urban slaves tended to be better fed and clothed than plantation slaves, but they also constantly faced the threat of violence and experienced a similar high rate of infant mortality. Many female slaves were raped; and in the south, many were forced to serve as concubines. On southern plantations, slaves often lived in families, but family units remained together according to owners' whims. Urban slaves were less likely to live with their families. Instead they were relegated to kitchens, stables, and laundries. Urban slaves did, however, have more control over their daily movements than those on plantations and farms.

Slavery was legal in all 13 colonies. When the American Revolution started, African slaves made up 20 percent of the population. Slavery had started in the American colonies in 1641 in Massachusetts. In Pennsylvania slavery had been established even before William Penn and his group of Quaker settlers arrived there in 1682. By the beginning of the 18th century, Pennsylvania's slave population had risen to around 19 percent. In the 1720s Pennsylvania suffered an economic depression, and the slave population declined to eight percent. During the following decade, Queen Anne's War signaled a return to prosperity, and slave prices dropped to record lows. Slave-owning proliferated in both urban and rural areas. By mid-century, urban slavery was on the wane; but in rural areas where slaves were considered essential, even the Quaker aversion to slavery was not sufficient to stop the number of slaves from multiplying eightfold.

AMUSEMENTS IN CITIES

Colonial newspapers served to entertain as well as inform. *The Boston News-Letter*, established in 1704, was the first colonial newspaper. *The Boston Gazette* was founded 15 years later. Newspapers in virtually every colonial town offered both foreign and domestic news, as well as editorials. Columns were filled with news of runaway slaves, local advertisements, crime reports, and political satire. The first political cartoon in colonial America was printed in the *New York Weekly Journal*. Afterward cartoonist John Peter Zenger was charged with libeling Governor William Cosby.

Religious activities formed the core of social activity in most colonial cities. Throughout the colonies individuals and groups used their own knowledge and interests to entertain and educate their neighbors. In Philadelphia internationally acclaimed astronomer David Rittenhouse built a mechanical model to detail the workings of the solar system, and Quaker botanist and naturalist John Bartram, who was designated by George III as "royal botanist," created a botanical garden that still exists today.

Native Americans were also avid gardeners. They created herb and fruit gardens centuries before the first European settlers came to America. Later

An 18th-century urban garden near Independence Hall in downtown Philadelphia. Wealthy colonials in cities built large homes, imported expensive furniture, and grew elaborate gardens.

on, immigrant gardeners combined elements of native gardens with English-style gardening to create herb and fruit gardens to surround their homes. Few of those gardens reached beyond the status of cottage gardens. Typical crops included cabbage, corn, and beans. Flowers were generally grown in front of houses or placed in windows. Popular flower varieties included hollyhocks, rosemary, pennyroyal, coriander, and sweetbriar. The most famous gardens in the individual colonies usually belonged to governors, including William Endicott of Salem and Governor John Winthrop of Plymouth. The historic gardens of Charleston date to 1682.

Gambling was a favorite activity in colonial America, and urban resident placed bets on horse races, cock fighting, dog fighting, wrestling, bear baiting, and ball games. Other popular amusements included playing cards and rolling dice. City resident of all ages took part in dancing, singing, and playing music. Where available and not prohibited, city elites frequented theaters. Because water and other beverages often presented health hazards, drinking alcohol was a way of life in the colonies. As might be expected, it was also turned into a social activity. Rum was the general beverage of choice. Members of the upper class also drank brandy and wine, while members of the lower classes were satisfied with hard cider and home-brewed beer.

PUBLIC SERVICES

Almost from the beginning, city officials became involved in providing basic services to local residents to ensure general safety and promote a reasonable quality of life. By the middle of the 18th century, class distinctions in America were becoming more clearly defined, and it became necessary to provide assistance to the poor to maintain stability. Increasing prosperity had provided the wealthy with the means to build palatial homes and fill them with furniture imported from Europe. As a result, crime became a major problem. Rioters frequently targeted the homes of the wealthy, even when their purpose of a riot was a product of growing hostility against the mother country. Punishments were often severe, and executions by hanging, burning, and drawing and quartering were attended by the public. Because sanitation was so poor during the colonial period, epidemics of yellow fever, smallpox, dysentery, typhoid, and typhus were common. Urban poor often lived in squalid, overcrowded conditions that served as breeding grounds for the growth of bacteria and heightened chances of spreading germs and contaminating others.

FIREFIGHTERS AND POLICE

The first recorded fire in North America occurred in the first settlement, Jamestown, Virginia. In January 1608 a raging fire destroyed most of Jamestown's wooden structures and stripped settlers of their meager possessions. As American cities grew and developed, it became clear that firehouses would be necessary to deal with fires that were common in daily life. In 1631 the city of Boston passed an ordinance outlawing wooden chimneys and thatched

Colonial Education

In early colonial America parents were responsible for educating their children. They had no government agencies to guide or hamper them. Local taxpayers and often private groups financed common schools. Specialized private schools included church schools, college preparation academies, dame schools, charity schools, and seminaries. Those who had the means relied on private tutors. The first common schools arose in Massachusetts to teach Calvinist Puritanism and preserve social order.

These schools were modeled on those of Martin Luther and the German princes. The first compulsory school law was the Old Deluder Satan Act of 1647. Over time, as New England prospered, the public schools became lax, and private schools appeared to teach commercial arts. By 1700 Boston's private schools outnumbered its public ones, and by the time of the Revolution many Massachusetts towns had no public schools.

roofs. In the 1670s in response to the activities of arsonists and a major fire, a local iron maker, Joseph Jynks, invented the first American water pump. When the pump proved unreliable, the city ordered a modern English fire engine, which was simply a wooden box with handles containing a direct-force pump. The first organized firefighting activities began in New Amsterdam (later New York). Governor Peter Stuyvesant appointed four fire wardens in 1648 and charged them with inspecting all chimneys to identify fire hazards and levying fines against those who refused to abide by anti-fire restrictions. Later on a volunteer fire watch was instituted, manned by eight prominent citizens known as the Rattle Watch who walked the streets at night to spot fires as soon as they broke out, notifying volunteers who set up bucket brigades to fight fires. By 1678 Boston had created its own firefighting team under the leadership of Captain Thomas Atkins. New York continued to serve as a model for firefighting technology, and Jacob Turck, who bore the responsibility for keeping New York's fire engines in repair invented the first American mechanical fire pumper. In Philadelphia, statesman and inventor Benjamin Franklin took a personal interest in firefighting, founding the volunteer Union Fire Company in 1736, and organizing the Philadelphia Contributorship in 1740 to insure homeowners against loss by fire.

Law enforcement in the colonies developed along English lines, with each city bearing the responsibility for policing its streets and neighborhoods. Night watches were established to patrol the streets and look for signs of problems and maintain order. Constables were elected at the local level, but governors appointed sheriffs who oversaw the entire law enforcement process. Colonial policing responsibilities included keeping slaves and Native Americans in line, maintaining public order, regulating community markets, controlling crimes such as vice, preventing public indecency, monitoring litter and pests, and protecting general community welfare. In southern states, posses were sometimes used to maintain control over slaves and search for runaways. Slave patrols were often large. Charleston's slave patrol, for instance, was comprised of 100 members.

CITY CULTURE

Even those Americans who railed against Britain politically believed the English set the standards for fashion and culture, and wealthy Americans regularly purchased such items as wigs, snuffboxes, books, and clothing materials from Europe. Despite strong ties to the English way of life, American cities developed their own identities. Immigrants came from around the world to lay claim to the vast opportunities offered in the colonies, swelling the American population from 250,000 in 1700 to 2.5 million in 1775. Not all of those immigrants had come willingly; nearly 20 percent of that population were brought to America as African slaves.

Large numbers of European immigrants used their educations, professional acumen, and work skills to help establish American cities, bringing parts of their own culture to each area in which they settled. European settlers who had enjoyed concerts, plays, and museums in their homelands were initially forced to settle for quieter entertainments such as impromptu home concerts and reading the few books and newspapers that were available. By 1750 seekers after knowledge and culture were more fortunate, since most cities had their own newspapers. Philadelphia even had its own lending library, established by local resident Benjamin Franklin.

Once theater companies were established, they became a major element in colonial culture. They were supported in large part by a network of Masonic lodges whose members included actors, theater managers, politicians, merchants, and art lovers. The fact that lodges owned their own theaters gave them total control over the plays that were performed on their premises, even when city leaders had banned the material elsewhere. After the American Revolution, theaters continued to display an English flavor, frequently highlighting the talents of actors who had honed their skills in Europe. The types of plays performed in American theaters varied according to city characteristics. Theater goers in port cities such as Norfolk enjoyed nautical themes. In cities that had been founded by the Spanish, religious themes were favored by missionaries who used theater to promote the teachings of their religion.

SOUTHERN THEATER

Southerners were considered more receptive than other Americans to the theater. The theater built in Williamsburg, Virginia, in 1716 is considered the first permanent American theater. Williamsburg's cultural offerings were improved greatly in 1752 when Lewis Hallam brought his London company to the city to perform William Shakespeare's *Merchant of Venice*. Hallam later opened in New York, where the city's first permanent theater was erected in 1732. Charlestonians built their first permanent theater four years later.

In some smaller American cities, particularly those where Puritan ethics were strong, journalists and members of the public sometimes considered the theater low-class entertainment, verging on the edge of immorality. Denied the opportunity to announce upcoming plays, actors in those cities were forced to deliver handbills to promote their work and attract audiences. In 1750 Massachusetts officially banned all theater. Nine years later Pennsylvania made producing and performing plays punishable by a fine of £500. In 1761 Rode Island also banned theater, and New Hampshire went so far as to deny actors admission to the colony because they were considered threats to morality. Despite such restrictions, theater continued to flourish in the colonies, and some cities officially authorized performances. In general larger cities tended to be more urban and progressive, placing fewer restrictions on performances.

Elizabeth Purdy
John Barnhill

Further Readings

Bridenbaugh, Carl. *Cities in the Wilderness: The First Century of Urban Life in America, 1625–1742*. New York: Oxford University Press, 1938.
Bridenbaugh, Carl. *Cities in Revolt: Urban Life in America, 1743–1776*. New York: Oxford University Press, 1955.
Edgar, Walter B. and Henry H. Lesesne. "Everyday Life in Colonial South Carolina." Available online, URL: http://www.itv.scetv.org/schistory/chapter9.pdf. Accessed June 2007.
Gilje, Paul A. *The Road to Mobocracy: Disorder in New York City , 1763–1834*. Chapel Hill: University of North Carolina Press, 1987.
Hashagan, Paul. "Firefighting In Colonial America." Available online, URL: http://www.ksffa.com/firefighting_in_colonial_america.htm. Accessed June 2007.
Hornblow, Arthur. "The First American Theatre." In *A History of the Theatre in America*. Philadelphia: J.B. Lippincott Company, 1919.
Kritzer, Amelia Howe. "Performance, Theater, and Culture in the Colonial Americas and Early United States." *William and Mary Quarterly Reviews of Books* (v.64/2, June 2007).
Lawrence, Lee. "Chronicling Black Lives in Colonial New England." *The Christian Science Monitor* (October 29, 1997).
Monkkonen, Eric H. *America Becomes Urban: The Development of U.S. Cities and Towns, 1780–1980.* Berkeley: University of California Press, 1988.
Nash, Gary B. *The Urban Crucible: Social Change, Political Consciousness, and the Origins of the American Revolution*. Cambridge, MA: Harvard University Press, 1979.
New York State Museum. "Albany: An Early American City," Available online, URL: http://www.nysm.nysed.gov/albany/earlycity. Accessed June 2007.
Turner, Tom. "American Colonial Gardens and Nineteenth Century Landscape Architecture." Available online, URL: http://www.gardenvisit.com/got/18/11.htm. Accessed June 2007.

CHAPTER 6

Rural Life

"My farm is small, my servants few, and good;
I have a little money at interest; I wish for no more."
— John Dickinson

PERMANENT COLONIZATION OF North America by the English began with the establishment of Jamestown in 1607. Over the next 100 years various individuals and groups with different motivations would help the establishment of British colonies in North America. By the early 1700s the early settlement phase of English colonization resulted in the foundation of 13 distinct colonies. Patterns of settlement in the northern, mid-Atlantic, and southern colonies predetermined the lifestyles of each area. Towns and cities were slow to develop in colonial America. By the outbreak of the American Revolution in 1776, the major cities of colonial North America were limited to Boston, Charleston, New York, and Philadelphia. However the colonies all remained linked by the fact that 90 percent of colonists were involved in agriculture, and they lived some type of rural lifestyle for much of the period between 1607 and 1783.

The settlement and growth of the Virginia colony was largely determined by the motivations and goals of the first settlers who arrived at what would be Jamestown in 1607. The men and boys who arrived in Jamestown under the leadership of Captain John Smith were interested in one main goal—the discovery of gold and riches similar to those treasures found by Spanish conquistadors in Central and South America. The original 104 inhabitants of Jamestown were slow to realize that the riches of Virginia would not be found in gold or silver. It took several years before the Jamestown colonists realized that Virginia's wealth would be found in its fertile soil. John Rolfe, the man who would one day marry the famous Pocahontas, arrived in Jamestown in 1610, where he introduced the idea of growing tobacco as a cash crop to the settlers in Virginia. Within two years Rolfe had made a substantial amount of money by exporting his tobacco crops to England, and by 1622 tobacco was Virginia's main cash crop.

Throughout the next century, growth and development of the mid-Atlantic colonies (Delaware, New Jersey, New York, and Pennsylvania) and the southern colonies (Georgia, Maryland, North Carolina, South Carolina, and Virginia) remained tied to the agricultural endeavors of the colonies. The New England colonies (Connecticut, Massachusetts, New Hampshire, and Rhode Island) fared very differently due to the legacy of their founders. A group from England called Puritans, but more commonly known as the Pilgrims, initially settled the New England area. In November 1620, 102 men and women arrived aboard the *Mayflower* and established Plymouth Colony close to where land had initially been sighted near Cape Cod. The men and women aboard the *Mayflower* had traveled to the colonies with the sole purpose of establishing a place where they could live in freedom to worship as they pleased. They immediately began to create a permanent settlement. The Pilgrims sowed fields and built settlements. Other English Puritans who immigrated to the safe haven of Protestantism represented by New England soon followed the example set by the Pilgrims. By 1691 the number of Puritans who were emigrating from England to North America was so high that the newly established Massachusetts Bay Colony eventually absorbed the earlier Plymouth settlement.

Key differences in the settlement patterns of the New England colonies, compared with the mid-Atlantic and southern colonies, helped in the creation and the development of a distinct type of rural lifestyle in each area. Geographically there was less land available in the smaller colonies of New England compared

An 18th-century view of the countryside, with farm buildings along the roadway in the mid-Atlantic region. Growth and development of these colonies were tied to agricultural endeavors.

Letters from a Farmer in Pennsylvania

by John Dickinson

"I am a farmer, settled after a variety of fortunes near the banks of the River Delaware in the province of Pennsylvania. I received a liberal education and have been engaged in the busy scenes of life; but am now convinced that a man may be as happy without bustle as with it."

Between December 1767 and February 1768 lawyer and plantation owner John Dickinson published a series of 12 letters in the *Pennsylvania Chronicle* regarding his opinions on the significance of the Townshend Acts. The British parliament had passed the Townshend Acts in July 1767 to raise money by taxing colonists in order to pay for a large war debt dating from 1763. Great Britain had accumulated a very large financial debt while fighting the French and Indian War between 1755 and 1763 that remained unpaid in the years immediately following the end of the war. Following pieces of legislation such as the Stamp Act, the Townshend Acts were Parliament's latest attempt to pay off the war debt. The Townshend Acts went into effect in November 1767, much to the dismay of many American colonists.

Many colonists, including John Dickinson, argued that the creation and implementation of the laws in a Parliament where the colonists were not directly represented was an insult to the basic civil liberties to which any Englishman was entitled.

Dickinson wrote his letters, collectively referred to as *Letters from a Farmer in Pennsylvania to the Inhabitants of the British Colonies*, in order to encourage protest by the colonists against the Townshend Acts. Penned under the pseudonym of "a Farmer," Dickinson most likely identified himself as a simple farmer in order to have his writings appeal directly to the majority of the colonial population that lived in rural settings.

The 12 letters written by Dickinson became widely circulated in both the colonies and Great Britain. It attained immense popularity as many colonists came to understand what they believed to be the natural rights to which they were entitled as subjects of King George III and citizens of Great Britain. While Dickinson's letters advocated colonists to take a stand against unfair legislation as represented by the Townshend Acts, Dickinson's writings never advocated a complete colonial split from British control. In the years directly preceding the outbreak of the American Revolution, Dickinson's writings became immensely popular as patriotic literature, despite the author's original intent.

An 1876 print titled "New England Kitchen—A Hundred Years Ago" shows a typical home, crowded with family members and full of activity and the hard work for which the Puritans were known.

to the large tracts of land available for settlement in the south. Small farms remained the standard in the north, while larger farms and plantations were normal in the south. However, the average family size of colonists living in a rural setting remained quite large in both the north and the south. Immigration rates also affected the development of rural life in colonial North America. Statistically settlers moved to New England in larger numbers than to the south for much of the 17th and early 18th century. The impact of such immigration patterns influenced the social development of rural life throughout colonial America.

Eventually northern colonies began to run out of land to grant newly arrived settlers. Because the ability to participate in many aspects of formal society in New England was tied to property ownership, a lack of land represented a serious threat to the social stability of the constantly growing population of New England. As a result the New England colonies were forced to look to other avenues of business in order to define citizenship and social standing. Large-scale farming was no longer a feasible goal for those wishing to make money as upstanding members of northern society. Instead the close proximity of the New England colonies to the Atlantic Ocean eventually resulted in a concentration on trade. Ports began to boom in fast-growing cities such as Boston. Monetary wealth became the new marker of social status in the north. The Yankee trader quickly replaced the colonial New England stereotype of the Puritan settler.

As for the southern colonies, 17th-century immigration patterns resulted in a severe shortage of labor in an environment that was founded on the idea of an agricultural economy. Southern landholders tried to compensate for this labor shortage with the use of indentured servants in the late-17th century. The rising costs involved with replacing indentured servants who had fulfilled their debt eventually made the large-scale importation and utilization of African slaves more cost effective for southern planters in the early 18th century. While the "peculiar institution" of slavery became more popular in the mid-Atlantic and southern colonies, it was by no means limited geographically to the south, as slavery was legal in all 13 colonies until well into the late 1700s.

Over the years large-scale production of cash crops became the sole pursuit of many colonists living in the mid-Atlantic and southern regions. As a result a true dichotomy developed in the nature of the rural lifestyle embraced by people living in the north, compared to those who lived in the south. While the total population of colonial North America reached approximately 275,000 people by 1700, the majority of all the colonists continued to remain united in their embrace of some type of rural lifestyle.

RURAL LIFE IN THE NORTHERN COLONIES

In the early 18th century the nature of a rural lifestyle in the northern colonies of New England was markedly different from the rural lifestyle embraced by their southern counterparts. Farmers who lived in Connecticut, Massachusetts, New Hampshire, and Rhode Island lived on small parcels of land in communities bound together by a common Protestant religion. The legacy of the Puritans who had originally settled in the area a century before was a religious work ethic that strongly influenced men and women who lived in New England during the early 1700s. The Puritans believed that men and women had to work hard in their life on Earth so that they could be rewarded for their labors in the afterlife. The Puritans also believed that in order to live a good life, one had to be able to read the Bible. High literacy rates among the educated farming families, combined with the influence of the Protestant work ethic on the northern colonists, ensured the continued success of many New England families.

New England families were extremely patriarchal. Men and women would usually not marry until the man owned a significant amount of land upon

A wool carding comb, one of the essential tools of rural life in colonial times.

Eliza Lucas Pinckney, Colonial Horticulturist

Eliza Lucas Pinckney was born around December 1722, on the island of Antigua in the West Indies to British Army Lieutenant Colonel George Lucas. She was the eldest of four children. Eliza spent several years in England during her childhood attending a finishing school where her studies included French, music, and botany. In 1738 Eliza and her family moved to a plantation at Wappoo Creek, just outside of Charleston, South Carolina. Shortly after Eliza's arrival in South Carolina, Eliza's father was recalled to his land holdings in Antigua. As Elizabeth's mother was suffering from illness, Eliza's father appointed her as trustee to administer the family's plantation and other lands in South Carolina. Eliza's mother died shortly thereafter, leaving Eliza as guardian to her three younger siblings.

Beginning in 1739 Eliza's father sent her several species of plants from the Caribbean so that she could conduct various horticultural experiments. One of the plant species that Eliza experimented with was a form of indigo. The indigo plant produces a vivid blue dye that was in extremely high demand by textile factories in England, and it would be an attractive new cash crop to Eliza if she could find a way to cultivate it in South Carolina.

Between 1739 and 1744 Eliza spent an extraordinary amount of time and effort trying to figure out a way to grow indigo successfully. Throughout the 17th and early 18th centuries, tobacco and rice had been South Carolina's primary cash crops. By the mid-1740s, the exhausted soil in South Carolina made it difficult to continue raising tobacco. The agricultural future of South Carolina looked extremely grim until Eliza successfully harvested her first indigo crop in 1744. She made huge profits from her indigo crops, which encouraged other planters to follow her example. Eliza's experiments eventually revolutionized agriculture in South Carolina.

On May 27, 1744, Eliza married Charles Pinckney, an older widower who was a friend of her father's. The Pinckneys had a happy marriage that produced four children. After her marriage, Eliza spent most of her time divided between her husband's home in Charleston, their plantation of Cooper River, and England. Over the years Eliza continued her horticultural experiments working with fig trees, hemp, flax, and silk worms. In 1758 Eliza's husband died unexpectedly from malaria, leaving his widow to look after their young children and his extensive land holdings.

When war broke out between the colonies and Great Britain in 1776, Eliza and her family sided with the Patriots. During the southern campaign of the war, British forces decimated Eliza's plantations in South Carolina, leaving the family financially ruined. Eliza died in 1793 in Pennsylvania while seeking medical treatment. Her contributions to South Carolina's agricultural future were so significant that by the time of her death in 1793, indigo was second only to rice among South Carolina's exports.

which he could build a house and plant fields. A woman would usually bring household goods as a part of her dowry, such as bedding and linens, kitchen utensils, and basic furniture including a table and chairs. A typical one-story New England farmhouse was constructed of wood with an attached chimney. Because it was usually difficult to obtain significant parcels of land upon which such houses could be built, couples had to wait to marry. As a result men and women in New England usually married at a much later age than their southern counterparts. The average age of a first marriage for men and women in colonial New England was in the early 20s. Men and women had fewer children because they married at an older age. The average family in colonial New England had between six and eight children. The infant mortality rate was lower and the average life span was usually longer for the northern colonists than for those in the south. This combined with a steady stream of male and female immigrants from Great Britain caused the population of the northern colonies to double for several generations in the late 1600s and early 1700s.

All members of the family worked hard to ensure the collective success of the family farm. Daily farm life was scheduled around the seasons, with planting and harvesting times marking important milestones for celebrations, marriages, and other family events. The farms of the northern colonies initially raised agricultural products imported from Great Britain such as wheat, barley, hops,

Two yoked oxen at the Howell Living History Farm in Lambertville, New Jersey, demonstrate how cattle were used as draft animals.

Northern farmers did not rotate the crops in their fields, and the rocky New England soil would be severely depleted after only a few harvests, particularly when corn (above) was grown.

and rye. After several years some farmers included native crops, such as corn, in their harvests. Northern farmers would only till certain fields each season, allowing some fields to remain unused and fallow in hopes of avoiding land exhaustion. Unfortunately as northern farmers did not rotate their crops, the already rocky New England soil would usually be severely depleted after only a few harvests, particularly when corn was grown. Hesitant to use animal fertilizers to replenish the soils, northern farmers did not make any progress at growing excess crops, until they realized crop rotation would work better than letting fields lie fallow.

By the early 1700s, land shortages combined with the difficulty that existed in producing large harvests forced northern farmers to turn to alternative business endeavors such as the forestry and fishing. Farmers who were unwilling to make the transition supplemented their crop harvests by raising livestock such as cows and pigs. By the mid-1700s farmers in areas like Massachusetts were using almost 90 percent of their land for pastures as opposed to crops.

Farmers were able to produce dairy goods such as butter, cheese, and milk, as well as salted meat, by raising livestock. Farmers who continued to grow traditional crops eventually abandoned the production of grain harvests. Instead crops such as tuber plants, which included potatoes, turnips, onions, and carrots, became quite popular. Farmers also seeded large apple orchards

The Atlantic Slave Trade

The first recorded instance of African slaves being purchased in the British colonies of North America occurred in 1619, when a Dutch ship arrived in Jamestown with 19 slaves for sale. The most common modern definition of slavery does not necessarily fit the historical context of the institution that dominated the early modern Atlantic world from approximately 1450 to 1850.

Throughout history the definition of slave has primarily meant one whose freedom was owned by another. Before the advent of the African slave trade, more commonly referred to as the Atlantic slave trade, the word *slave* was not synonymous with one's race. Slavery was indicative of a social status, the place in society to which one was entitled. Atlantic world slavery changed this notion so much that it varied extremely from other forms of slavery previously practiced.

Throughout the 17th century British colonists purchased African slaves in small numbers. The two most common forms of slave management were via the task system or via the gang system. A slave ordered to work via the task system was given a certain amount of tasks to complete each day. With their owner's permission, slaves serving under the task system often spent their free time learning a skilled trade or working for another person for a fee. Task system slaves could earn their own money, which might eventually go toward buying their own freedom.

The alternative form of slave management was the gang system, a much more brutal system that offered no money or chance for freedom. By the beginning of the 18th century indentured servitude became a less cost-effective source of labor for colonists. It was cheaper for colonists to import African slaves whom they would own for life. In order to ensure the constancy of a work force, many colonists who owned slaves eventually turned away from the continued use of the task system and embraced the gang system.

In September 1739 a group of disenfranchised African slaves under the leadership of a slave from Angola named Jemmy rebelled against their owners. This slave uprising, known as Stono's Rebellion, was the first recorded violent slave revolt in the history of British North America. Although the owners quickly put down the rebellion, the memory of Stono's Rebellion bred fear and distrust between white owners and African slaves. Early the next year the state legislature of South Carolina passed a harsh slave code called the South Carolina Negro Law of 1740, making it illegal for slaves to earn their own money or to learn to read.

Slave owners were also granted the power to kill rebellious slaves to protect the greater social good. While there was never another major slave revolt in the colonial era, such harsh measures as represented by South Carolina's example proved indicative of how the institution of slavery would be governed in North America during the antebellum period.

that would allow for the production of such goods as cider and vinegar. As time passed and northern farmers moved from subsistence farming to excess crop production, markets developed to facilitate trade. The northern markets eventually grew largest in settlements with access to the ocean. As a result port cities like Boston grew and prospered in an astonishingly short period. The close proximity of the northern farms to ports where their goods could be traded to other colonies and Great Britain eventually led to the birth of the merchant class and town life in New England by the mid-1750s.

RURAL LIFE IN THE MID-ATLANTIC AND SOUTHERN COLONIES

By 1700 colonists living in the mid-Atlantic and southern colonies had made a firm commitment to establishing an economy based solely on agriculture. Following the example of Virginia colonists who grew tobacco as a cash crop for export, people who lived in the other southern colonies tried to find cash crops to grow successfully on their various lands.

The mid-Atlantic colonies, often seen as the breadbasket of colonial North America, focused on growing grains such as wheat. With their close proximity to the New England colonies where trade began to boom in the mid-18th century, colonists in the mid-Atlantic colonies dabbled in some forms of trade that contributed to the growth of port cities like New York and Philadelphia. Such trade attracted skilled artisans and laborers to emigrate to New York and Pennsylvania from places like Germany and the Netherlands. However most colonists remained firm in their commitment to agricultural endeavors.

The population of the southern colonies remained somewhat small compared to the boom growth rates of New England. Immigration trends aside, weather contributed significantly in keeping the southern population small. The extreme heat of the southern climates made it very hard for people from Great Britain to adapt to living in places like Virginia, the Carolinas, or Georgia. The warm weather also attracted disease-carrying insects in the wet climate of the south. Diseases such as cholera, dysentery, malaria, small pox, and yellow fever resulted in high mortality rates. Social isolation was also an issue, as the huge tracts of land available for settlement resulted in farms spreading out over many miles. Geographic isolation eventually resulted in a type of social isolation whereby one's circle of friends and enemies was often limited to close neighbors. The social culture of the South eventually developed a strict hierarchy that could be broken down into three very distinct classes.

The members of the most wealthy and influential class were known as planters. The planter class represented the smallest of three classes according to population. Planter families owned huge tracts of land that they often subdivided into more than one plantation. The planters would build large Georgian mansions on the plantations and spend huge amounts of money to furnish their houses with the best possible goods imported from Europe. The planter families often purchased large numbers of slaves to work their lands. Successful crop harvests resulted in large profits from the sale of tobacco, rice, and indigo. The members of the planter class were often descended from families that had settled in the colonies from the earliest periods. They also owned parcels of land that were centrally located for easy access to methods of transportation, so their goods could easily be sold at ports like Charleston. As a result the planter class was seen as the most socially elite group in the south. They exercised the most political power in colonies like Virginia and the Carolinas.

The members of the second level in the social hierarchy were known as yeoman farmers. Yeoman farmers owned plots of land that were smaller than plantations. While yeoman farmers planted the same crops as planters, they often could only afford to own a limited number of slaves to work their lands. As yeoman farmers were often descended from colonists who came to North America after the initial waves of settlement, the parcels of land that they owned were further inland than the lands claimed by the planters. This meant that any excess crops that the yeoman farmers wanted to sell demanded overland transport to market. The costs of transporting their goods cut into an already small profit margin.

The third and lowest class in the social hierarchy of the white settlers of the south consisted of tenant farmers. Tenant farmers often rented land from other owners. They worked very small parcels of land and conducted subsistence farming. Tenant farmers rarely owned any slaves, forcing them to conduct all the farming labor themselves. The parcels of land that tenant farms might try to purchase from other landholders were often located on the colonial frontier. As a result, their holdings were at greater risk for attack from native tribes than any other group.

By the late 1600s and early 1700s African slaves represented a distinct social class. Although in the early 1600s, African Americans brought in by traders from the Caribbean islands were treated as indentured servants, patterns of discrimination, both informal and legislated, began to emerge. By late in the 1600s, African-American servants were held to lifetime bondage. To ensure that mixed-race children of such slaves would remain slaves, laws began to define the condition of children as that of their mothers, since nearly all inter-racial children were fathered by white men and African women. As a consequence of these and other laws, the number of free Africans in the colonial south remained very small, while the number of slaves increased both through the survival of births over deaths and through the continued importation of slaves from the Caribbean.

Discontent from the yeoman and tenant farmers ultimately caused the first major colonial rebellion in British North America. Between the summer and fall of 1676 a yeoman planter from Virginia named Nathaniel Bacon marched on the colony's capital of Jamestown with an armed group of rebels. Bacon represented the discontented yeoman and tenant farmers from the Virginia frontier, also known as the backcountry, which remained relatively unprotected from

Indian raids. The colonial legislature in Jamestown refused to allow the western yeoman and tenant farmers to defend themselves against Indian attacks by any means necessary. Bacon and other yeoman and tenant farmers resented this policy. They felt the tidewater gentry, who were members of the colonial legislature, were dictating unfair legislation. For three months Bacon and his men ravaged the colony in protest, even burning Jamestown to the ground. The rebellion ended when Bacon died from what others described as a "bloody flux" on October 23, 1676.

Bacon's Rebellion marked the first major clash between the various classes of the southern elite. It ultimately determined that some type of concessions by the planter class to the yeoman and tenant farmers were necessary to keep the peace. The planters responded to the social threat by further isolating their elitist group from the other two classes. They also supplemented their own small numbers by importing slaves at such increasing rates that, by the mid-1700s, African slaves outnumbered white southern colonists by a ratio of two to one.

In 1763 Great Britain claimed victory over France when the Treaty of Paris was signed, officially ending the French and Indian War and radically changing the nature of colonial North America. Great Britain forced France to cede large chunks of territory to the English, including portions of Canada and the Louisiana territory. Great Britain also gained control of the Spanish colonies of East and West Florida. British colonists living in the original 13 colonies were overjoyed, until they learned of a provision in the peace treaty that prevented their expansion into the new British territories, except for East and West Florida. The British had bought peace with various Indian tribes by forbidding settlement west of the Appalachian Mountains in the Proclamation of 1763.

When the colonists heard of the limitations placed upon them by Parliament, combined with a series of legislative acts designed to raise colonial taxes to pay for the debt accumulated during the war, the age of the American Revolution was born. The era of the imperial crisis with Great Britain and her colonies lasted from 1763 until 1783. During this time the nature of rural life in North America changed little.

It was not until the outbreak of the American Revolution that many simple farmers, the true practitioners of rural life in colonial America, served as members of various colonial militias. Members of the militias, often viewed as crude, rebellious, and unreliable by the regulars of the Continental Army, played key roles in several major battles of the war, including the skirmishes of the famed minutemen at Lexington and Concord, as well as General Washington's key victory at Yorktown in October 1781. After achieving peace in 1783, the farmers returned home to rebuild their lives and build the new American nation—one firmly founded on principles espoused by those who favored the rural lifestyle in colonial America.

Deborah L. Bauer

Further Readings

Adams, James Truslow. *Provincial Society, 1690–1763*. New York: Macmillan Co., 1927.

Alden, John Richard. *The South in the Revolution, 1763–1789*. Baton Rouge: Louisiana State University Press, 1957.

Dudley, William, ed. *American Slavery*. San Diego, CA: Greenhaven Press, 2000.

Durant, Thomas J., Jr. and J. David Knottnerus, eds. *Plantations Society and Race Relations: The Origins of Inequality*. Westport, CT: Praeger, 1999.

Gipson, Lawrence Henry. *The British Isles and the American Colonies: The Northern Plantations, 1748–1754*. New York: Alfred A. Knopf, 1960.

Kulikoff, Allan. *From British Peasants to Colonial American Farmers*. Chapel Hill: University of North Carolina Press, 2000.

McDonald, Forrest, ed. *Empire and Nation: Letters from a Farmer in Pennsylvania (John Dickinson) and Letters from the Federal Farmer (Richard Henry Lee)*. Indianapolis, IN: Liberty Fund, 1999.

Otto, John Solomon. *The Southern Frontiers, 1607–1860: The Agricultural Evolution of the Colonial and Antebellum South*. Westport, CT: Greenwood Press, 1989.

Ravenel, Harriott Horry. *Eliza Pinckney*. New York: C. Scribner's Sons, 1896.

Robinson, W. Stitt. *The Southern Colonial Frontier, 1607–1763*. Albuquerque: University of New Mexico Press, 1979.

Tunis, Edwin. *Colonial Living*. Cleveland, OH: World Publishing, 1957.

———. *Frontier Living*. Cleveland, OH: World Publishing, 1961.

Ward, Harry M. *Colonial America, 1607–1763*. Upper Saddle River, NJ: Prentice Hall, 1991.

CHAPTER 7

Religion

THE
NEW TESTA-
MENT OF OVR
Lord Ieſus Chriſt, Tranſlated out of
Greeke by *Theod. Beza.*
WHEREVNTO ARE ADIOYNED
briefe Summaries of doctrine vpon the Euange-
liſts and Acts of the Apoſtles, together with the methode
of the Epiſtles of the Apoſtles, by the ſaid
THEOD. BEZA.

"Say nothing of my religion.
It is known to God and myself alone."
— Thomas Jefferson

COLONIAL RELIGION WAS marked by simplicity in worship and preaching, and a strong sense of fellowship, which bound the congregants together. This is not to say they did not have schisms, divisions, or moral failures in their groups, but they did produce a remarkably rich religious experience in the New World. American colonial church history is noted by historians around the world and students at home for three great epochs: the Salem witchcraft trials, the Great Awakening, and the role of religion and the quest for religious freedom on the part of the revolutionary generation.

Anglicans came to the New World in 1607 under the sponsorship of the Virginia Company. In the early 18th century the church grew rapidly, largely due to two missionary societies, the Society for the Promotion of Christian Knowledge (SPCK) and the Society for the Propagation of the Gospel in Foreign Parts (SPG). The Anglicans established institutions of higher learning in New England, such as King's College in New York (now Columbia University), and the College of William and Mary in Williamsburg, Virginia. When the Revolution began the Anglican clergy opposed the efforts of the Patriot Party, and many of their clerics supported the crown at great risk, exiled to Canada, or stayed after the disestablishment of the church after the war.

The worship of the Anglican churches was formal, but usually of the low-church Calvinist form without the wearing of vestments (usually dressed in

"The Witch No. 3" by George Walker depicts the Salem witchcraft trials, in which 14 women and five men (two victims shown in the stockade above) were put to death on the gallows.

The Salem Witchcraft Trials

The English had long believed in witches and spectral creatures, and the Puritans believed in them as well. A tragic episode based on this belief occurred in Salem (modern Danvers), Massachusetts, in 1692. A few girls testified that a slave named Tituba and other village outcasts had placed them under a spell. Tituba belonged to the Reverend Samuel Parris, an unpopular cleric, who decided to investigate the issue. Many historians feel that Parris simply tried to use the accusations as a way to deter criticism of his pastoral failings. Tituba accused several local women in the community as practitioners of the black arts, which resulted in community emotions reaching a fever pitch. Parris and others declared that the girls had sold their souls to Satan.

In the end 14 women and five men lost their lives on the gallows, and poor Giles Cory, an elderly gentleman, suffered death by crushing with large stones in an effort to extract a confession. The excitement began to wane when the accusers railed against some of the most revered members of Salem, and it became clear something was amiss. The idea of spectral evidence received condemnation by distinguished clergy such as the father of Cotton Mather, the venerable Increase Mather, who urged caution all through the trials.

Though 150 souls awaited trial, the governor disbanded the special court, and the remaining prisoners were released. For over a decade after the horrific experience, Salem pondered what should be done to make amends for the obvious wrongs of the witchcraft hysteria. In 1696 the trial judge, Samuel Sewall, admitted he erred in his judgments, and Cotton Mather suffered denunciation for his role in helping stir up the hysteria with his writings about the affair. The Assembly reversed the convictions of the executed, and in 1697 the Massachusetts General Court called on the community to conduct a day of atonement to repent of the wrongs done. In 1711 many of the victim's families received financial compensation.

The Quakers

When the first members of the Religious Society of Friends (Quakers) arrived in the New World shortly after the founding of the denomination in 1652, they did so not only with a desire to both find religious freedom for their own persecuted denomination, but also to spread their faith throughout Colonial America. While the Quakers were not unique among early Americans in their desire to create an ideal religious community, they were unique in their relations to other religious groups and Native Americans.

Led by their belief in the presence of an inner light or "that of God" in every person, Quakers attempted to create a society that respected all persons, avoided violence, advocated freedom of religion, and were known for their fair dealings with Native Americans. Though Quakers lived in Rhode Island, North Carolina, Pennsylvania, and western New Jersey, their most notable presence was within William Penn's "Holy Experiment" of Pennsylvania. Persecuted and frequently jailed in England, Penn obtained a charter for Pennsylvania in 1681, and there sought to create a community founded upon Quaker ideals, in which other groups could peacefully coexist. Though Quakers faced significant persecution in Massachusetts throughout the colonial period, they remained the majority in the Pennsylvania assembly until 1755. Their commitment to pacifism and opposition to slavery, though always present within the denomination, set them apart during the Revolution. After the war Quakers expanded their reform efforts to include prison reform, Native American rights, temperance, and women's suffrage.

black) and built the worship around preaching rather than the liturgy. Sabbath-keeping was common among the parishioners, and like other colony groups, drinking and gaming were forbidden on the Lord's Day, though gossip and business dealings went on as usual.

The Congregationalists, Baptists, Dutch Reformed, Catholics, Lutherans, Presbyterians, Jews, and Quakers soon came to establish either traditional or simplified worship services in freedom and peace. Though the Anglicans and Congregationalists soon became "established" or official churches in their colonies, other groups came amid them such as the Moravians, Amish, and Mennonites, who enriched the religious pluralism of the colonies.

MEETINGHOUSES AND CHURCHES

Most of the church meetinghouses built before 1680 were small, crude, and uncomfortable. Most churches were no more than 20 feet by 40 or 50 feet, and built of wood. An example was a wood structure in Sudbury, Massachusetts in 1643 that had a thatched roof measuring 20 by 30 feet. Sudbury

The First Church in Salem, Massachusetts, was built in 1634.

built three such structures, but in 1688 the citizens built a church with a permanent roof and a finished exterior. After 1680 the churches become more sophisticated. In New England, the meetinghouse, located in the center of the village, lay a short distance from the homes of most parishioners. The meetinghouse was all-purpose as it served as the townhall, public building, and in the event of an Indian attack, an impromptu fortress.

The narrow wooden benches upon which the worshippers sat consisted of seats without back supports, though they were not pews. Later in the colonial period the Puritans required congregants to purchase a pew, and they received assignments according to their social position. It was not unusual for the elderly and hard of hearing to sit close to the front. Most of the early churches had only one window behind the pulpit. As the preachers preached in greatcoat and gloves in the winter gloom, worshippers pounded their feet to stay warm. Most Puritan churches held two services on Sunday. The first ran to noon, and the second an hour later after people returned home for a cold lunch. Cooking a hot meal would constitute work on the Lord's Day. It was during this hour that children received catechism of the first service.

DISTINGUISHED CHURCHES AND THE LORD'S DAY

Once churches became established and the colonies wealthier, the church buildings became more elaborate and distinguished. They grew larger, more refined in architecture, and more aesthetically pleasing. Regional variations abounded. Churches in Virginia and Maryland constructed after 1680 were long and narrow, with English and Flemish brickwork with zigzag patterns in the exterior halls. In South Carolina artisans built square stucco buildings, such as the Anglican church St. James Goose Creek in 1706.

Before the Great Awakening church buildings could not afford steeples or bells. Congregations that possessed bells placed them on wooden stands on the ground and frequently did not build steeples for several years until they had the funds to do so. After 1680 church renovation became commonplace. New England churches featured smoothly polished pews, finely carved pulpits, mahogany baptismal fonts, and silver communion cups. Jewish synagogues followed similarly.

In all the colonies Christians observed Sunday as a day of rest. The Dutch, however, treated Sunday as a day of frolic and leisure during which the taverns

A Chronology of Colonial Religion

1607 Anglicans come to the New World with the Virginia Company.
1620 William Bradford and the Separatists settle in Plymouth, MA.
1623 Puritans settle New Hampshire.
1628 Dutch Reform ministry begins in New Amsterdam, now New York City.
1630 Puritans led by John Winthrop settle Massachusetts Bay. Winthrop exhorts the settlers to establish a "city upon a hill" that God will bless.
1634 Maryland established as a haven for Catholics by Lord Baltimore.
1636 Nominal Baptist Roger Williams founds Rhode Island as a place of religious freedom.
1636 Thomas Hooker and fellow Puritans found Connecticut.
1638 Lutherans begin ministry in the colonies at Wilmington, Delaware.
1640 Presbyterians begin their ministry at Southampton, on Long Island.
1644 John Clarke establishes first lasting Baptist work in Rhode Island.
1649 Catholics in Maryland pass The Toleration Act guaranteeing all Christians who believe in the Trinity freedom of worship.
1654 First Jewish congregation begins in New Amsterdam with 53 refugees from Recife, Brazil.
1662 Congregationalists institute the Half-Way Covenant in New England.
1674 Quakers arrive in West Jersey and establish a proprietary colony.
1682 William Penn receives a Royal Charter to establish a colony for Quakers, but guarantees religious freedom to all who settle there.
1692 Salem Witchcraft Trials begin in Salem (now Danvers), MA.
1701 Church of England's Society for Propagation of the Gospel in Foreign Parts forms in England.
1706 First Presbytery forms in Philadelphia.
1707 First Baptist Association is established in Philadelphia.
1714 Massachusetts Assembly reverses the Salem witchcraft trial verdicts.
1730 Amish settle in Pennsylvania.
1739 George Whitefield, English Calvinist itinerant preacher, arrives in the colonies and in 1740 begins the first preaching tour of the colonies.
1740 Gilbert Tennent publishes *The Danger of an Unconverted Ministry.*
1741 Presbyterians split over the awakening into the New Side (those supporting the Great Awakening) and the Old Side (those in opposition).
1745 Gilbert Tennent and the New Side faction of Presbyterians form the Synod of New York.
1769 First Methodist preachers arrive in the North American colonies.
1776 John Wesley withdraws Methodist clerics from the colonies in support of the Crown.
1779 Thomas Jefferson writes his Bill for Establishing Religious Freedom in Virginia.

The First Great Awakening

Church historians have long defined revivals as bringing about religious and moral change in individuals, while awakenings change not only the behavior, but also the world-view of entire groups. The Great Awakening changed American church life in ways that are still felt in the 21st century. It is believed that the revivals that began the Awakening started among the Dutch in New Jersey through a Reformed minister, Theodore Jacob Frelinghuysen, who arrived in the colony in 1720. Imbued with German Pietism, the belief that the Christian life required a dynamic and active experience and devotional life, Frelinghuysen began to preach that conversion was necessary for salvation and that the actions of one's life should reveal an inner change. Gilbert Tennent of Pennsylvania (1703–64), a Presbyterian, became a friend of the Dutch pastor, and learned about devotion from him. Soon Tennent was preaching on the same themes in Pennsylvania.

In Massachusetts Jonathan Edwards (1703–58) noted in the 1730s that his parish at Northampton seemed in a state of spiritual decline. He was also troubled by the looseness of the youth in the community, and the cold spiritual atmosphere and attitude among the adults. After making a conscious effort to revive the youth, he began preaching a series on justification by faith, and revival broke out in his church. The Awakening grew in strength when George Whitefield (1714–70), a friend of John and Charles Wesley's, arrived in America in 1739. Whitefield began the first of seven preaching tours in America, in which he preached to thousands.

Both secular and church historians have debated as to why the Awakening occurred and its impact upon the colonies. It may be a coincidence, but the outbreaks of enthusiasm came about after an outbreak of diphtheria, which took the lives of many in New England. Indeed, epidemics would make 18th century colonials think about their eternal destination. Nevertheless, such reasoning can never fully explain the intensity and impact of the religious upheaval.

The Awakening produced a great increase in church membership and attendance, and the Baptists proved to be the greatest beneficiaries of the revivals with their membership increasing at least fourfold after 1740. It served to deepen the piety of the colonists, and it also resulted in the founding of several institutions of higher education such as the College of New Jersey (Princeton) by Presbyterians in 1746, Rhode Island College (Brown) by Baptists in 1764, and Queens (Rutgers) established by the Dutch Reformed in 1766. Finally, some historians argue that the Awakening democratized the churches and laid the nationalist foundation and fervor that erupted into the American Revolution.

remained open and inhabitants of the villages played. The English colonists took the day seriously. In 1611 the English in Virginia forbade gaming on the Sabbath, even in the privacy of one's home. Furthermore it was required that colonists attend services twice on Sunday. Absence could result in flogging or death. By the 18th century mandatory service was no longer required, and the punishments abandoned. The Virginians also used the day as time to enjoy gentle and quiet recreation. In New England the day continued with observation in the old manner. The Puritans forbade all non-essential activities on the Lord's Day, and they continued the Old Testament observance of beginning the Sabbath at sundown on Saturday. The Puritans levied fines for infractions such as smoking tobacco, playing quoits, and even picking strawberries. One poor soul fell down a dry well and waited while his rescuers debated about whether not they should help him on the Sabbath.

The Calvinists sought to end the Yuletide observance, which they viewed as pagan. William Bradford halted playing games on the day, and Massachusetts Bay enacted a five-shilling fine for anyone brazen enough to celebrate with fun or frolic the birth of Christ. Outside of New England, Christmas celebrations continued, but not to the length they enjoyed in Europe. In the backcountry, the people acknowledged the birth of Christ with gunfire. Other holidays, such as saints' feasts, St. Valentine's Day, May Day, and the rites of harvest, withered away and did not return until well into the 19th century.

The sermons in New England served as the focal point of the service of worship. The Puritan sermon lasted approximately one hour, and prayers could last that long as well. Preachers had hourglasses next to the pulpit and they often preached through two or even three rounds of sand. Those who fell asleep received a tap on the head from a stick (for men) and a rabbit's foot on the face for women to keep them awake. The sermon structure consisted of stating the doctrine in one sentence, and that in turn was broken down into smaller manageable parts. The pastors preached in the famous plain style, without oratorical flourishes, and with few illustrations from outside sources. Illustrations came from the agricultural life of the people or artisans. The conclusion consisted

Christ Church in Philadelphia, founded in 1695, was the first parish of the Church of England (Anglican) in Pennsylvania.

of "uses" or how one could make the sermon contents useful in everyday life. The sermon served as a devotional tool, an ethical lesson, and for many, an educational event as well. The worshippers found themselves drawn into the great battle between good and evil. It served as a shaper of values for those attempting to build the "city upon a hill." The idea was for the message to be understood by all in attendance. Therefore sermons could be directed toward youth, women, and servants, or to themes such war or epidemics. The method of Peter Ramus, an influential French humanist, found acceptance in New England. The preacher gave the text, explication of the doctrines, list of proofs, and the application, which climaxed with the address. A great deal of evangelical preaching today has its roots in the Puritan-Separatist Congregation style of the 16th through 18th centuries.

The jeremiad, a sermon based on the warnings of Jeremiah in the Old Testament book of Lamentations, was a popular style with pastors and itinerants. The sermonic style concerned warnings of impending doom if repentance was not forthcoming on the part of the hearers. If the hearers did not repent soon, disaster, as in the exile of the Jews into Babylon, was sure to come amid much wailing and remorse. One famous sermon, "Sinners in the Hands of an Angry God" by Jonathan Edwards, delivered in 1741, proclaimed: "There is no want of power in God to cast wicked men into hell at any moment. Men's hands cannot be strong when God rises up. The strongest have no power to resist him, nor can any deliver out of his hands. He is not only able to cast wicked men into hell, but he can most easily do it. Sometimes an earthly prince meets with a great deal of difficulty to subdue a rebel, who has found means to fortify himself, and has made himself strong by the numbers of his followers. But it is not so with God. There is no fortress that is any defence from the power of God." It is debatable as to how effective that type of preaching was, but no doubt some individuals did heed the warnings.

The 600-year-old baptismal font in Christ Church was sent to Philadelphia in 1697 from London.

By the 18th century the worship services improved. The two services moved closer together so that members could get home by dark, and new churches were erected to accommodate an expanding population. The first churches could not offer comforts for the congregants attending faithfully. It was common

Missions were established along the California coastline between 1769 and 1823.

California Missions

Established by the Franciscan Order to introduce Christianity to the natives, the California missions were a group of Spanish outposts along the Pacific Coast, established between 1769 (with San Diego) and 1823 (San Francisco Solano). The fact that so many California towns bear the names of saints is due to the mission period. The Spanish introduced livestock and foreign produce to the area, and set up its first industries.

Originally intended to be turned over to native control after 10 years, as had been done in Mexico, the California missions remained in Spanish control for a much longer period than that. They never became fully self-sufficient, and required financial support from Spain for as long as the country held the region. Missions were established based on the area meeting a number of criteria, including ample ground on which to raise crops and let herds graze, and a local population that was not too hostile and seemed tractable by missionaries. Spanish religious, political, and financial concerns were intertwined, in mutual service to one another. Ideally the natives would congregate at the mission, and through the efforts of the clergy, would be converted not only from pagans to Christians, but from an undisciplined state to an orderly civilization. Once baptized young women were supervised to safeguard their virtue until marriage thereafter, and young men were expected to labor on behalf of the mission, not to roam the countryside as they pleased. The work day was six hours long, divided by a mid-day meal and a two-hour siesta. In return meals and clothing were provided, often of better quality than the locals were accustomed to—but after providing for them, a great deal of surplus goods remained, from which the Spanish made their profit.

African-American Religious Practices

From the arrival of the earliest slave until the Revolution, religion served as a tool for survival and inspiration, as well as an instrument for oppression within the African-American population. Adherence to vestiges and practices of traditional African religions such as Santeria and Candomblé allowed slaves to continue to remember and honor their lives before enslavement. The West African religions in practice focused on a world in which spirits were constantly at work and no distinction existed between the sacred and the profane. However the belief in a supreme deity and a notion of good and evil melded well with forms of traditional Christianity as Christian slaveholders used religious conversion as a justification for enslavement.

Usually drawn to the emotionalism of more evangelical groups such as the Methodists and Baptists, Christian African Americans developed their own forms of worship that incorporated traditional African religious practice, including the use of spirituals, distinctive forms of preaching, and shouting in worship. Such practices were further strengthened by the revivalism of the Great Awakening and came to influence the practice of nonslave Christians. Though Christianity was often used by whites to further the subjugation of African Americans, and limitations were often placed on African-American worship, baptism, and religious instruction, religion ultimately became a means of managing and overcoming suffering. Once greater freedom was achieved, African Americans would form their own denominations, thus continuing the influence of African traditional religion, and the emphasis on religion as a vehicle for liberation, even after slavery had ended.

for wine and bread to freeze in winter months and the roads to the meetinghouse were often abysmal. Nooning houses were constructed near the place of worship to serve as a spot whereby the families could enjoy warmth as they partook of their noon meal before attending the afternoon service. The facilities contained several fireplaces to help thaw the cold bodies of the faithful.

In all of New England and in the middle and southern colonies, the Sabbath was also a social time for families and friends, which helped alleviate the hardships of colonial life. Inside the meetinghouse, men and women sat together in pews, rather than in separate sections as in earlier times.

The Sabbath was not the only occasion for worship. During the week, churches conducted fast-day lectures, catechism classes, and youth and women's meetings. The 18th century was austere, but not as much as the 17th century. Weddings and funerals became worship events, and both became more elaborate as the century progressed. Pastors also took worship to the people by offering specific sermons for political events such elections and warfare.

In the Chesapeake region of Maryland and Virginia, the Sabbath, though observed, received a lighter emphasis. The Anglicans also conducted two services, one in the morning and one after a luncheon break. During the worship, the priests could perform baptisms and weddings. Stray animals, gusty winds, and late arrivals disturbed services. The chief difference between the Congre-

John Peter Gabriel Muhlenberg (1746–1807)

A German-educated cleric and ordained as a Lutheran and an Anglican, Muhlenberg ministered to German-American congregations in Virginia. When the American Revolution began, Muhlenberg exhorted his congregation that there was "a time to preach and a time to fight, and now is the time to fight!" On January 21, 1776, he preached his farewell sermon and at the close of the worship service, removed his clerical garb to reveal the uniform of a military officer. He thundered from the pulpit a climax of the oration: "There is a time to pray and a time to fight, and that time has now come!" He recruited 300 men from his parish and formed the nucleus of the 8th Virginia Regiment, mostly Germans residing in the Shenandoah Valley.

The "fighting parson," John Peter Gabriel Muhlenberg.

After defending the coasts of South Carolina and Georgia, Muhlenberg received promotion to brigadier general in the Virginia Line, through which he served at Brandywine, Germantown, and Monmouth. It was while on campaign in Georgia that he contracted the liver disease that would eventually end his life. Though the Virginia Line received orders to return south and defend Charleston, Muhlenberg remained and assisted Baron von Steuben with the defense of Virginia. During the Yorktown Campaign, Muhlenberg led a brigade in Lafayette's Division on the south bank of the James River that attacked one of the two British redoubts. He was brevetted a major general in September 1783, and promptly retired from the army in November of that year. After the war he could not bring himself to return to the ministry he left behind in Woodstock, Virginia, because "it would never do to mount the parson after the soldier." He worked in politics for the Democratic-Republicans and for the federal government until his death from liver disease in 1807. Muhlenberg remains a prime example of a "fighting parson."

The Old Swedes Church in Swedesboro, New Jersey. Originally Lutherans met in a log cabin on this site in 1703. This church was built in 1784 and now houses an Episcopal congregation.

gational Puritans and Separatists of New England and the Anglicans lay in the Anglican insistence on using the *Book of Common Prayer*. The Anglican Church structures appeared to stress the validity of the prayer book, with the font for baptism, the pulpit, and the table providing the liturgical focus. The communion table was often at the east end of the building, with the font on the west, and the pulpit somewhere in the middle along the wall, but often, like the Puritan houses of worship, in the middle. The pulpit was elevated and consisted of two or three levels or decks: a reading deck for the clerk at the lowest level, a second deck for the pastor to read scripture, and many times a third deck from which the sermon was preached. Seating was flexible so that parishioners could turn to see an appropriate view of the service.

The church service followed the prayer book to the letter, which provided a lengthy order of service, much longer than today. If the Eucharist communion was not offered on a particular Sabbath, the service contained a metrical psalm. In addition the services included opening sentences that called the hearers to repentance, the General Confession, the Absolution, the Lord's Prayer, other liturgical prayers, and scripture lessons from the Psalms and Old and New Testaments. If the minister administered the Eucharist on communion Sunday (three or four times yearly) he included additional scripture texts, offerings, Confession, Absolution, perhaps an additional hymn, and the taking of the communion cup and bread. One historian noted that due to the size of flagons for use in the service, each participant received at least a quarter of a pint of fermented wine. The sermon that followed could be quite short, like a modern devotional service of about an hour, or could be hours long.

MUSIC IN WORSHIP

Both the dominant groups, the Calvinists and the Anglicans, used metrical psalms without musical instruments. A deacon in New England or the church clerk in Virginia announced the tune (about 40 named tunes existed for the hymns at that time). The leader would sing out a line and the congregation would sing it back in call and response pattern. Lyrics came from the *Bay Psalm Book,* the first book printed in British North America in 1640. Anglicans used the 1696 *Psalter* by Tate and Brady. Anglicans, if they could afford it, used a barrel organ and choir, but the Puritans of New England viewed the use of such modes as reminders of popery.

Judaism in the Colonies

Some 5,000 of the Jews expelled from Spain at the end of the 15th century emigrated to the Americas. They had faced, and continued to face, persecution in Europe and in the Muslim world. The New World provided the same hope for a fresh start as it did for the Pilgrims in Massachusetts, as well as the freedoms intrinsic in available land and less-entrenched local culture. Jews from Portugal also emigrated to Brazil—it was the 23 Brazilian Jews who moved to New Amsterdam in 1654 who are actually considered the first Jews to reside in what is now the United States. It is possible that Spanish Jews were already living in parts of what is now the American Southwest or Texas.

When the Revolutionary War broke out 2,000 Jews were living in the colonies, nearly all of them Sephardic Jews from the Iberian peninsula, of Spanish or Portuguese descent. Despite the situation in Europe, there was no native antisemitic sentiment in the New World—when it eventually developed in the next century, it was part of a broader anti-immigrant movement, especially centered on immigrants from southern and eastern Europe.

Though early Jews had to restrict their religious practices to their homes, in the 18th century they were able to buy land to build houses of worship just as Christians could, in many of the colonies. Jews were instrumental in the settling of Philadelphia, Baltimore, and Charleston. By the end of the 18th century South Carolina had become home to the most Jews in North America, mainly because of its guarantee not to abridge the right of any religious group to build a church—a guarantee that thus eased the creation of the Jewish community.

John Witherspoon (1723–94)

Born at Gifford, Scotland, and educated at the University of Edinburgh, Witherspoon served as a Presbyterian pastor until 1768, when he left his parish at Paisley for the presidency of the College of New Jersey (Princeton University). Under his leadership, the college flourished, but the American Revolution halted its advance. Although Witherspoon did not approve of pastors entering politics, circumstances in the colonies caused him to rethink his position.

Beginning in 1774 he served as a county delegate and member of the Somerset County Committee of Correspondence, attended political conventions, and led in the movement to arrest the Tory Governor William Franklin. In June 1776, when chosen as delegate to the Continental Congress, he urged that body not to delay in declaring independence, and he was the only clergyman to sign the Declaration of Independence. His sermon, preached at Princeton in May 1776, *Dominion of Providence over the Passions of Men*, was the first of many such written discourses in which Witherspoon wrote in defense of American liberty.

Witherspoon held a seat in Congress almost continually from 1776 to 1782, served on over 100 committees, and took an active part in the debates on the Articles of Confederation. In addition, he helped organize the executive branch and form alliances with foreign governments. He played a role in drawing up instructions for the peace commissioners responsible for negotiating terms with Great Britain. After the conflict Witherspoon earned the title of the "political parson." Witherspoon spent his remaining years rebuilding the College of New Jersey.

By the 18th century as the colonials realized that Rome could not harm them, and when financial resources allowed, other modes of musical expression came to fruition. Robert Tufts, a Harvard graduate, published in 1715 *An Introduction to the Singing of Psalm Tunes, in a Plain & Easy Method, With A Collection of Tunes in Three Parts,* in which he taught singers to sing by notes. Needless to say, this resulted in much of what churches experience today as a "worship war," in which the reactionary element saw regular unified singing as "papist," and the pastors and youth who enjoyed the New Way. Organs entered Anglican worship in the 18th century and in the Congregational bodies in the 19th century.

CLERGY NEEDED

Outside of New England clergy remained in short supply throughout the 17th century. The majority of clerics received advanced degrees. Historian

Patricia U. Bonomi, in *Under the Cope of Heaven*, debunks the myth that clergyman who wanted to come to the colonies had little formal education. In fact in Virginia alone, in 1726, 23 of 42 rectors had attended university, 12 at Oxbridge colleges and others at Scottish universities or Trinity, Dublin. Many clergymen had attended Oxford or Cambridge universities, while some had studied at William and Mary, where most of the native-born ministers enrolled. The average tenure of a rector was 15 years, and many served in one post until their deaths.

Despite negative stereotypes, there are scant moral scandals or lapses in character or ethics. However a great number of the clerics fought with parishioners over salaries. Most clerics practiced what today is known as "tent-making" or "bi-vocational" ministry in that they worked at another occupation such as medicine, law, teaching, farming, or a trade. Many pastors settled for taking a part of their pay in firewood and produce. The clergy living in such a manner had the advantage of helping them relate to the problems of their members and their struggle for existence on the frontier. The duties of the colonial pastors did not differ from pastors in the 21st century. In remote rural areas, the pastors administered catechisms, preached, taught, visited the sick, and counseled.

The pastoral life in New England was difficult enough, but in the south, it required a great amount of stamina. Due to the long distances between parishes, most ministers had to become itinerants, or traveling preachers. In Britain a parish was five square miles, but in Virginia or South Carolina, it might cover 60 to 100 square miles and contain only a few hundred members. In the settled areas and in the backcountry, a church might be a barn or another building used as church. Because of the scarcity of trained clergy, layman often filled the role of lay preacher or Bible reader in local parishes lacking pastoral leadership. The state of affairs made for a tremendous amount of conflict, because when a pastor did arrive, due to the lay leaders lack of willingness to relinquish control, surrendering that authority to the new minister sometimes met with severe opposition.

Jim Baugess

Further Readings

Ahlstrom, Sidney E. A *Religious History of the American People*. New Haven, CT: Yale University Press, 2004.

Bailyn, Bernard. *The Ideological Origins of the American Revolution*. Cambridge, MA: Belknap Press of Harvard University, 1967.

Bonomi, Patricia U. *Under the Cope of Heaven: Religion, Society, and Politics in Colonial America*. New York: Oxford University Press, 2003.

Boyer, Paul and Stephen Nussbaum. *Salem Possessed: The Social Origins*. Cambridge, MA: Harvard Univeristy Press, 1974.

Butler, Jon, Grant Wacker, and Randall Balmer. *Religion in American Life: A Short History*. New York: Oxford University Press, 2003.

Butler, Jon. *Religion in Colonial America*. New York: Oxford University Press, 2000.

Demos, John Putnam. *Entertaining Satan: Witchcraft and Culture of Early New England*. New York: Oxford University Press, 1982.

Gaustad, Edwin S. and Leigh Schimdt. *The Religious History of America: The Heart of the American Story from Colonial Times to Today*. San Francisco, CA: HarperCollins, 2002.

Karlsen, Carol F. *The Devil in the Shape of a Woman: Witchcraft in Colonial New England*. New York: W.W. Norton Press, 1998.

McLoughlin, William Gerald. *Revivals, Awakenings, and Reform: An Essay on Religion and Social Change in America*, Chicago, IL: University of Chicago Press, 1978.

Mol, J.J. *The Breaking of Theological Traditions: Theological Convictions In Colonial America.* Berkeley, CA: The Glendessary Press, 1968.

Morison, Samuel Eliot. *The Intellectual Life of Colonial New England 4th ed*. New York: New York University Press, 1970.

Noll, Mark A. *Christians in the American Revolution.* Grand Rapids, MI: Christian University Press, 1977.

Purvis, Thomas L. *Almanacs of American Life: Colonial America to 1763*. New York: Facts on File, 1999.

Wolf, Stephanie Grauman. *As Various as Their Land: The Everyday Lives of 18th Century Americans*. New York: HarperCollins, 1993.

CHAPTER 8

Education

"An investment in knowledge always pays the best interest."
— Benjamin Franklin

EARLY EDUCATION IN the New World centered on the inculcation of virtue and piety. The Puritans and Separatists that settled in New England desired to found, as John Winthrop stated, "a city upon a hill," in which the settlers would begin a society built on biblical precepts. The Puritans desired to educate the young so that they could be proficient in the reading and interpretation of the Scriptures. Other colonial settlers in the middle and southern colonies had mixed motives for coming to the New World. However, even in those regions, religion played an important part in the educational process. The 1642 school law demanded that parents educate their children, or the government would do it for them.

The Massachusetts School Law of 1647 established the first organized school system in the New World. The purpose of the law was to prevent the advent of barbarism among the Puritans of New England. In keeping with the ideal of education for the purpose of spiritual growth and devotion, the written text tells the purpose of the act in succinct terms: "It being one chief project of the old deluder, Satan, to keep men from the knowledge of the Scriptures, as in former times by keeping them in an unknown tongue, so in these latter times by persuading from the use of tongues." The law required every township in the jurisdiction that contained 50 households to appoint a teacher to instruct all the town's children to read and write, and the local teacher was to receive wages at the expense of the community. When a community reached 100 families, a grammar school was required to instruct youth for possible university education. If the town with 100 families did not provide for a grammar school education for its youth, the selectmen issued a fine of £5 issued until the community implemented the law. In most of the colonies outside New England, mandatory attendance laws did not exist.

TYPES OF SCHOOLS

Dame Schools and Petty Schools were the earliest schools in the colonial period, in which women of any married status taught young children in her home for meager fees or gifts. Some of the students were mere toddlers; therefore, the dame schools served as a form of early daycare. Since the teachers had very little formal training, the education received by the very young scholars was minimal in scope and content. The curriculum included reciting the alphabet, Bible

Ezekial Cheever, Classicist and Schoolmaster

In a day when most schoolmasters were part-time instructors due to pastoral responsibilities, Ezekial Cheever (1614–1708) found his calling in the pursuit of educational excellence. Born to a spinner in London, and educated at Emmanuel College at Cambridge, he left England in 1637 and arrived in Boston in June. In 1638 he settled in New Haven, Connecticut, as schoolmaster. Hailed as a godly man by his peers, he was appointed to high political office in his community, and while there, also preached in the local parish church.

In 1650 he moved to Ipswich and as schoolmaster there enhanced the reputation of the Free School. He was so successful there that he moved to Charlestown, where he stayed for nine years. His most successful tenure was at the Boston Latin School where he received £60 per annum, including "possession and use of ye schooled-house." Though a strict disciplinarian, his talent and reputation imbued his young scholars with a sense of awe toward his immense ability. He served as a schoolmaster for 78 years—38 of those in Boston. He taught until his death at age 94.

Cheever's greatest work was in the field of the classics and Latin. His most famous literary work, a text *Accidence, a Short Introduction to the Latin Tongue*, went through 20 reprints and was republished again in 1838. Cheever's greatest accomplishment as a teacher is reflected on the number of his young scholars that attended Harvard, including his most famous pupil from the Boston Latin Grammar School, Cotton Mather, who eulogized him in an elegy by writing, "Do but that name Cheever, and the echo straight, Upon name good Latin will repeat."

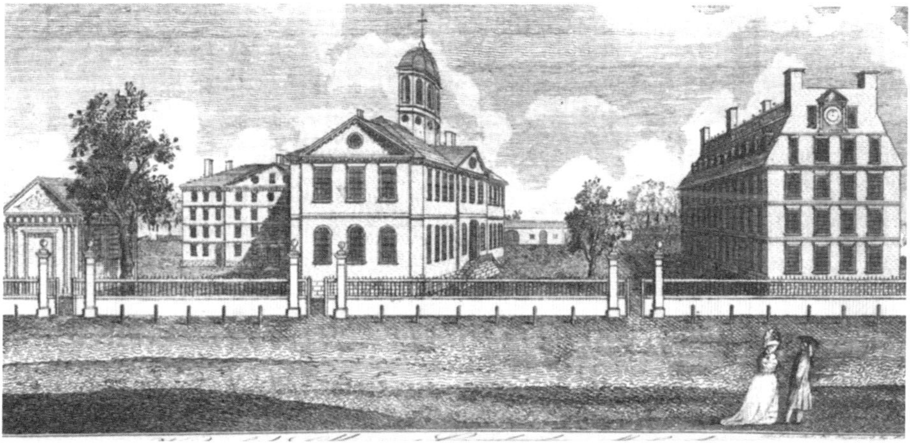

A late 18th-century print shows several buildings on the Harvard College grounds, (left to right) Holden Chapel, Hollis Hall, Harvard Hall, and Massachusetts Hall.

verses, reading, writing, and elemental arithmetic. Girls received the traditional domestic training of the day, but they too learned the skills of reading and writing. The classroom textbooks for the dame schools could be hornbooks—paddle shaped devices with the syllables, Model Prayer, and alphabet. A common teacher's book was Edmund Coote's *The English Schoole-Maister* (1596), which served as answer key and manual for the instructor. The instructional method was rote memorization because of the scarcity and expense of materials.

The purpose of the dame school was to prepare boys for the Latin Grammar School, but for girls, the dame school served as their total educational experience. Even in the dame school, the teacher taught, served as a model, and led in hands-on instruction of domestic tasks as the young girls learned to read, write, understand, and memorize Bible passages. The southern planters often founded petty schools, based on the dame school model. Once the planters secured a tutor, the tutor taught the resident children in the plantation house, along with some neighbor children. In addition to local homes, churches, or small buildings could serve as petty school facilities.

Young men, in preparation to attend Harvard, attended Latin Grammar Schools. In keeping with the ideals of the Renaissance, they taught a curriculum based on classical learning. Such an education would assist in creating a leadership class of high moral character. By 1700, 39 such schools existed in New England. Most of the Latin Grammar Schools were located in the mid-Atlantic colonies. The instructors needed to teach in the grammar schools were required to be highly educated and proficient in the Greek and Roman classics. Therefore most teachers were ministers. In addition to teaching the Bible, as was required in every phase of learning in the colonial period, they also needed vast knowledge of the Bible languages of Koine Greek and Biblical Hebrew.

Other subjects, taught if the instructor had acquired proficiency, were geography, history, and mathematics.

The southern colonies, much more rural and isolated than their neighbors to the north, used old field schools, constructed upon a worn out tobacco field and staffed by local Anglican ministers. Private subscriptions maintained the staff and furnished supplies. The local community hired and fired the teachers. Because of the agricultural cycle in the south, old field schools remained open only a few months a year.

AFRICAN AMERICANS AND NATIVE AMERICANS

For Native Americans education was almost always the result of efforts of religious organizations trying to convert them to Christianity. Before natives could be considered ready for conversion they had to be able to read the Bible and religious literature. Many missionaries went to Native American villages to teach reading and writing, thereby making it possible for the children to remain with their families and at the same time giving them skills to become interpreters. Some natives, such as those recruited by Eleazar Wheelock for his Indian Charity School, were taken from their villages to be educated in English-style schools. Most of these found the separation from their native culture difficult and rejoined their native tribes. However some became fluent in both cultures and were able to live in both worlds.

Supporters of education for blacks in the colonial period included those with economic interests in seeing African Americans acquire trade skills, and those with religious and charitable goals such as missionaries, who regarded literacy, or at least the ability to read the Bible, as necessary for conversion. Since skilled labor was scarce in 18th-century America, masters found it necessary to train some of their slaves in a trade. Slave men and women either learned these skills from other slaves, or served apprenticeships under white craftsmen. As far as reading and writing were concerned, slaves usually received these skills under the direction of a religious group.

EDUCATION FOR THE POOR

The Anglican Church had long supported education for the poor and orphaned. An organization within the Church of England, the Society for the Propagation of the Gospel (SPG), raised funds and provided teachers (usually young ministers) for the colonies to educate their less fortunate. The SPG distributed educational materials and printed books on various academic disciplines as well as religious tracts. Apprenticeship, or the learning of a trade under a master craftsman for a period of several years, was a way in which to make the poor and orphans less dependent and more educated. Parliament issued the Poor Law of 1601 which, in keeping with the biblical injunction that if a man does not work he will not eat, ordered that anyone between the age of 12 and 60 who lacked means of support was to be bound out or given over to a master craftsman for seven years. Each parish had to appoint persons to oversee that the poor and orphaned did receive an indenture to tradesmen.

The American colonies passed similar laws, but instruction in religion was included. In addition the American colonial authorities were empowered to round up the lazy, orphaned, or those with absent parents, and send them to the workhouse and receive instruction in some useful enterprise. The problem that plagued the colonials was the practice of Londoners dumping their poor and sometimes shiftless onto the colonies. In 1705 the Virginia Assembly passed an act requesting all parents to take responsibility for the instruction of their young and demanded masters to teach apprentices to read and write.

SCHOOL LIFE

Discipline could be harsh in colonial schools. Whipping posts, often with leather straps, found frequent use for those students who were unruly or made mistakes. The student felt the sting of a rattan, a leather strap attached to a wicker stick. "Whispering sticks" were inserted in the mouths of students to prevent them from whispering in class. On occasion, the whispering sticks contained strings for tying the stick to the student's head. Slit sticks used for pinching students' noses remained on the students for long periods. Teachers used a ferule, a staff generally used for non-disciplinary functions, to strike or "cane" a student. Some teachers utilized the dunce cap if young scholars failed to complete lessons. The ridiculous looking cone-shaped hat, placed on the head of the student, who then sat in a corner on a stool, served to humiliate and embarrass the offending child.

Placing a dunce cap on the head of a student, who then sat in a corner on a stool, served to humiliate and embarrass the unruly child.

A TYPICAL SCHOOL DAY

Children in New England enjoyed the best teachers and facilities of the colonial era, but even those were one-room schools with a teacher's desk raised above the students on a platform. A fireplace was present to provide heat when needed, and each school had several windows. Usually they were clapboard structures. Log schools dominated the landscape in the middle colonies, and in the south the buildings used for teaching students consisted of abandoned farm buildings or sheds. The school day was long and tedious, and the school week was Monday through Saturday. In the mornings, the students practiced grammar drills, and in the afternoon they studied the classics of Greek and Roman literature. Each Friday they reviewed material and completed examinations. On Saturday the young scholars worked on translation in writing. The grammar school education began at age seven or eight and lasted seven years. The first Latin Grammar School was the Boston Latin Grammar School, opened in 1635, and its sole purpose was to ready young men for Harvard, especially in the field of ministry or law. The students received instruction in the mornings in subjects such as Bible studies, Latin, arithmetic, and writing. A copybook contained pithy moral lessons that the student would write in the book, which the schoolmasters hoped would inculcate good moral character in young pliable charges.

Students wrote with quill pens, dipped in an inkwell.

After lunch and a brief recess, the children returned for their recitations. The students recited Latin, Bible verses, and various narrative on other subjects. Books and paper were expensive; therefore, much learning was oral. If the students had access to books, they often possessed the *New England Primer*. The primer, first printed in 1690 by Boston printer Benjamin Harris, remains the most well-known and oft quoted text of the era. It was the most successful textbook printed in early America. Although the book went through a few revisions in the 200 years of use in classrooms, mostly it remained intact throughout. It held the title "primer" because it was a first grade reader in the late 17th and early 18th centuries, though it is doubtful most first-graders in the 21st century could understand its content or have familiarity with the values stated within its pages. Watt's hymns, the alphabet, the phonetic and pronunciation syllables, and simple prayers open the work. The alphabet exercise began as follows: "In Adams fall, we sinned all," and completed with the following: "Zaccheus, He did climb the tree Our Lord to see." All of these accompanied woodcut drawings, which amplified the points the students learned.

The Westminster Shorter Catechism taught basic theological lessons, as did the inclusion of the Model Prayer, and the famous children's prayer, "Now I Lay Me Down to Sleep." The Puritans wasted no opportunity to teach letters or phonics, but they always made the best use of their resources and taught values simultaneously. In addition students used hornbooks, revolving alphabet books, and battledores—short illustrated primers secured with a flap. The paper, foolscap, was large, rough, and often not ruled properly. The students wrote with quill pens, which they dipped in an inkwell to write. The quills held little ink, so the student had to insert the quill many times. The study in writing, Latin, and history served to prepare a student for college, but most did not attend school beyond the elementary grades. High schools did not exist at the time. Therefore the students that did attend college enrolled as early as 12 years of age. The teachers taught as many as 40 children in the one-room structures, and that meant teaching several students at different grade levels. The teacher had to maintain tight control on student behavior or chaos would ensue.

COLLEGIATE EDUCATION

Harvard College, the first institution of higher learning in the colonies, came into existence in 1636. According to the author of *New England's First Fruits* (1643), after immigrants settled in they looked after a "way to advance learning and perpetuate it to prosperity, dreading to leave an illiterate ministry to

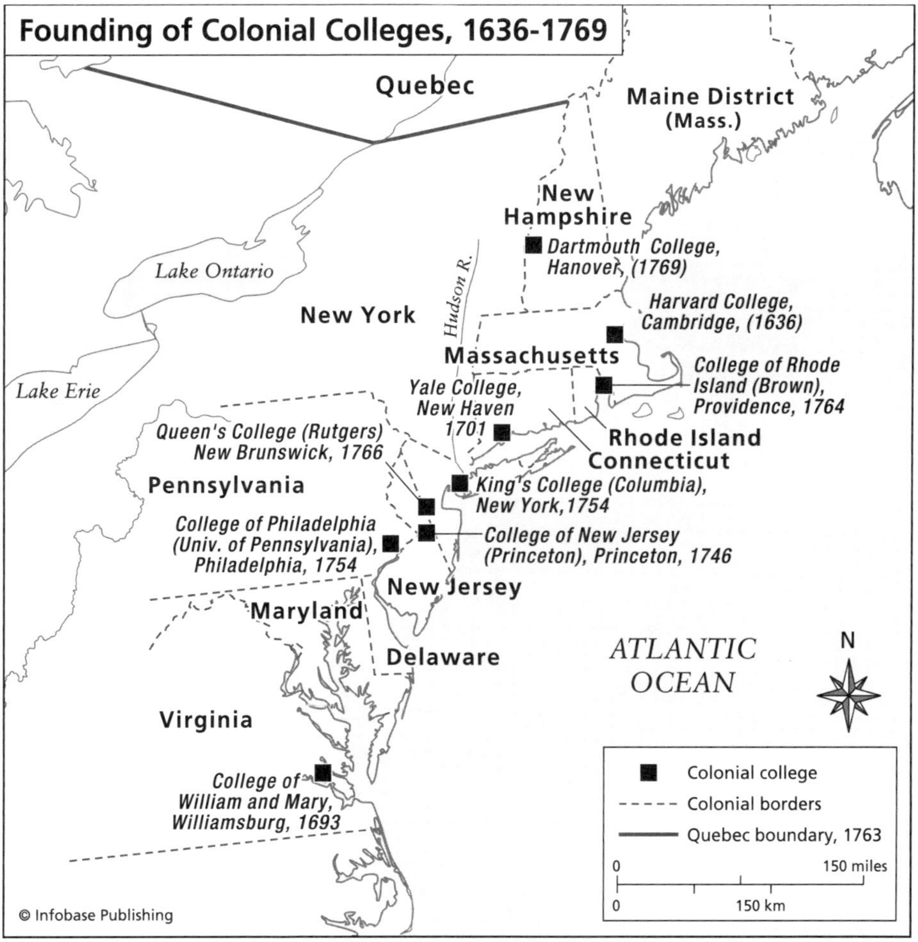

Cotton Mather, Educational Activist

A portrait of Cotton Mather.

The son of Increase Mather and Maria Cotton, the young Mather lived a life of the mind throughout his earthly pilgrimage. Mather learned to read before his formal schooling began. At age 18 he received his M.A. from Harvard.

Though he served as pastor in Boston for several years, his literary output and his work on educational pursuits were equally prodigious. He wrote *The Christian Philosopher* (1721) in which he argued that science worked in the service of the Creator.

He was much concerned with the education of not only collegians, but also of children. Like all the Puritans in New England, he believed that to build a true wilderness Zion, an educated population well-versed in divinity must became a reality. In *A Father's Resolutions*, an exhortation consisting of 21 resolutions, Mather instructed the heads of household in the 10th resolution concerning education as follows: "I will be solicitous to have my children expert, not only at reading handsomely, but also at writing a fair hand. I will then assign them such books to read as I may judge most agreeable and profitable; obliging them to give me some account of what they read; but keep a strict eye upon them, that they don't stumble on the Devil's library, and poison themselves with foolish romances, or novels, or plays, or songs, or jests that are not convenient." Like most Puritans, he sought education as a divine instrument in the service of the Lord, offering classes for blacks and Native Americans in 1717.

Mather, though learned if not brilliant, did not always succeed in his educational endeavors, especially after he suffered rejection as a candidate for the presidency of his alma mater, Harvard. His fortunes soon changed. By the end of the 17th century many local pastors, dissatisfied with the religious direction of Harvard, which they felt was in a state of spiritual decline if not apostasy, desired to start a college in Connecticut. Mather threw himself into the work to establish the new institution. He wrote a wealthy benefactor in England, Elihu Yale, and asked him for funds to establish a college; furthermore, Mather promised that if Yale endowed the new institution it would bear his name. Yale, deeply moved by the solicitations, relented and sent three bales of Indian goods, a parcel of books, and a portrait of King George I. The merchandise brought £500 at a sale, and as Mather promised, the college took the benefactors name, which it bears today.

Mather, often remembered for his role in the Salem witchcraft trials, died unrepentant, and for many today, his actions during that tumultuous period taint the record of an otherwise stellar career.

the churches when our present ministers lie in the dust." Fortunately, John Harvard, a clergyman, came to the rescue. Harvard gave one half of his estate totaling approximately £1,700 toward building the college facility, and his library. It was for the propagation of the gospel and to train pastors that Harvard came into being. In addition the new college was to make available classical learning to the layman, much like Oxford or Cambridge.

OTHER COLLEGES

A royal charter established William and Mary College in 1693. The founders stated that the purpose of the college was "for the advancement of learning, promoting piety, and provision of an able and successive ministry in this country, it hath been thought fit that a college of students of the liberal arts and sciences be erected and maintained." Unlike Harvard, which was Puritan in orientation, William and Mary aligned with Anglicanism. Yale came into being because of dissatisfaction with Harvard. Many in New England came to believe that Harvard was not following Puritan principles. Many in Connecticut wanted a college in the colony, and many of the Harvard faculty even prayed that Connecticut could also have an institution of higher learning.

The College of New Jersey (now Princeton), founded in 1746 by Scot Presbyterians, desired to promote classical learning and seminary curricula. Many of the Presbyterians studied in academies known as log colleges. The most notable log college at Neshaminy, Pennsylvania, run by Reverend William Tennent, was more like a modern Bible institute, but with the inclusion of classical languages. The Old Side Presbyterians did not like the idea of a log college run by a single pastor, and the synod decreed that the ministers completing the log college curriculum must pass an examination written and administered by the synod. A schism ensued, and the New Side revival-minded Presbyterians founded what is now Princeton. The pastors that Princeton produced carried Evangelical Calvinism and classical learning to the western frontier.

King's College (now Columbia) received its charter in 1754, and even though the charter required an Anglican presidency, board members came from various denominations. The college did not establish a theological faculty or department. Likewise the University of Pennsylvania, founded in 1755, stressed the secular in education. Most colleges in the colonial period possessed denominational ties. Soon other denomination colleges sprang up all over the colonies. Rhode Island College (later Brown) was founded by Baptists in 1764; Queen's College (Rutgers) was founded by the Dutch Reformed Church in 1766; Dartmouth was founded by Congregationalist pastor Eleazar Wheelock in 1769.

BACHELOR DEGREE

The curriculum in the colleges prepared the young scholars for work in the clergy, law, or public service. A prime example is that of the three-year plan of study at Harvard for bachelor degree candidates, based on the model of

Benjamin Franklin on Education

A lifetime of learning and observation culminated in Franklin's 1749 publication, *Proposals Relating to the Education of Youth in Pennsylvania,* in which he outlined his ideas for educating youth in an "academy." His academy later became the Academy and College of Philadelphia, later renamed the University of Pennsylvania. He sought to provide a practical education because he considered the classical studies at Harvard as producing "fops."

Franklin based the arguments in his pamphlet on the works of Milton, Locke, and other contemporaries in the field of education. Franklin lamented that no academy existed in Pennsylvania, and that the lack of learning would cause a deficiency of good character resulting in moral catastrophe for the colonies. He urged the wealthy to institute a charter for the establishment of an academy, maintain it with their frequent presence, and encourage the youth to pursue excellence in their studies. In keeping with his practical bent and his scientific curiosity, he recommended building the academy site near a stream, but on high ground, and near the local fauna and plant life. The rectors should write and speak the English language in the proper manner, and hire tutors as needed. The students needed to receive physical training, instruction in self-control, and to live on an adequate but lean diet. "They should be taught every Thing that is useful, and every Thing that is ornamental," wrote Franklin, "But art is long, and Time is short." He concluded that young scholars must learn "those Things that likely to be most useful and most ornamental." In addition, all should learn to write "in a fair hand" and "Drawing, by Imitation of Prints, and some of the first Principles of Perspective."

Emmanuel College at Cambridge, England. A class day for all three years began at 8:00 A.M., with logic and physics until 2:00 P.M., and then students participated in disputations, or practice in argument and debate. A moderator introduced a proposition, and the object was for the participants to rebut the thesis of the proposed topic with as much oratorical flourish as possible. Masters set aside Wednesday for Greek studies, Thursday for Hebrew, and Friday was reserved for declamations or recitations using allusions from ancient literature, and rhetoric (persuasive speaking and writing). Saturday was reserved for catechetical divinity, and the study of history and plants.

In all three years at Harvard, students maintained a commonplace book. Dr. Samuel Johnson defined a commonplace book as "A book in which things remembered are arranged under general heads." It served as a device to aid one's memory for later use. The owner of the commonplace book would record sayings, anecdotes, verses, lectures, quotes, and restatements of remarks that made an indelible impression on the compiler. The use of the common-

Massachusetts School Law

Massachusetts in 1642 became the first colony to require the education of children with the passage of the first compulsory school law. This law was further expanded in 1647 when Massachusetts passed a law requiring every town with a population of 50 families to provide a schoolmaster:

It being one chief project of that old deluder Satan to keep men from the knowledge of he Scriptures, as in former times by keeping them in an unknown tongue, so in these latter times by persuading from the use of tongues, that so at least the true sense and meaning of the original might be clouded by false glosses of saint-seeming deceivers, that learning may not be buried in the grave of our fathers in the church and commonwealth, the Lord assisting our endeavors.

It is therefore ordered that every township in this jurisdiction, after the Lord has increased them to the number of 50 householders, shall then forthwith appoint one within their town to teach all such children as shall resort to him to write and read, whose wages shall be paid either by the parents or masters of such children, or by the inhabitants in general, by way of supply, as the major part of those that order the prudentials of the town shall appoint; provided those that send their children by not oppressed by paying much more than they can have them taught for in other towns.

place book was to aid students in remembering information they might need later in disputations of declamations.

William Smith (1727–1803) became provost of the College of Philadelphia at the invitation of Benjamin Franklin. As the college was non-sectarian, he liberalized the curriculum in 1756 by limiting the classical languages to a third of the curriculum, allowed another third for science and math, and the remainder for logic, ethics, metaphysics, and rhetoric—a skill highly valued in the colonial era. Students read and studied the classics, but they also examined current works as part of their educational experience.

Those desiring a career in the bar "read" law through the auspices of an experienced lawyer for whom the legal student served as clerk. Many students journeyed to London and studied at the Inns of Court. It was not until after the French and Indian War that the College of Philadelphia (now University of Pennsylvania) and King's College (Columbia) attempted to create departments of medicine, but they were not of the highest standard. Medical students, like the legal scholars, learned hands-on with another physician.

Jim Baugess

Further Readings

Altenbaugh, Richard J. *The American People and Their Education: A Social History.* Upper Saddle River, NJ: Pearson Education, 2003.

Barck, Oscar Theodore, Jr. and Hugh Talmage Lefler. *Colonial America.* London: Collier-Macmillan Limited, 1968.

Brands, H.W. *The First American: The Life and Times of Benjamin Franklin.* New York: Doubleday, 2000.

Cremin, Lawrence A. A., *American Education: The Colonial Experience, 1607–1783.* New York: Harper & Row, 1970.

Franklin, Benjamin. *The Autobiography of Benjamin Franklin*, ed. by Leonard W. Labaree, et al. New Haven, CT: Yale University Press, 2003.

Gould, Elizabeth Porter, *Ezekiel Cheever, Schoolmaster*. Boston, MA: The Palmer Co., 1904.

Hawke, David Freeman. *Everyday Life in Early America*. New York: Harper & Row, 1989.

Isaacson, Walter, ed. *A Benjamin Franklin Reader*. New York: Simon & Schuster, 2003.

Middlekauff, Robert "Mather, Cotton," *American National Biography*. New York: Oxford University Press. 2000.

Morison, Samuel Eliot. *The Intellectual Life of Colonial New England*. New York: New York University Press, 1955.

Pulliam, John D., *History of Education in America*. Columbus, OH: Charles Merrill Publishing Company, 1976.

Smith, Wilson, ed. *Theories of Education in Early America: 1655–1819.* Indianapolis, IN: Bobbs-Merrill Company, Inc., 1973.

Spring, Joel, *The American School: 1642–1985*. New York: Longman, 1986.

Thompson, Merritt M., *The History of Education*. New York: Barnes & Noble, Inc., 1966.

CHAPTER 9

Science and Technology

"As we enjoy great advantages from the inventions of others, we should be glad of an opportunity to serve others by any invention of ours..."
— Benjamin Franklin (who never patented his inventions)

THE DEVELOPMENT OF American natural philosophy in the 17th century occurred under difficult circumstances. Being diverse and sparsely settled the colonies were initially inhospitable grounds for what is now called science and technology. The original 13 colonies, as independent members of the emerging British Empire, imported their intellectual influences largely within the context of British developments.

In addition the colonies were organized to serve the interests of British mercantilism. This meant that colonial trade and commerce operated on dependent terms that favored the mother country. Other European influences did emerge, but these were also largely filtered through the prism of a young empire.

The economic development of the colonies also varied considerably. New England, the mid-Atlantic colonies, and the south were very different in terms of education, religion, geography, infrastructure, and social makeup. Population growth was relatively slow during the 17th century, with estimates suggesting that by the 1650s the entire colonial population was but 50,000, and most of these settlers were in New England.

Agriculture was the means of both colonial survival and wealth. Many farms operated at a subsistence level, particularly if they were located away from rivers and ports. The plantation economy characterized the south. This economy was increasingly tied after 1619 to the "peculiar institution" of slavery which soon became codified in colonial statutes.

Another prominent feature of the colonial economy was the use of the indentured labor system. Indentured servants made up a considerable percentage of the overall population, with some estimates suggesting as many as a third to a half of the workforce fell under this category. Many were unskilled, but for those with skills, conditions and terms could be negotiated. Such skills were important in building local technologies.

The indentured servants were later joined, following the passage of the Transportation Act of 1718, by a steady stream of forced immigrants. These transported settlers were convicted of many different types of crimes; being a debtor was prominent among them. Over the course of the century they could be found in at least nine of the original 13 colonies. The expansion of slave labor in the southern colonies eventually replaced the indentured system and the Revolution ended criminal transport. In South Carolina for example, slaves came to outnumber whites, sometimes by a two-to-one margin.

Steady population growth occurred throughout the colonial period, reaching approximately 250,000 people by 1700 and almost two million by 1760. This population level, along with rising standards of literacy and commercial development, created a better background for the establishment of a colonial scientific and technological environment. Improved social and economic conditions increased scientific and technological possibilities and made for more profitable colonial enterprises.

The rise of early colonial cities also provided a focal point for intellectual pursuits. By the mid-18th century Boston's population was 15,000, New York City had 16,000 to 17,000 people, and Philadelphia numbered approximately 20,000. These urban settings in time became centers for the exchange of ideas and opened the way for experiments in all areas of endeavor.

SCIENTIFIC REVOLUTION

Within this colonial context during the 17th century, the western world was undergoing a scientific revolution. This was a time of substantial change that created the basis for a modern worldview that eventually transformed the nature of colonial and European life. The emerging scientists of this era helped confirm previous discoveries as found in the work of Copernicus (1473–1543), Kepler (1571–1630) and Galileo (1564–1642). The basis for such change came through the introduction of early formulations of what would later be called the scientific method. Inquiry rose to new levels. This approach involved careful observation and subsequent experimental analysis to create hypotheses which, in turn, led to further testing, reassessment, and revised conclusions.

The end of decades of destructive European warfare, the consolidation of Protestantism in northern Europe, and the subsequent reduction of papal controls allowed for greater personal freedoms. These emerging scientific thinkers could then explore ideas without the fear of condemnation, or even worse, brutal persecution. In essence the scientific revolution discovered that the universe was subject to the laws of nature, and these laws could best be understood through the application of the tools of observation and human reason. This step took science out of the medieval realm that relied on classical thought, magic, and superstition. There now were new ways and methods of doing things. What also occurred was a change in the nature of the questions asked of the natural world.

The scientific revolution is difficult to date precisely, as is the idea of actual science, which at this time remained undefined as part of an all-embracing natural philosophy. In terms of specific starting places for fields of science, it can be argued that cosmology and astronomy launched the initial inquiries of this period which, with the refinement in mathematical knowledge as the century progressed, led to developments in physics and concurrently anatomy and physiology.

John Winthrop, the Younger

John Winthrop, the Younger (1606–76) reflected the changing nature of colonial life as a consequence of the scientific revolutions of the period. Winthrop was born in England and educated at Trinity College, Dublin, and arrived in Massachusetts in 1631. He was the son of John Winthrop, the first governor of Massachusetts Bay Company. Through his Massachusetts base he ventured forth in 1635 to establish a new colony along the Connecticut River, eventually founding a settlement that took the name New London. By the 1650s he became an important force in Connecticut politics, becoming governor, a post he would hold from 1659 until his death. In 1662 he secured a new Royal Charter for the colony.

Winthrop was a physician as well as a politician and treated the ailments of numerous Connecticut settlers. He also applied himself to practical scientific and technological matters, starting an iron works, exploring for mineral deposits, as well as investigating evaporation as a method of reclaiming salt from sea water.

He built a sizable library, made use of a telescope to explore the heavens, and began a lengthy correspondence with the emerging scientists of England. His work gained the attention of the Royal Society, which elected him a fellow during his 1661–63 visits. In addition to papers, he sent the society numerous New World natural specimens, including milkweed pods.

Winthrop had elevated the stature of colonial learning, and his diverse interests made him an example of the new era of observation and discovery. His mill in New London, Connecticut, is still standing as a symbol of his early technological efforts.

In most of the colonial period, what is usually thought of as scientific progress did not arise in the colonies, and the discoveries and developments in Europe filtered to the colonies through publication, often some years after their first appearance. On the other hand the discovery of new plants, animals, birds, and native peoples in the New World greatly stimulated the development of fresh thinking in Europe. Meanwhile in both Europe and in the colonies, daily life involved the application of technical developments in such fields as ship-building and design, the powering of mills, improvements to agriculture, the use of tools and implements, and the construction of buildings. By the late colonial period, a handful of innovative individuals in the colonies began to make contributions to both science and technology.

SCIENTIFIC METHOD

The idea of a scientific method owes much to the work of thinkers such as Francis Bacon (1561–1626) in England and Rene Descartes (1596–1650) of France, who helped develop the inductive and deductive methods for organizing our reasoning processes. Significant applications of the experimental method were pursued by people like William Harvey (1578–1657), whose work helped explain the mysteries of the circulation of blood. These methods provided the means for more detailed scientific experiment, producing along the way many false avenues as well, and these in themselves opened the ground for further study and correction.

The Britain of which the American colonies formed a key part (the United Kingdom as a country would not emerge until after Scottish unification in 1707) led the way in many of the era's scientific developments. The Civil War of the 1640s unleashed greater freedom of thought, which continued after the Restoration. This was best symbolized in 1660 by the establishment of the Royal Society of London for the Promotion of Natural Knowledge, which represented another major step forward. The organization's motto of *nulla in verba* (nothing based on words) reflected a new scientific approach that stressed the importance of experimental results. The leading scientists of the period sought out Royal Society membership, and this over time produced members drawn from the American colonies.

This new breed of researchers included Robert Boyle (1627–91), Robert Hooke (1635–1703), and most significantly, Sir Isaac Newton (1643–1727). Boyle saw a purposeful world operating under God's mechanical laws that could be discovered through careful experiment. He worked to give birth to modern chemistry, and along with Robert Hooke improved air pumps, important in creating vacuums. In addition he formulated Boyle's gas laws, which uncovered the relationships between gas volumes and pressure.

Robert Hooke became the first curator of experiments with the Royal Society and made major contributions to our understanding of natural processes in a number of areas. He built upon the work of others to enhance microscopic magnification, examining the plant cell in the process. He formulated laws of elasticity, developed an idea for a universal joint, and improved telescopes and barometers, examined fossils, and created a balance wheel essential for watches and clocks. The one area that he could not overcome was his stormy relationship with the greatest scientist of the age, Newton.

Isaac Newton's life bridged the centuries, and his considerable endeavours influenced scientific understanding from this time on. His work did much to build a world of laws and gave a seeming order to the universe. Overcoming an unpromising personal start in life, Newton developed the mathematical tools that were essential for the advancement of all science, as well as the properties of motion and matter. Along with Christian Huygens (1629–95) in Holland, Gottfried Leibnitz (1646–1716) in Germany, and Robert Hooke, Newton was instrumental in creating the mathematics that could explain such areas as circular motion, volume, and gravitation. Newton began his advances in this area in 1666 when he was just 24 years old. He formulated (Newton provided a more fully developed description in 1671) a new mathematics now known as calculus, which became the language of science. He is therefore generally seen, along with Leibnitz, as a key force in the invention of calculus.

In his most important work, *Principia Mathematica* published in 1687, he outlined his three laws of motion and built his universal law of gravity that explained how the planets stayed in their orbits. Other work included theories of light and optics, which made modern astronomy possible. Newton's contributions to the scientific revolution spread far and wide and created in the process a dominant vision that revealed that the same natural laws governed the heavens and earth.

During this era Newton's friend Edmund Halley (1656–1742) made significant contributions to astronomy. In his youth he formulated a star catalogue of the southern hemisphere based on his St. Helena observations. In time he became famous for his study of comets and their trajectories. He also mapped the world's winds, made longitudinal calculations, studied global magnetism, and created mortality tables. His prominence was enhanced further with his appointment as Astronomer Royal in 1720.

Sir Isaac Newton developed the mathematical tools essential for the advancement of all science, as well as the properties of motion and matter.

The wide spectrum of ideas uncovered during the 17th century made their way to the American colonies throughout the century, particularly as circumstances

Scientist David Rittenhouse

David Rittenhouse (1732–96) was born in Pennsylvania and became one of America's most noted colonial scientists. He was also an avid patriot and committed revolutionary. In 1756 Rittenhouse built the first telescope and observatory in America. In 1767 he constructed an orrery, which provided a mechanical model for studying the sun, moon, and planets. He was an important member of the American Philosophical Society (founded in 1745 by Benjamin Franklin to promote inquiry in the sciences and humanities) and upon the death of Franklin, Rittenhouse became society president.

During the Revolutionary War he used his engineering expertise to aid the colonial cause by producing gun powder, cannons, and protective devices such as harbour chains. In 1783 he put his optical skills to work to make a pair of spectacles for George Washington.

changed to allow for greater concerns besides simple survival. The rise of Puritan New England, and later Quaker Pennsylvania, given their support for education as an essential for bible studies, also opened the doors to other inquiry as well.

These early colonial settlers were generally constrained by practical necessity. In some rarefied quarters there were sufficient transfers of knowledge in natural philosophy that English methods entered the American context. The establishment of the Boston Latin School in 1635 for younger students as well as Harvard College in 1636, William and Mary in 1693, and Yale in 1701, provided examples for future educational establishments in the Americas. Access was restricted by gender, race, class, and location, but a growth in the importance of education did take root. The south though was slower to develop what would eventually be called public education. American colonial life also proved very receptive to the works of John Locke (1632–1704), whose codification of the idea of observation and experience as a basis for the empirical model would prove very influential in education and politics. He transcribed the tenets of the scientific revolution into more practical terms, and these were well received by the colonial educational elite.

American colonials also imported the standard technologies of the era such as guns, cannons, furniture, and plowshares, along with the pigs and cows, which allowed them to build a permanent agricultural base. In this agricultural society Americans were soon planting wheat, rye, oats, sugar cane, rice, cotton, and tobacco in order to produce for their own needs and harvest surpluses.

THE ENLIGHTENMENT

The Enlightenment, much like the scientific revolution, is generally identified as a product of the 18th century, yet precise dates and overlaps between centuries make definite chronologies difficult. This "age of reason" would nevertheless have a major influence on the flowering of American colonial life during the 1700s. Increases in population and prosperity created a sense of distinction and independence of thought and deed. The old political, social, and religious absolutism that characterized European society, although it was sometimes tried, was more difficult to translate to American shores, where there was an abundance of unfettered or virgin land and fewer social constraints.

Further there was no embedded feudal elite with dominant control over land and life. In addition institutional religion was difficult to impose in an environment that had been receptive to so many religious exiles seeking various forms of freedom of worship. By the 18th century Puritan control in New England had waned as the church itself matured. Protestantism of the English model expanded notions of freedom of speech and press and this increased an

Thomas Jefferson on the Superiority of Science to Politics

From *The Writings of Thomas Jefferson*, an excerpt of a letter from Jefferson to David Rittenhouse:

Writing to a philosopher, I may hope to be pardoned for intruding some thoughts of my own, though they relate to him personally. Your time for two years past has, I believe, been principally employed in the civil government of your country. Though I have been aware of the authority our cause would acquire with the world from its beginning known that yourself and Dr. Franklin were zealous friends to it, and am myself duly impressed with a sense of the arduousness of government, and the obligation those are under who are able to conduct it, yet I am also satisfied there is an order of geniuses above that obligation, and therefore exempted from it. Nobody can conceive that nature ever intended to throw away a Newton upon the occupations of a crown. It would have been a prodigality for which even the conduct of Providence might have been arraigned, had he been by birth annexed to what was so far below him. Cooperating with nature in her ordinary economy, we should dispose of and employ the geniuses of men according to their several orders and degrees.

I doubt not there are in your country many persons equal to the task of conducting government: but you should consider that the world has but one Rittenhouse, and that it never had one before. The amazing mechanical representation of the solar system which you conceived and executed has never been surpassed by any but the work of which it is a copy. Are those powers then, which being intended for the erudition of the world are, like air and light, the world's common property, to be taken from their proper pursuit to do the commonplace drudgery of governing a single state, a work which may be executed by men of an ordinary stature, such as are always and everywhere to be found?

exchange of values that gradually undercut autocratic religious powers as well as the absolutist controls of the monarchy and the aristocracy.

The thought that was emerging during the 18th century built upon the discoveries of the 17th-century natural philosophers who applied rational thought to understand the physical world. During the 18th century the same processes would be applied to society where reason would become the basis for authority. The French *philosophes* such as Voltaire (1694–1778), Montesquieu (1689–1755) and d'Alembert (1717–83) challenged old institutions including the church; they saw reason to be a better tool for understanding than slavish systems, whose authority relied on concepts such as divine right.

The idea of a fountain of modern knowledge inspired other French thinkers, such as Denis Diderot (1713–84) and his group of encyclopedists, to build a central reference base for understanding the world. This base became the *French Encyclopedia,* published between 1751 and 1785. Likewise, Samuel Johnson (1709–84) in London was inspired to write his *English Dictionary* to codify and better explain the meaning of language. Diderot's friend Jean Jacques Rousseau (1712–78) also examined the importance of reason in ordering society and saw mankind in its natural state as essentially good, and argued that the betterment of society could come about through a social contract that better served the people's interests than the *ancien regime* with its absolutist state.

Although there were differences in interpretation and emphasis, in general the Enlightenment offered an idea of progress that appeared optimistic in its belief in a better and more positive future. How this was to be achieved was through a system of empiricist thought as expressed by philosophers such as David Hume (1711–76). It was argued that when rational approaches were applied to the formation of society, what emerged was a nation-state that would challenge intolerance, censorship, and dogmatism of all sorts. In this new society the individual, particularly in the form of a growing merchant middle class, had certain rights as well as needs that should be better protected. Hume's fellow Scot and friend, Adam Smith (1723–90), furthered this debate in his *Wealth of Nations* (1776), an analysis that formed the basis for modern economics and created a system which raised the status of the individual. For Smith, increasing individual

Denis Diderot created the French Encyclopedia, *published between 1751 and 1785.*

Other Representatives of the American Enlightenment

John Bartram (1699–1777) provides another example of an individual rising in colonial society without the benefit of much formal education. He would make a sizable contribution to the development of science, and with Benjamin Franklin was an early proponent of the American Philosophical Society.

Coming from a Pennsylvania Quaker farming background, it is not surprising that Bartram's interest in plants began at an early age. In order to learn more about the identity, nature, and workings of the plant world, he created, beginning in the 1720s a botanical garden and specimen collection. He introduced perhaps as many as 200 new species to many collectors in both Britain and Europe. His reputation was such that in 1765, King George III appointed him Royal Botanist.

John Bartram's son William (1739–1823) was inspired by his father's work and, in turn, became a colonial naturalist, collector, and botanist of distinction in his own right. William's book of travels, published in 1791, established his reputation as America's most widely traveled scientist. Later he joined with his brother to preserve his father's botanical garden and in time published the nation's first plant catalog.

Jane Colden (1724–66) was born in New York City, the daughter of Cadwallader Colden, a medical graduate of the University of Edinburgh and a prominent member of colonial-era New York society. Jane Colden manifested an early interest in science and demonstrated special ability in botany. She is best represented in her illustrated 1757 catalog of several hundred local plants.

Following marriage in 1759 to William Farquhar, her scientific output seemingly decreased, but some of her work on plant classification was later published in Scotland. Jane Colden is now credited as America's first significant female scientist, a role that was deemed unusual even in an enlightened 18th century.

Benjamin Banneker (1731–1806), like Jane Colden, was a figure outside the typical norms of colonial society, and his achievements were noteworthy given the obstacles of the day. Banneker was born in Maryland, the son of a former slave, and later became a tobacco planter.

He gained a rudimentary education through a local Quaker school and possessed considerable mathematical talents, eventually building clocks and calculating the details used in the almanacs of the day. In his later years he developed an interest in astronomy, predicting eclipses, and briefly assisted Andrew Ellicott's initial boundary survey of the District of Columbia north of the Potomac in 1791. Banneker also exchanged correspondence with Thomas Jefferson in regard to the issue of slavery and black inferiority and for this he is often remembered.

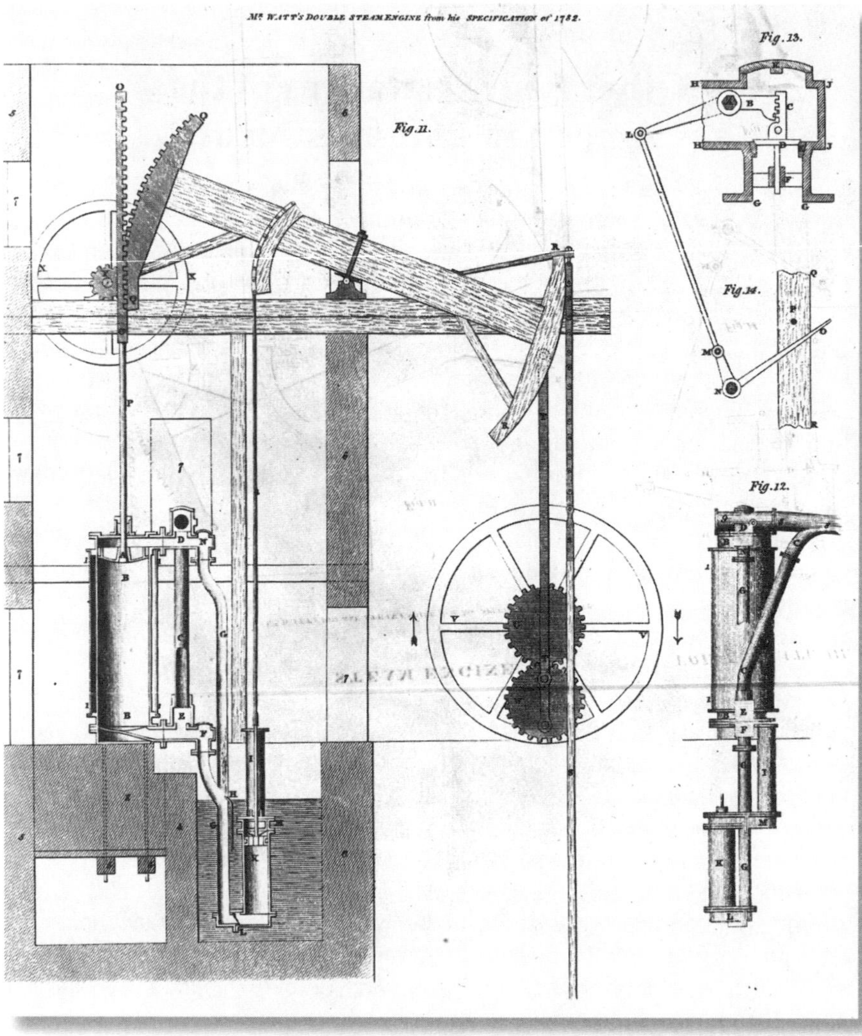

James Watt's double steam engine from his specification of 1782. Watt had improved Newcomen's steam engine, making possible important industrial developments.

freedom worked hand-in-hand as a force that brought wealth, prosperity, and knowledge to society and the nation.

Within the American colonies during this century, many distinguished members of the American social and political elites were influenced and informed by Enlightenment developments and beliefs. The influences, generally more English than French, could be seen in the works of Jefferson (1743–1826), Washington (1732–99), Paine (1737–1809), Franklin (1706–90) and many others. Such individuals in time challenged the existing political order by drawing their terms of reference from the Age of Reason itself. What emerged was a call for inherent freedoms, an appeal to natural law, criticism of old institutions of church and monarchy, and a commitment to a Deist view of a mechanical universe that left man to pursue through self-determination his rights to both property and independence. These attitudes created a positive environment that saw real practical benefit in understanding the surrounding natural world.

As the years passed the transfer of ideas accelerated and a more predictable and mechanically understandable world entered a wider public consciousness. New technological possibilities came into being, which changed the very nature of life in England, Europe, and the American colonies. As the century progressed these changes made possible the Industrial Revolution, the impact of which is still being felt today.

The inventive output in the period was truly prodigious. Thomas Newcomen (1664–1729) created an atmospheric steam engine in 1712, which set the stage for further development. The sextant appeared in the 1730s, developed by John Hadley (1682–1744) in England and Thomas Godfrey (1704–49) in America, which allowed for improved navigation. Benjamin Huntsman (1704–76) produced modern steel in England in the 1740s; and the Leyden jar, which is an early electrical capacitor, was developed in 1745 by Dutch inventor Pieter van Musschenbroek (1700–48). In 1747 James Lind's (1716–94) experiments with citrus fruits for the British Royal Navy uncovered a method of prevention of scurvy. James Hargreaves (1720–78) introduced in England in 1764 his Spinning Jenny, which allowed for cheaper cloth production, setting the stage for a revolution in factory textiles.

By 1765 James Watt had improved Newcomen's steam engine, making possible important future industrial developments in transport and other areas. For example in 1785 Edmund Cartwright (1743–1823) used Watt's steam engine to power a loom, which made mass clothing production a reality. In addition important developments also came about through the more accurate prediction of longitude, a problem solved by John Harrison's (1693–1776) fourth chronometer in 1761.

FOOD PRODUCTION

In other areas such as agriculture great strides were made in improving food production. This freed people from the land, allowed for the growth of cities, provided trade surpluses, and produced workers for the Industrial Revolution. Crop rotation in the form of the Norfolk system became more common, and Jethro Tull's (1674–1741) mechanized seed drill revolutionized yields, and formed a key part of American colonial agriculture.

In Georgia in 1733, the first commercial garden, the Trustees Garden, was planted with the purpose of studying plants for their productive possibilities. In the area of animal breeding, experiments improved the quality of livestock. Between the 1760s and 1790s George Culley and others produced animals with better traits. Breeds that are today recognized as Angus, Jersey, and Hereford

The Conestoga wagon could carry eight tons and was likely designed by German or Dutch settlers in Pennsylvania.

cattle, as well as Leicester Longwool sheep entered the local landscape. In the study of nature, which created the bases for modern biology, the Comte de Buffon (1707–88) in France provided major insights into natural history, as did Carl Linnaeus (1707–1778) of Sweden who provided a systematic scheme for ordering and classifying both plants and animals, which would have a significant impact upon scientific developments in the 19th century. Their work was supported by the likes of Gilbert White (1720–93). His *Natural History and Antiquities of Selborne* of 1793 detailed important botanical relationships that stimulated the curiosity of other naturalists.

Enlightenment ideas were richly nourished in 18th-century colonial America. The colonies rapidly developed in ways that would challenge British attempts at mercantilist control and imperial dominance. American trade and considerable maritime shipping interests increased native wealth, and advances in agriculture were producing the surpluses needed for trade. In addition there were rising industries, such as mines and mills, producing the raw materials necessary for a more technological society.

With its vast resources and abundant land, particularly in the west, American economic promise and wealth encouraged maximum inventiveness to bring these products to market. In order to meet the demands of expansion, better transport was necessary, and the Conestoga wagon served this purpose. Developed in the 1720s, reputedly by German Mennonites or possibly by Dutch settlers, the Conestoga took its name from Conestoga Creek in Pennsylvania. With its heavy frame, large wheels, and broad base, the wagon could carry eight tons and was pulled by large teams of oxen or mules over rough terrain.

If the wilderness was to be tamed, improved weapons were required, and the flintlock rifle was a tool that proved its value in the repeated French and Indian wars of the period. Its greater accuracy brought food to the table and kept the British at bay during the Revolutionary War. Lancaster, Pennsylvania, gunsmiths developed the rifle during the 1730s. With an increased barrel length, .50 calibre ball, and light weight, the long rifle was an invaluable frontier weapon that was often identified with Pennsylvania and Kentucky. It would remain in use until the 1840s when it was replaced by cap and ball percussion rifles.

Massachusetts-born Eli Whitney (1765–1825) symbolized the importance problem solving had on 18th-century science and technology. He is credited with promoting the advantages of interchangeable parts in the process of musket production. Although developed later at the Springfield Arsenal, the concept he advanced became crucial to the American system of manufactures. His development of the Cotton Gin, patented in 1794, would bring him fame, but not wealth, or the social consequences he intended.

During his travels in the south he saw the enormous difficulty associated with the removal of seeds from the round cotton bud. At this time the institution of slavery appeared to be in terminal decline and was hardly profitable. Inadvertently Whitney's invention provided the means for the revival of slavery in the south for it separated the seeds from cotton so successfully that 50 pounds of clean cotton could be produced in a day. The plantation cultivation and production of cotton brought wealth to the southern plantation owners and provided an export crop to feed the emerging textile mills of Britain and New England. Although both the system of interchangeable parts and the cotton gin came well after the end of the colonial period, they both were American developments and built on the 18th-century approach to technical problem solving.

The triumph of Enlightenment thinking in America found particularly noteworthy representatives in Thomas Jefferson (1743–1826) and Benjamin Franklin (1706–90). Both men advanced science and technology immeasurably. Jefferson and Franklin were enormously successful in multiple fields, including invention, politics, philosophy, and science. Franklin is perhaps better known as a scientist, but Jefferson was equally interested in improvements in technology and production.

Thomas Jefferson saw success in invention, politics, philosophy, and science.

Jefferson's political career saw him at age 33 write the Declaration of Independence, and later become governor of Virginia, Minister to France, secretary of state under George Washington, vice president during the John Adams administration, and finally president. His commitment to American expansion saw him engineer the Louisiana Purchase in 1803, and his belief in the advancement of knowledge made him an instrumental force in the founding of the University of Virginia in 1819.

Yet Jefferson was a keen observer of the natural world and an accomplished architect and mathematician. He corresponded with the leading scientists of the day, created impressive gardens to study plants on his plantation, Monticello, and made improvements in agriculture such as applying Newtonian principles to plow design. Jefferson's devotion to learning also saw him explore the fields of meteorology and palaeontology. He invented better methods for excavating archaeological sites, including Indian mounds. Jefferson's accomplishments made him stand out in an age of many impressive individuals, and he inspired invention and the search for knowledge in others. His selection as third president of the American Philosophical Society was for Jefferson as important as any of his many achievements.

FRANKLIN'S CONTRIBUTIONS

The premier American colonial scientist of the 18th century was Benjamin Franklin, who like Jefferson combined success in numerous endeavors. His polymath skills epitomized Enlightenment virtues. Born in Boston under humble circumstances, Franklin rose an apprentice printer to great success as a printer/publisher in Philadelphia, America's leading colonial city. He believed in self improvement and promoted it at every opportunity. He was also fervent in his support for the revolutionary ideals of individual liberty, which in time made him a leading light of the Revolution.

Franklin's *Pennsylvania Gazette* spread the news of the day, and his *Poor Richard's Almanac* provided practical advice on worldly conditions, including how to advance in the world. The need to open the world of opportunity to others led him to start a lending library, the Library Company of Philadelphia, to promote public access to knowledge. Other civic works included the establishment of the first fire department in 1736 and the first fire insurance company in 1752.

Benjamin Franklin rose from being an apprentice printer (depicted in the painting above) to become the premier American colonial scientist of the 18th century.

His inquisitive nature also drew him to the observations and experiments that would make his name as an inventor and scientist. His studies of physics and electricity brought him to the attention of the Royal Society, and subsequently led to his invention of the lightning rod in 1752. Franklin's belief in colonial scientific promotion contributed greatly to the successful establishment of the American Philosophical Society, of which he became first president.

Franklin's curiosity found an outlet in inventions such as the Franklin stove, the catheter, the glass armonica (a musical instrument), odometer, and bifocals (which he produced in 1780); all instruments designed to improve the human condition. He contributed to the Declaration of Independence and worked tirelessly for the Continental Congress, serving an important diplomatic role in France that helped secure French support for the war with Britain. After independence, through his role as postmaster general, he worked towards unifying the nation.

Like Jefferson, Franklin was a man for all seasons and made his mark as both a patriot and intellectual. His virtues far exceeded any personal vices as was seen in his early abolitionist convictions, and his service as president of the Pennsylvania Society for Promoting the Abolition of Slavery.

PRAGMATIC SCIENTIFIC APPLICATIONS

Developments in science and technology by the close of the 18th century had made America economically stronger and more independently minded. The needs of the new country, its abundant resources, and its new-found political path allowed it to forge pragmatic scientific applications to fit its own idea of progress. Advances were seen in the large emerging cities along the eastern seaboard with their permanent brick and stone classically influenced Georgian architecture. The material culture reflected the products of maturing artisans whose decorative arts, silverware, finished furniture, and manufactured products were of increasing quality, as were the creature comforts that were designed to make life more bearable.

The crude conditions of early colonial life had become more refined, that is, for those who could afford it. The shovel, dung fork, hoe, scythe, and sickle still remained the essential technologies of an agrarian society, but quality was improving and the emerging Industrial Revolution was bringing prices down through advances in metallurgy. Apothecaries became more common and these brought the rewards of the new chemistry and botanical medicine to the public at large.

By the close of the 18th century the American population was approaching an impressive four million people, of whom approximately 760,000 were African Americans. The size of the country and the availability of land allowed for lower population densities than in other countries, and this would prove of enormous benefit. Americans were growing taller, richer, and had higher fertility rates than other lands, an important bonus given the steady threats of disease and war. Science and technology lay behind the advances, accomplishments, and possibilities necessary for survival and expansion, and success bred further expansion. The construction of the Wilderness Road in the 1770s through the Cumberland Gap penetrated the Appalachians, and allowed access to the western territories of Kentucky, Tennessee, and the Ohio Valley. By 1796 the application of existing technology made even this primitive pioneer enterprise an all-weather road, and thus symbolized how triumphs in engineering and technology could increase the prosperity of an entire nation. The scientific and technological transfers of the 17th and 18th century set the groundwork for the explosion of American science and industry in the 19th century.

THEODORE W. EVERSOLE

Further Readings

Beale, Otho T. and Richard Shryock. *Cotton Mather, The First Significant Figure in American Medicine*. Baltimore, MD: John Hopkins University Press, 1954.

Brasch, Frederick E. "The Newtonian Epoch in the American Colonies." *Proceedings, American Antiquarian Society* (XLIX, 1939).

Cohen, I. Bernard et al., eds. *Puritanism and the Rise of Modern Science*. New Brunswick, NJ: Rutgers University Press, 1990.

Eggleston, Edward. *The Transit of Civilization from England to America During the 17th Century*. New York: Appleton and Co., 1901.

Hoffman, Nancy and John C. Van Horne. *America's Curious Botanist: A Tercentennial Reappraisal of John Bartram*. Philadelphia, PA: American Philosophical Society, 2004.

Hindle, Brooke. *The Pursuit of Science in Revolutionary America, 1735–1789*. Chapel Hill: University of North Carolina Press, 1956.

James, Edward T. et al., eds. *Notable American Women, 1607–1950*. Vol. 1. Cambridge, MA: Harvard University Press, 1971.

January, Brendan. *Science in Colonial America*. London: Franklin Watts, 1999.

Klein, Randolph S. *Science and Society in Early America: Essays in Honor of Whitfield J. Bell, Jr*. Philadelphia, PA: American Philosophical Society, 1986.

McGaw, Judith A. *Early American Technology: Making and Doing Things from the Colonial Era to 1850*. Chapel Hill: University of North Carolina Press, 1994.

Shields, David S. *Oracles of Empire: Poetry, Politics and Commerce in British America, 1690–1750*. Chicago, IL: University of Chicago Press, 1990.

Stearns, Raymond F. *Science in the British Colonies of North America*. Urbana: University of Illinois Press, 1970.

CHAPTER 10

Entertainment

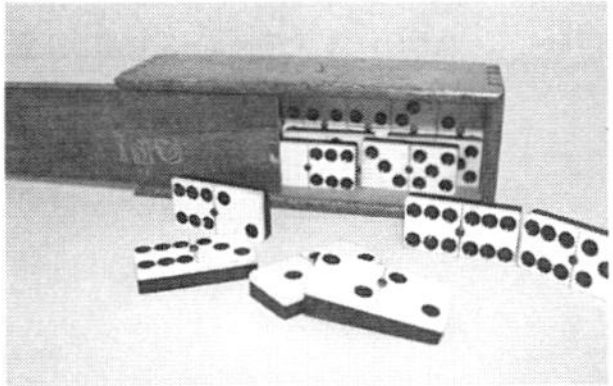

"I examined my heart, and findinge it needful to recreate my minde with some outward recreation, I yielded unto it, and by moderate exercise herein was much refreshed."

— John Winthrop

BECAUSE MAKING A living in the new world was time-consuming and energy-draining, the earliest settlers in America had little time and energy for activities related to leisure and entertainment. Leisure time, which is the sort of spare time most associated with entertainment and sport, was in short supply, as was leftover energy after the demands of the day and the week were met. The short supply of time and energy persisted through most of the American colonies, from early settlement up to the Revolutionary War. Despite little time and energy, colonists found ways to enjoy themselves and share moments of leisure with their families and communities.

Early settlers of the colonies along the eastern seaboard brought with them both family customs and community habits of celebrating seasonal festivals. These festivals were born out of rural life in England and were especially common in New England. Many of the English colonists focused on a stricter religious observance and had a unique view of celebrations, sport, and play.

The primary source of entertainment and play in the colonial era was the family. One of the chief joys of parents has always been playing with their children and teaching them along the way. No doubt the early colonists felt this way, but what each deemed appropriate for play and for teaching varied quite a bit from colony to colony. The content of play and teaching was influenced both by religious persuasion and the sort of community in which the

Colonial leisure activities sometimes involved items such as a ball-and-cup toy, naughts and crosses (tic tac toe) boards made of twigs and small tree branches, and decks of playing cards.

family lived. Children were generally free to play and to grow up in a carefree manner up until the age of about six, at which time they were expected to begin taking on a serious round of household or work chores.

When a newborn joined a colonial household, a parent or an older sibling might make a baby rattle from a dried out gourd or a hollowed out piece of wood. That parent or sibling might also sing the child to sleep, comforting themselves and the rest of the household with the sound of familiar lullabies brought across the ocean.

As a child grew older, someone might make a whirligig to delight and amuse the young baby, and it often worked to fascinate older children as well. The materials needed were simple and included a button or a round piece of bark or thin disc of wood scrap, and some thread, twine, or leather thong. Several pieces of twine were threaded through holes in the button or bark, and when they were pulled tight or snapped together, the disc would turn and also make a whirring sound. Doing this in front of the fire would cast shadows and add to the fun as well. Tops made of wood, soft cloth dolls or poppets, and corn shuck dolls were toys parents enjoyed making and giving to their children.

Parents did not necessarily give toys as Christmas gifts. In some areas, notably those settled by the stricter members of the Puritan belief, Christmas was not observed, though in those colonies there were celebrations of thanksgiving and of harvest. These were usually distinct from each other and other sorts of community gatherings based around seasonal observance, both religious and secular. Though the religious celebrations were based heavily on activities such as preaching and worship, they also provided a chance for community members to gather and meet each other, which offered a sort of public entertainment for the adults, as did the preaching.

Through the early days of the colonies, most entertainment and celebration took place within the family and with nearby neighbors. The early settlements in North America had much more in common with the rural countryside of medieval England than they did with 17th-century London. Public events were rarely spontaneous, and common places for people to gather, such as public houses or town squares, developed slowly in most areas.

Indentured servants and slaves had less chance for free time than even the working farmer or tradesperson, but generally enjoyed the same sort of activities. Those with more wealth, especially landowners in the southern colonies, were less tied to filling their days with household tasks. Women might spend their time making quilts or socializing with family members or teaching children. Men might hunt or gamble with friends or discuss politics. If neighbors were nearby, calling on them was a form or entertainment, and if homes were widely separated, going for visits and receiving guests to stay in the home were also ways to enjoy society.

SHARING FAMILY ACTIVITIES

The focus for relaxation and entertainment was within the home. Playing with children and helping them learn could help adults find lighter sides of the demands of daily work. For the women, planting and caring for food and herb gardens, cooking, keeping the house in good order, making and maintaining clothing, caring for children, and keeping track of household stores were among the things that filled their days. For the men, farming the larger fields and crops, hunting for food, keeping the home and household buildings in repair (and building them when necessary), and possibly pursuing a skill or trade such as shipbuilding, furniture making, or blacksmithing were among the jobs they had to do. All this was done by daylight, too; a flickering candle or firelight was too dim to allow pursuit of these chores after dark.

Skill at working with cloth or working in wood, cleaning, tending to crops, and cooking were some of the family work children learned. Children began to take on work of the family early, and the amount of time available for play depended on such variables as period, social status, and religion.

GAMES

Children might play naughts and crosses (tic tac toe), all hid (hide and seek), and draughts (checkers). If someone in the family had a fiddle or a whistle, or knew how to read or how to carve in wood, it's likely that they taught their children these things, although in some families only boys would be encouraged to learn such things.

Colonial Holidays

Christmas was a religious holiday observed with services in Church of England and Roman Catholic areas, but was definitely not celebrated in strictly Puritan areas to emphasize their turning away from the practices of other beliefs. Family visits and perhaps a special meal might be commonly held on the day in other Protestant areas. It was not, generally, a day for celebrating children or childhood, as it is often seen today.

New Year's Day, and sometimes the 12 days of Christmas between December 25 and the Feast of the Three Kings on January 6, was often celebrated with balls, dances, fireworks, and parties of young revelers going from house to house in cities looking for a holiday handout of food, drink, or coin.

February second, known also as the feast of Candlemas, was the midpoint of winter and as with today's groundhog's day rituals, people looked for signs of spring and prognosticated the course of the coming crops from the conditions on that day.

Valentine's Day customs have endured through time. Superstitious colonial women believed that the first person one saw on Valentine's Day would be a partner in marriage. They also had the custom of writing names on scraps of paper and then putting them in a bowl of water. The first name to rise to the top would be the one to marry.

Even in the Catholic colonies, Easter wasn't marked as a major holiday, although Dutch colonists in New York colored eggs with natural dyes on the day, using beet juice for red and purple shades, and onion skins to make bright yellow. Bringing another custom from across the seas and from ancient times, some colonists set up maypoles and performed maypole dances at the beginning of that month. An ancient fertility ritual, this practice was not considered proper in many places, but May being a month of the beginning of spring in many areas, the custom became transmuted into spring festivals as time went on.

Though not formally marked on the calendar, the end of harvest and gathering were celebrated with feasts and thanksgivings both sacred and secular. This occurred from the end of August through October. All Hallows Eve on October 31, All Saints' Day on November 1, and All Souls' Day on November 2 were variously observed as days of church attendance.

Though the New England colonies, because of their Puritan, Pilgrim, and Quaker religious beliefs and their ideas of proper society, did not celebrate many of the holidays celebrated in other colonies, they had their own holiday—Thanksgiving. This was observed in solemn church service and separately, usually, on other days with social feasting and festival. Thanksgiving did not become a national holiday until the time of the Civil War, when President Abraham Lincoln, hoping to encourage national unity and lift a divided nation's spirits, proclaimed it so in 1863.

READING

Reading material and literacy were both somewhat limited in the early days of settlement, but most men and some women could understand enough to read the Bible. For many households the Bible was their entire library, sometimes supplemented by a practical book such as an almanac. Those were the sorts of books the first immigrants usually brought with them. Some of the wealthier colonists brought or imported more, though.

In 1638 minister John Harvard donated 400 books to the college that would be named after him, and the first printing press in what is now the United States was begun, also in Cambridge in the Massachusetts Bay Colony. It printed broadsides and broadsheets, one- and two-sided pages often dealing with news of the day, and chapbooks, which consisted of a 16 or 32 pages and were roughly six by four inches in size. These might be religious books, spellers, or history narratives, and as separation from England drew closer, political writings. The first book printed in the North American colonies was the *Bay Psalm Book* in 1640.

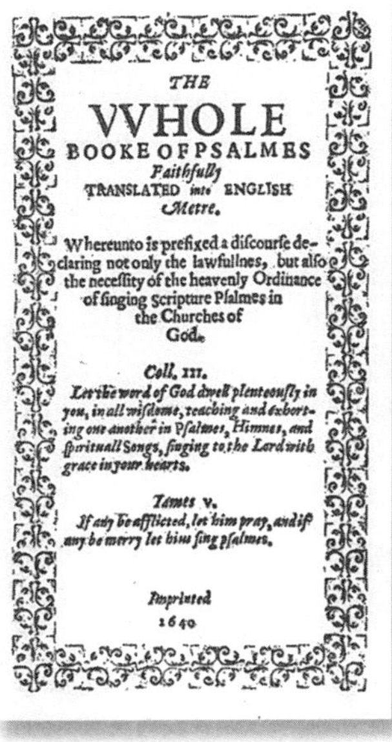
THE VVHOLE BOOKE OF PSALMES Faithfully TRANSLATED into ENGLISH Metre.

Whereunto is prefixed a discourse declaring not only the lawfullnes, but also the necessity of the heavenly Ordinance of singing Scripture Psalmes in the Churches of God.

Coll. III.

Let the word of God dwell plenteously in you, in all wisdome, teaching and exhorting one another in Psalmes, Himnes, and spirituall Songs, singing to the Lord with grace in your hearts.

Iames v.

If any be afflicted, let him pray, and if any be merry let him sing psalmes.

Imprinted 1640

One of 11 surviving copies of the Bay Psalm Book. *Richard Mather and two other ministers transformed the Psalms into verse to be sung in churches.*

Reading books for leisure was not widespread, even through the time of the Revolutionary War, mainly because there was not much leisure time. For the most part books were for improving one's faith, for academic learning, or for practical reference. Broadsheets, however, were more topical and found wider audiences, serving the function later taken over by newspapers. They helped spread news and information, gossip and rumor, which kept local communities informed and also helped carry news between widely separated settlements and colonies in America.

MUSIC

Another function of broadsheets was to share songs, poems, and limericks. As with books, some colonists found room for a violin, whistle, or a packet of sheet music in their sea baggage, while others found the means to import these once in North America. Other portable instruments like flutes, tabors (a type of drum), and small pipes also made their way across the ocean. Still others drew music out of what was available, coming up with gourd banjos, all sorts of drums, rattles, and wooden spoons for percussion, and of course lifting their voices in song, whether it was a lullaby to lull a child to sleep, a rousing song shared by men over drink, or a story of the old homeland—a ballad passed along and remembered. For the wealthy there might be music teachers, usually those trained in Europe who traveled from town to town and lived with upscale families long enough to school the young gentry on light harpsichord or flute and often a bit of dancing. This was most often true of the southern colonies, as the religious ideas of Puritan, Pilgrims, and Quakers in the north equated music with worship.

COMMUNITY ENTERTAINMENT

In places where religious observance was varied, such as the southern colonies of Maryland and Virginia, or some New England communities, community festivals celebrating spring or harvest, or Christmas or another religious holiday were more common. Later political events and militia training also provided time for community exchange.

Even in the early days of settlement, when physical conditions for the colonists were at their most harsh, and even in the areas of strictest religious observance, there were times for people to come together for public gatherings. However, in certain colonies the idea that these would have been considered entertainment and sport would have been not only frowned upon, but shocking. The importance of sharing in community was recognized, though, both for

A Currier & Ives nostalgic print titled "Harvesting the Last Load." Planting, harvesting, and storing the fruits of the harvest for the winter were all occasions of celebration.

The First Thanksgiving (Really)

The colonists went to church and gave thanks on the first Thanksgiving. They sat down together to a big meal of turkey and dressing, pumpkin pie and potatoes. They were mostly dressed in black with starched white collars as they were every day . . . not likely. Much of the long-accepted view of the celebration is based not on fact, but on mid-Victorian romanticism of the past.

That first celebration in 1621 at Plymouth, Massachusetts, was a harvest feast. These were quite separate from church-based observances of prayers and thanksgiving, and the people in Plymouth at the time would not have thought that the two were related, or thought it right to combine them. The Wampanoag people who joined the English colonists for this three day celebration of feasting would not have been invited to a church service. Native Americans incorporated spirit-based thanksgiving into their everyday lives, so they too would not have thought of making a special event to combine with the feast.

The menu probably included turkey, but not roasted with stuffing. The colonists didn't have the right type of ovens for that preparation, nor to bake pies and cakes. What they very likely enjoyed was an everyday dish of stewed pompion, the term in those days for pumpkin, and all kind of squash combined with butter, vinegars, ginger, and salt.

For meat they had several types of wild fowl. Fish was on the menu, as was deer, brought by the Wampanoag. There was no corn on the cob; the sort of corn they grew then was for corn meal or perhaps corn porridge. The kernels were tough and hard. They had cranberries, but not cranberry sauce, as there was honey but no sugar. As it was a celebration, if someone had managed to brew beer from the barley the settlers had grown, children and adults would both drink it, along with water. Dried or fresh apples and berries were probably on the menu as well, along with beans and nuts, but not potatoes, which had not yet been introduced into New England.

This meal was eaten outside, as there was no building in Plymouth large enough to hold the approximately 50 colonists and their 90 native visitors. According to custom, it is likely that men sat at the table while women served them, and children either waited on the adults or ate after their elders were finished. Those starched white collars and black clothes were not likely present either. Time and supplies for making collars and cuff and keeping them white were limited, and were in any case for wealthy and leisured citizens only. In the colonies most clothes were in hues supplied by natural dyes, which might be shades of brown, grey, red, and green, depending on the location and the time of year.

The only remaining accounts of that first celebration are *Mourt's Relation: A Journal of the Pilgrims at Plymouth* (published in 1622) and Governor William Bradford's *History of Plymouth Plantation* (published in about 1642).

Beyond the 13 Colonies: New Spain, New France, and New Russia

From the Atlantic coast of north Florida to Mobile Bay in Alabama, from the bayous of Louisiana to the dusty missions of San Antonio, from outposts in northern New Mexico to northern California and in the forests and the snows of Alaska, there were other colonists in North America in the 17th and 18th centuries. Like their counterparts along the eastern seaboard, they too found themselves making lives and homes in places far from familiar territory, facing unfamiliar landscapes, unexpected challenges, and limited resources.

Most of the Spaniards in the new world were military men or priests, so were many of the French. Some were traders, and some very few women came along to the early settlements. Games of chance, drinking bouts, and contests of military skill were typical entertainments in the largely male military garrisons. Within the missions, reading and studying were common.

French and Spanish colonists had much more interaction with native populations than did the English colonies, and gradually there were intermarriages and common law relationships across the races. Though there were well established centers of culture in Mexico to the south by the mid-16th century, even the most direct routes between those places and the settlements to the north in what would be come New Mexico were at least a six month journey. People there had to depend on themselves for entertainment, which on the side of sport often took the form of horse racing, foot races, or various games of chance. Both the Spanish and native cultures of the area valued the visual aspect of things, and this mostly found practical expression through the building and ornamentation of churches and the decoration of items used in everyday work. Music and singing, whether it be drums and whistle to accompany military parades, fiddles to provide dance music, or the guitar to accompany singing, were also part of life in these areas.

Further to the north, in what would become Alaska, merchants from Russia were making homesteads. Some of the traders brought their families with them. Facing similar frontier conditions as other early settlers, these 18th-century families drew on their own resources for entertainment, teaching children in similar ways, though in different languages and customs than other early settlers. Making games out of planting and hoeing the cabbage and potato crops, teaching children how to fish for salmon, and how to keep the log houses in order, were both chores and sources of fun for parents and children. Holiday feasts of the Russian Orthodox church were observed, and there were trading days with the native population that sometimes called for feasting and games as well. Drawing on what was available to them, as all early settlers did, the Russian people in this far outpost also created a new drink with which to entertain themselves: fermented cranberry juice.

In a painting by J.L.G. Ferris, George Washington greets his family at Mount Vernon upon his return from hunting. Hunting was also a form of entertainment in colonial times.

the human necessity of community and the practical matters of meeting marriage partners and collaborating on community projects. This was as true in the small villages typical of the northern colonies, as it was in the more scattered settlements in across the southern colonies.

These community events were often set in motion by a seasonal festival or a church observance. Planting, harvesting, and storing the fruits of the harvest for the winter were all occasions of celebration. There were also church-declared days of thanksgiving or fasting, times of special religious observance, and time set aside for militia training, as well as events such as communal building projects, and in some cases events such as weddings and funerals.

Each of these provided entertainment in the sense of giving people in a largely rural and sometimes isolated society the chance to talk, to connect, and to meet new people or keep up with friends. Conversation and the exchange of news was a big part of entertainment. So was food, usually prepared by the women and shared on makeshift tables set up by the men.

There would be time for games or sport at these gatherings, as well,most often spontaneous rather than planned. Children might find a barrel hoop and make a game of rolling it over uneven ground from one place to another. Men might compete at marksmanship with guns or perhaps bow and arrow, or in a modified version of marksmanship, with pitching stones or pebbles at a target, or at ninepins or bowling. Children might play at hop frog (leap frog), or set up races or play hide and seek. For children and adults, especially adult women whose participation in sports or games was frowned upon by most levels of society at the time, the simple joys of taking a walk with a friend or sharing stories and songs around the table sufficed for good entertainment.

THEATER, REVIVALS, AND HUNTING

There was theater in the colonies, but both the distrust of that sort of entertainment by religious groups and the geographic isolation of small communities slowed the growth of playhouses and theatrical companies in the colonies. In fact, almost all the colonies prohibited theater at one time or another, and in those two that did not, Maryland and Virginia, the reception for actors and troupes was not warm. Several plays were published in the colonies in the first part of the 18th century, but they were satirical pieces intended more for publication than performance. As the century drew on, several ballad operas were staged, the first in Charleston, South Carolina, in 1735. Shakespeare was produced in the colonies, often under the umbrella of a college or educational situation to avoid the strictures of those who did not approve. Even in those parts of the colonies that did not rule out theater for religious reasons, it was still often seen as a waste of time, or a diversion for the leisured upper class. As the Revolutionary War approached, this attitude became more pronounced, with the Second Continental Congress passing a resolution in 1775 to ban plays along with cock fighting, gaming, and what were seen as other sorts of dissipation.

Revivals, which could hardly be seen as dissipation as they were meant to spread religious faith, were also a potential source of entertainment, that would grow in popularity during the 19th century. The first religious revivals in the colonies were held in the Delaware Valley area in the 1720s. Popular English evangelist preacher George Whitfield drew crowds when he traveled through the colonies 10 years later.

Hunting was also a form of entertainment, whether it was pursued mainly for the sport of chasing game, or to feed the family and community. New forms of game unfamiliar to the early colonists added to the enjoyment of pursuit, as did the fact that in the colonies there were not the social and class restrictions often associated with hunting back in England. Small game and fowl were most often hunted, along with deer. Along the waters, fishing was also a form of recreation as well as a way to feed one's family.

LIFE AT THE EDGE OF THE WORLD

As the first waves of colonists worked to establish themselves at the edge of the North American continent at the beginning of the 17th century, they found time for a bit of entertainment and play with their children and socialized at church. From England they brought with them the tradition of seasonal festivals marking the turn of the agricultural year, and when their circumstance permitted, they celebrated these in the New World, enjoying feasting, games, and fellowship. Three quarters of the way through the 18th century, as the Revolutionary War approached, there were more people in the colonies, but it

The larger cities had a playhouse and several taverns where men could go for conversation. The City Tavern in Philadelphia above was constructed in 1772–73.

was still a largely agrarian society. News was shared through broadsheets, and plays could sometimes be seen at colleges, while the larger cities such as New York and Boston each had a playhouse and several taverns where men could go for conversation. Seasonal and church-related festivals were still common, and as feelings began to run toward independence, time for militia training and town meetings also took on the trappings of entertainment with people gathering to socialize as well as to conduct business.

Kerry Dexter

Further Readings

Archiving Early America. "Primary Source Material from 18th Century America." Available online, URL: http://www.earlyamerica.com. Accessed May 2007.

Aveni, Anthoni. "Once Around the Colonial Seasons." *Journal of Colonial Williamsburg* (Holiday, 2006).

Bordessa, Kris. *Great Colonial American Projects You Can Build Yourself*. Chicago, IL: Nomad Press, 2006.

Breen, T.H. *Puritans and Adventurers.* New York: Oxford University Press, 1980.

Breig, James. "Early American Newspapering." *Journal of Colonial Williamsburg* (Holiday, 2006).

Egloff, Keith and Deborah Woodward. *First People: The Early Indians of Virginia*. Charlottesville: University Press of Virginia, 1992.

Earle, Alice Morse. *Child Life in Colonial Days*. Stockbridge, MA: Berkshire House Publishers, 1993.

Jennings, Francis. *The Invasion of America.* Chapel Hill: University of North Carolina Press, 1975.

Loftin Snell, Tee. *The Wild Shores: America's Beginnings.* Washington, D.C.: National Geographic Society, 1974.

Roberts, Russell. *Holidays and Celebrations in Colonial America.* Glasgow, Scotland: Mitchell Lane Publishers, 2006.

Samuel, Charlie. *Entertainment in Colonial America*. Eugene OR: PowerKids Press, 2003.

Tunis, Edwin. *Colonial Living.* Baltimore, MD: Johns Hopkins University Press, 1999.

CHAPTER 11

Crime and Violence

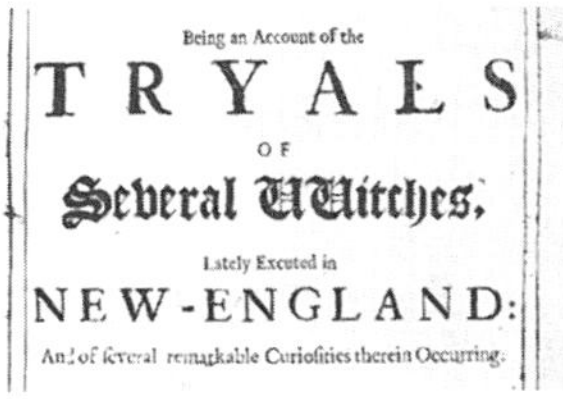
Being an Account of the
TRYALS
OF
Several Witches,
Lately Excuted in
NEW-ENGLAND:
And of several remarkable Curiosities therein Occurring.

"If any person within this Government shall by direct exprest, impious or presumptuous ways, deny the true God and his Attributes, he shall be put to death."
— Colonial Laws of New York, 1665–75

CRIME AND VIOLENCE became an increasingly common part of the everyday lives of the American colonists. Common crimes of the 17th century included victimless crimes such as public intoxication, or drunkenness, improper sexual activity, avoidance of taxation or military duty, counterfeiting, swearing, and criticisms of public officials. Treasonous speech was a serious offense. Moral violations were considered crimes and were met with swift and harsh punishment. Theft, such as burglary and highway robbery, and murder were less common in the early colonial period but would appear with increasing frequency by the 18th century. The theft of valuable items such as horses and farm animals was also a serious offense. Slander was punished harshly due to the value of a person's good reputation in colonial times. Thefts, drunk and disorderly behavior, prostitution, pick-pocketing, and a flourishing black market plagued urban areas. Arson, embezzlement, and fighting were also problems.

Piracy was a common crime during the early colonial period. Pirates were especially active along the American Atlantic coast and in the Caribbean during the latter 17th century. Early colonists often welcomed their arrival in port, as they provided black market goods at bargain prices. They also often spent freely on lavish wining, dining, and drunken good times while ashore, benefiting the local economy. Thus their activities were often aided through the bribery of corrupt local officials and by merchants seeking to avoid the Trade and Navigation Acts of the British government. New York and Charleston were well-known early pirate haunts. The free spending, however, was combined with stealing and looting sprees. As pirates began to capture colonial ships, public opinion became more hostile, and colonial efforts to combat piracy stepped up. The pirates' reign in the region had died out by the mid-18th century and the center of pirate activity shifted elsewhere.

In the early colonial period, morality was closely interrelated with crime and punishment. Most colonial Americans viewed crime as a form of sin, and the punishment of moral crimes was built into the legal codes. Historian David Flaherty observed that the homogenous nature of colonial society in the 17th century helped legally enforce morality. Examples of crimes the colonists considered moral violations included swearing, public drunkenness or other disturbances of the peace, absence from church services, inappropriate behavior on the Sabbath, gambling and card playing, and unacceptable sexual relations such as adultery, premarital sex, rape, and bearing children out of wedlock. Blasphemy, or denying the existence of God, worshipping more than one God or a different God, were all against the law. The strict moral codes of the Massachusetts Bay Puritans were the most well-known example of the colonial legislation of morality. The Connecticut Blue Laws in the 1650s also mixed the moral and civil aspects of crime and punishment, declaring, among many other laws, that "No woman shall kiss her child on the Sabbath or fasting day."

Those charged with crimes of a moral nature faced public confession in the church, public punishment, and scorn as a means of rehabilitation. The public ridicule criminals endured also helped to keep moral order by serv-

The Puritans and Moral Crime

Among the Puritans in the Massachusetts Bay Colony, those who did not conform to the religious and social order were treated as criminals and outcasts. Crime threatened the ideal religious society the Puritans had traveled to America to shape as they desired. Criminals were threats to both God and society, and Puritans viewed them as instruments of the devil. The legislation of morality and harsh punishment of moral violations helped maintain the Puritan social order.

Religious leaders often preached sermons that emphasized the danger of offenses against God to not just the individual, but to the entire society. Colonial America's first written laws, produced by the Massachusetts Bay Colony in 1648, codified moral offenses for all to see. Extreme violators, such as those that directly challenged the church's doctrines or leaders, were banished from the colony. Roger Williams, Anne Hutchinson, and the Reverend Thomas Hooker were the most well-known people to face banishment.

ing as cautionary tales for those tempted to stray from the community's accepted behavior. The law could be, in the words of historian Lawrence Friedman, "bossy, parental, and moralistic." The public was also expected to do their part in maintaining moral order by shunning those who violated its codes.

A 1774 print shows two American revolutionaries tarring and feathering the tax collector, with a gallows In the background.

LAW ENFORCEMENT

The colonial legal system was based on English Common Law, but it was also tailored to local conditions as well as local social and religious beliefs. Laws and their enforcement varied from colony to colony. Colonial law enforcement was decentralized and authority was distributed among a variety of officials as well as the public itself. A more uniform system would not be created until the late 18th century. The key law enforcement figures in the colonies were the mayors in urban areas, and the county sheriffs in rural areas. Constables and marshals aided the mayor and were responsible for making arrests and carrying out punishments. County sheriffs enforced the laws in addition to other duties, such as tax collection and the supervision of elections. Many towns and cities supplemented these officials with night, and sometimes day, watches. The watchmen looked for crimes while also keeping an eye out for other threats to public safety, such as fires or riots. The militia would supplement these forces in times of war or riot.

Colonial citizens considered preventing and responding to crime a public responsibility. Men who were freemen or citizens were called upon to serve terms as constables or marshals and to serve as night watchmen. They were not paid for their services, and those who refused to serve a term as constable could be fined heavily. Anyone witnessing a crime was expected to aid the victim. Those who did not do so faced liability in certain areas. On the other hand, informants who reported criminal acts to authorities often received a reward, such as a portion of any fine that was collected. Colonial newspapers aided in crime prevention by alerting the public when known criminals had been spotted in the area.

Colonial courts performed a variety of functions and were an important part of colonial society. When courts were in session, the entire population of the area was usually in attendance and the atmosphere was often festive and social. The local courts and justices of the peace were the most central figures in the life of the average colonial American. Those accused of crimes who appeared before a court were entitled to trial by jury, but most defendants requested that a judge hear their case. Higher courts would hear cases involving more serious crimes such as murder and treason. Lawyers were unpopular throughout much of the colonial period, and some colonies even passed laws barring them from practicing. By the 18th century however, lawyers would become more professional and more popular. Those convicted of crimes often faced harsh and public punishments.

Most punishments were physical in nature and meted out in public due to a shortage of prison space and the desire to use punishments as a form of deterrence and public shaming in the hope of rehabilitation. The town square was the most common site for public punishment. The punishment of children was largely considered a family responsibility and usually occurred at home. Some older children or children accused of more serious crimes did appear before the courts. Those most likely to be involved were slaves, orphans, and apprentices. Whipping was the most common form of physical punishment, and many town squares had whipping posts for such occasions. As an alternative, the criminal was sometimes tied to a horse cart and run through the streets.

Most town squares also had wooden devices such as the pillory, with holes through which the prisoner placed his head and hands while he stood, and the stocks, where the prisoner sat with ankles bound. Those in the pillory or stocks remained for the duration of their sentence, facing bad weather, taunts, and being pelted with rotten fruit. Colonials used the chair-like device known as a ducking stool to dunk prisoners under water; the Bilbo to hold a prisoner in chains, often upside down; and the wooden horse as a punishment for military offenders. Other physical punishments included placing the tongue on a cleft stick or running it through with a hot wire, cutting off the ears or nailing them to a pillory, and slitting the nose. Repeat offenders could be permanently branded with a letter symbolizing their crime.

A print of a colonial woman being punished in a town square on a whipping post, a common method of punishment.

Non-physical but public forms of punishment included requiring the repayment of stolen property, often at two to three times its value, public repentance before the church, fines, disenfranchisement, mock hangings, and the wearing of badges of shame, such as letters representing the crime committed. In many cases, fines provided a way for those who could afford them to avoid any type of physical punishment for their crime. Those who could not pay fines suffered physical punishments or were bound out as servants. Although probation was not used in colonial times, many colonial courts allowed criminals or known troublemakers to pay bonds as guarantees of future good behavior. Prison terms were rare in colonial America.

Convicted criminals could also face banishment or the death penalty, but colonial officials only used these punishments in extreme cases. Those offenses that warranted the death penalty varied with location and time period. Fewer crimes were classified as death penalty offenses in the colonies than in Britain. Murder and piracy were the crimes most likely to result in a death sentence. Like other forms of physical punishment, the execution was usually carried out in public to serve as a deterrent to future offenders. Hanging was the most widely used capital punishment. Others included stoning or crushing a person under heavy weights and burning at the stake. Entire communities, including women and children, attended executions in large numbers and were expected to learn a lesson from the spectacle.

In the hierarchical colonial society, wealthy criminals often received different treatment than their poorer counterparts. The types of punishment received often varied by class, with the lower class usually suffering harsher punishments. For instance, the wealthy often avoided physical punishment through pardons or the paying of fines. Poorer criminals could not afford the fines and were not often pardoned. Crime historians Frank Browning and John Gerassi note that in the Massachusetts Bay Colony, for example, the law exempted gentlemen who owned property from whippings by 1648. Punishment also varied by gender.

Colonial Jails

Prison terms were rare in colonial America, with colonial jails (also called gaols) serving as holding cells rather than as sites of punishment or rehabilitation. Most criminals avoided jails because their services were needed in a land of limited population; colonial Americans believed a person's time would be better spent at work. Spending the funds required to build jails and support prisoners in idleness did not make sense to the colonial mindset. Most criminals spent limited time in jails when awaiting trials or punishments. Only debtors and vagrants faced lengthy sentences. Debtors were housed with other criminals and were frequently allowed to leave during daylight hours to work off their debts. Colonial jails were also noted for their flimsy, haphazard construction, and jailbreaks were quite common. The first stone prison was not erected until 1722 in Philadelphia.

Insufficiency of Evidence Against Witches

The names of Increase Mather and his son Cotton are forever tied with the 17th century Salem witch trials. While Increase Mather never doubted the existence of witches, he was disturbed by the use of the testimony of what he termed "bewitched" accusers in the trials. Reprinted below is an excerpt of his 1693 tract *Cases of Conscience Concerning Evil Spirits Personating Men* where he argued on behalf of a more scientific approach to obtaining proof to ensure that justice was done.

Let me here premise two things:

1. The evidence in this crime ought to be as clear as in any other crimes of a capital nature. The Word of God does nowhere intimate that a less clear evidence, or that fewer or other witnesses may be taken as sufficient to convict a man of sorcery, which would not be enough to convict him were he charged with another evil worthy of death. If we may not take the oath of a distracted person, or of a possessed person in a case of murder, theft, felony of any sort, then neither may we do it in the case of witchcraft.

2. Let me premise this also, that there have been ways of trying witches long used in many nations, especially in the dark times of paganism and popery, which the righteous God never approved of, but which (as judicious Mr. Perkins expresseth it in plain English) were invented by the devil, that so innocent persons might be condemned and some notorious witches escape. Yea, many superstitious and magical experiments have been used to try witches by. Of this sort is that of scratching the witch . . . yea, and that way of discovering witches by tying their hands and feet, and casting them on the water to try whether they will sink or swim. I did publicly bear my testimony against this superstition in a book printed at Boston eight years past.

Women were often punished more harshly for the same crime as men, and the lower classes were more likely to receive a death sentence.

CRIMES OF INDENTURED SERVANTS AND SLAVES

During the 18th century discontentedness and crime among indentured servants became an increasing problem. From the beginning of the colonial era, many indentured servants had been former convicts shipped from England. Other servants had been the victims of kidnappers who roamed the streets of British cities looking for easy marks to ply with drugs or heavy drinks before capturing them. In the early colonial years most colonies accepted any available laborer regardless of their background, and most servants were hard workers who planned to gain their freedom and land when their terms of indenture expired. For this reason servant crimes and rebellions were less common in the early colonial period. During the 18th century however, both servant crime and colonial resentment toward the British for the practice of sending their poor, troublesome, and criminal to the colonies began to escalate.

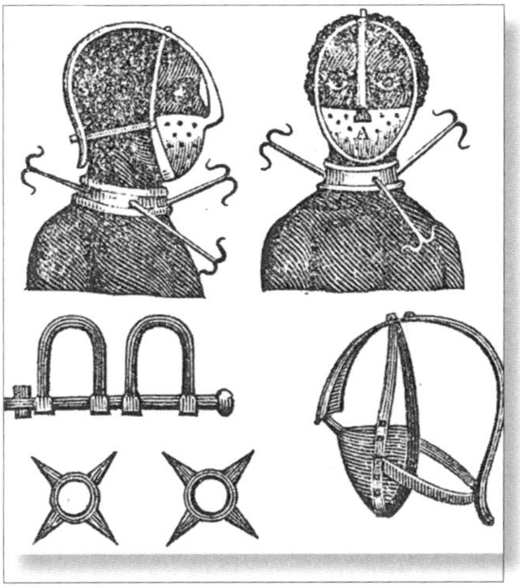

An illustration of the iron masks, collars, leg shackles, and spurs used to restrict slaves.

Parliament disallowed late 17th-century attempts by Virginia and Maryland to legislate against the British practice of sending convicts to the colonies, increasing colonial anger. Many servants no longer held to the promise of buying land upon their freedom as the colonial population grew and land shortages developed, particularly in the New England area. Behavioral problems, crime, and escape became more and more common, and newly arrived British convicts often took the blame. For example historian William K. Polk noted that the 1751 *Virginia Gazette* published an article on the rise of violent crime in the colony, and cited the arrival of great numbers of British convicts as the chief cause. Punishments for servants usually included whippings, fines paid to their masters, or additional time being added to their terms of indenture. Masters were sometimes punished for abuse of servants or apprentices.

Southern colonists also viewed slaves as another potentially explosive source of crime and violence in the 18th century. The first Africans had arrived in the American colonies in 1619 at Jamestown, Virginia. Most of these early Africans, however, served finite terms as indentured servants. These terms gradually lengthened during the course of the 17th century and grew to include the enslavement of children. Extended servitude as a form of punishment for African-American servants for the same crimes committed by white servants were often much longer. By the 18th century American slavery had become a legal reality. During the late 17th and early 18th centuries the rapid growth in the slave population led to ever-increasing fears of slave crimes and rebellions.

Slave owners sought to keep tight control over their slaves through increasingly harsh slave codes and punishments for violators. In 1682 Virginia became the first colony to enact such a code. It served as a model on which many other colonies patterned their own slave codes. Slave patrols roamed areas of the south to ensure slaves obeyed the codes and to capture runaways.

Free African Americans, who whites often viewed with deep suspicion, also faced laws restricting their movement and forbidding them from carrying weapons. Those who worked in certain professions were forced to pay taxes in many colonies, and others required them to have white guardians. Miscegenation, or interracial marriage, was against the law in many colonies, including Maryland and Virginia. Free African Americans also often faced accusations of aiding fugitive slaves or inciting and planning slave rebellions.

Slaves were often accused of insolence, deliberately working at slow speeds, deliberately performing tasks incorrectly, faking illness or injury, breaking tools, drunkenness, and stealing. More serious accusations included deliberate self-injury, attacks on one's overseer or master, running away, and plotting or inciting slave revolts. Court cases against slaves followed special procedures. Slaves did not have the right to a trial by jury and were tried in the county courts even when accused of felony crimes. Even free African Americans were forbidden from testifying against white defendants or serving on juries.

Common penalties took the form of harsh, often brutal physical punishments, included whippings, branding with hot irons, ear cropping, nose slitting, and castration. Punishments were usually conducted in front of other slaves to serve as a deterrent. Slave drivers and overseers viewed harsh punishment as a reinforcement of their authority. On the other hand an owner or overseer's mistreatment of a slave frequently went without punishment. For example it was legal to kill a slave either during the course of punishment or apprehension of a fugitive. Masters also often sexually exploited their slaves without penalty.

In the 17th century victimless crimes such as fornication and drunkenness were two to three times as common as victim crimes. As the 18th century progressed, however, assaults, murders, thefts, and other victim crimes became more frequent, as did smuggling and the black market. Crime itself became more common, more professional, and more sophisticated. Criminals formed counterfeiting rings and gangs of thieves. Crime reporting also became more common as the number of colonial newspapers increased and crime stories found their way into the headlines. As colonial officials openly worried about the growth of crime, public punishments became more common and harsher in nature. Punishments involving mutilation, such as branding and ear cropping, were used more frequently during the course of the 18th century.

A print depicts the events of January 25, 1774, when Boston Commissioner of Customs John Malcom was tarred, feathered, and hanged.

Impostors known as "confidence men" found the fluid nature of colonial society and its reputation as a place to start anew as an aid to

Tom Bell: Infamous Confidence Man

Tom Bell was the most infamous of the colonial confidence men of 18th-century America. According to historian Carl Bridenbaugh in *Early America*, Bell was featured in more than 100 newspaper articles between 1738 and 1755, making him one of the most well-known people in the colonies. Like many confidence men, he traveled extensively to conduct his scams, and utilized an extensive list of aliases. Although he occasionally held legitimate jobs as a shopkeeper, mariner, and schoolteacher, he made most of his living as a criminal impostor. He would use his education, knowledge of high society, taste for fine dress, wits, daring, and fabricated tales of troubles to gain the confidence of his victims.

One of his most famous exploits began by chance, when a stranger remarked on his remarkable likeness to the Reverend John Rowland of Boston. He decided to impersonate Rowland and stayed with a nearby family. On the way to deliver a Sunday sermon he borrowed the family's horse to return to their house where he had conveniently forgotten his sermon notes. He then made off with their horse, as well as some money and other items, forcing the real Reverend to clear up the misunderstanding, but not before great legal trouble and damage to his reputation.

By 1743 Bell had escaped from imprisonment in Rhode Island and Philadelphia. On February 10, 1743 Benjamin Franklin published a large article about Bell in the *Pennsylvania Gazette*, adding to his renown and warning the public of his tricks. His appearance and manners became well-known, hindering his ability to successfully carry out future scams. Bell was eventually caught and hanged on April 21, ending almost two decades of criminal exploits.

their criminal careers. Common terms for confidence men included sharpers, mumpers, swindlers, charlatans, rogues, and vagabonds. Many of them came from lower- or middle-class origins and used sometimes-elaborate schemes and fake identities to cheat their victims. These identities usually involved an alias and a story of a high-class person down on their luck. Others tried to pass themselves off as pastors because of the high standing of religious figures in colonial society.

In the years preceding the American Revolution, the growing crisis between the colonies and Britain led to increasing episodes of mob violence in colonial America. Rebellions against authority were not new to the colonies. Nathaniel Bacon and his followers had conducted a campaign of violence against Virginia Governor William Berkeley in 1676 until Bacon died and Berkeley restored order. Berkeley hanged 37 of Bacon's followers for their actions. Political rebellions had become common by the mid-18th century, with notable examples including Leisler's Rebellion in New York, the Paxton

Boys in Philadelphia, the Green Mountain Boys in Vermont, and the Regulator Movement of the Carolinas. Colonial mobs also acted in vigilante fashion to capture criminals or escaped slaves.

After Britain's victory in the French and Indian War, Parliament began passing legislation imposing stricter rules and new tax policies on the colonists, sparking the crisis leading to the outbreak of the Revolution. Loyalists who remained faithful to the British and British officials who sought to enforce the new regulations tightening control over the colonies found themselves the targets of threats and violence. Such mob action was widely tolerated and sometimes spun out of control, as during the 1770 Boston Massacre and the 1773 Boston Tea Party. Ultimately the ideals born of the American Revolution would come to reshape American attitudes toward crime and punishment in the post-Revolutionary period.

MARCELLA TREVINO

Further Readings

Andrews, William, and Henry M. Brooks. *Curious Punishments of Bygone Days*. New York: Frederick, 1960.

Bridenbaugh, Carl. "'The Famous Infamous Vagrant,' Tom Bell." *Early Americans*. New York: Oxford University Press, 1981.

Browning, Frank and John Gerassi. *The American Way of Crime: From Salem to Watergate A Stunning New Perspective on American History*. New York: G.P. Putnam's Sons, 1980.

Bullock, Steven C. "A Mumper among the Gentle: Tom Bell, Colonial Confidence Man." *William and Mary Quarterly* (v.55/2, 1998).

Chapin, Bradley. *Criminal Justice in Colonial America, 1606–1660*. Athens: University of Georgia Press, 1983.

Daniels, Christine, and Michael V. Kennedy. *Over the Threshold: Intimate Violence in Early America*. New York: Routledge, 1999.

Friedman, Lawrence M. "Notes Toward a History of American Justice." In *American Law and the Constitutional Order: Historical Perspectives*. Lawrence M. Friedman and Harry N. Scheiber, eds. Cambridge, MA: Harvard University Press, 1988.

Lynch, Jack. "Of Sharpers, Mumpers, and Fourberries: Some Early American Impostors and Rogues." *Colonial Williamsburg: The Journal of the Colonial Williamsburg Foundation* (Spring 2005).

Oliver, Willard and James Hilgenberg. *A History of Crime and Criminal Justice in America*. Upper Saddle River, NJ: Pearson, 2006.

Polk, William K. *The Birth of America: From Before Columbus to the Revolution*. New York: HarperCollins, 2006.

CHAPTER 12

Labor and Employment

"Remember that time is money."
— Benjamin Franklin

THE AMERICAN COLONISTS believed that work benefited the entire community, not just the individual. Economic motives for colonization included the unemployment and underemployment rampant in Britain, and the labor market helped determine patterns of immigration during the colonial period. Securing a place for surplus laborers was a key reason to colonize America. Potential colonists were attracted by the higher wages, more plentiful work, lower cost of living, and greater potential to attain land in the New World. During the early colonial period, the heavy labor required for successful colonization combined with religious dictates supportive of hard work to ensure that colonial Americans were a hard-working people. Almost everyone who could work labored either at home on the family farm, or in one of the developing colonial industries.

Families provided one of the key sources of labor throughout the colonial period, especially on farms. This labor was supplemented with hired workers, when necessary. In the Chesapeake and southern colonies, labor-intensive crops would lead to the institution of a system of indentured servitude in the 17th century, and slavery in the 18th century. Master craftsmen worked at a variety of trades, and trained newcomers through a system of apprenticeship. Seaport towns and cities employed numerous colonists in the merchant and maritime industries. Goods were produced for both household and market consumption at both the local and international levels. Colonial America was largely rural and most colonial Americans worked in the seasonal business of agriculture, whether subsistence or commercial.

AGRICULTURAL WORKERS: FARMERS, INDENTURED SERVANTS, SLAVES

Many agricultural workers were simply members of farm families growing food for their tables, as well as surpluses that could be sold on the market. Many farm families supplemented their income with livestock, the production of dairy products, and participation in domestic industries such as cloth weaving. The seasonal nature of farming also allowed farmers the opportunity to work in other areas during down periods in the agricultural cycle. Colonial Americans brewed a variety of alcoholic beverages from fruits and grains, both domestically and commercially. The distilling of rum was the largest such industry and was a key component of the slave and fur trades. Colonial housewives made cornmeal and other items at home, often producing surplus for sale or for neighbors. Colonial gristmills employed workers in the manufacture of wheat and other types of flour. Bakers produced ships' biscuits and bread.

In the New England region, children were the main labor force on family farms, as large-scale agriculture and labor-intensive crops did not take hold in much of the area's rocky soil. Large landowners in the rich farmlands of the river valleys of the northern and middle colonies often employed seasonal surplus labor, frequently providing room and board in addition to wages. Farmers in the Chesapeake and southern colonies grew labor-intensive crops that quickly resulted in labor shortages. Indentured servitude proved to be the solution to 17th-century labor shortages, as well as the main method of emigration to America for those who lacked the funds to pay for their ship's passage.

Indentured servants signed contracts outlining a set term of service and freedom dues. The most common terms of indenture were four to five years, with seven years being the maximum allowed for all servants except criminals, debtors, and those illegally kidnapped and brought to America. Masters legally provided room and board for their servants and could not inflict punishments considered cruel and unusual. Servants were

Colonial women baked bread in outdoor ovens. This oven was found in Jamestown, Virginia, and appears to have been used between 1650 and 1690.

A painting by Sidney E. King, commissioned by the National Park Service, showing the harvesting of tobacco at Jamestown, Virginia, in about 1650.

required to work faithfully and not marry during their indenture. Courts extended terms of service for violators or for runaway servants who were captured. Servants were the property of their owners and could be bought and sold at will; a few were even lost at card games. Many were also required to refrain from certain behaviors such as gambling. Freedom dues were agreed-upon items that masters would provide their servants after their periods of indenture had ended, which frequently included such items as clothing, corn, tools, land, guns, and livestock.

Most early indentured servants arrived in the Chesapeake colonies of Virginia and Maryland, where tobacco was a profitable but labor-intensive crop. The London Company of Virginia or individual planters in need of labor would pay the transportation costs of emigrants who signed an indenture contract before their departure. Most early indentured servants were single males from England. They helped drain swampland, clear and plow fields, and plant and cultivate crops, as well as helping to run the household. Skilled workers served shorter terms of indenture and worked in craft shops. Early servants went through a period known as seasoning, where mortality rates from fevers such as malaria in the swampy Chesapeake were quite high. Masters and servants often worked and lived side by side. Those who survived their indenture would receive their freedom dues and seek to start their own small farms, as land was more readily available in the early colonial period.

During the 18th century indentured servants began arriving from Ireland and other European nations and came as family groups, balancing the ratio between the sexes in the Chesapeake region. Many of these latter indentured

A photograph of a newspaper advertisement from the late 1700s for the sale of slaves at Ashley Ferry near Charleston, South Carolina.

servants were known as redemptioners. Redemptioners were those who owed their passage to a merchant or ship captain and did not have indenture contracts before setting sail for America. Many had been lured by the merchants' promises of America as a golden land of opportunity. Those who did not have someone in America to pay their passage were sold to the highest bidder upon reaching the colonies.

Mortality rates had decreased dramatically, but land was less readily available, so those later servants who finished their indentures had more trouble securing good land, and some even chose to return to their homelands. Indentured servants became less common by the 18th century as the southern colonies switched to the use of African slaves as their main source of labor. Slaves were not much higher in price, gradually came to serve for life, could be treated more harshly, could not blend into society as runaways, and did not represent future potential competitors.

The first Africans arrived in the mainland American colonies in 1619 aboard a ship that landed in Jamestown, Virginia. Many New England merchants and shippers participated in the transatlantic trade that brought Africans to the New World. Most of the early Africans to arrive were sold as indentured servants and went through the same seasoning process as their European counterparts. African indentured servants faced additional legal restrictions, such as not being allowed to bear arms. Females worked in the fields alongside males. Their terms of indenture became longer than those of white indentured servants, and gradually were replaced with the lifetime bondage of slavery by the end of the 17th century.

Some Africans were able to obtain their freedom through completion of their indentures, manumission by their owners, or purchase. A few, like Anthony Johnson of Virginia, even owned land and indentured servants of their own. In 1665 Johnson and his family moved to Maryland and leased a 300-acre plantation. Africans, even those who were free, faced a degraded status due to the color of their skin and their non-Christian religions. Most colonies passed laws not allowing interracial relationships or marriages. Even freed Africans faced discrimination and legal restrictions, as they were viewed as a bad example to slaves.

In the late 17th and early 18th centuries slavery became a legal institution. The number of imported slaves and their prices greatly increased, as they became the preferred source of labor in the southern colonies. Natural increase raised their numbers even farther, as the children of slave women also became legally bound to the institution. Most slaves lived in the southern colonies, although they could also be found in the northern and mid-Atlantic colonies. New England slaves lived mainly in urban seaports and served in wealthy households, shipyards, and shops. Slaves in the northern and mid-Atlantic regions lived under less harsh slave codes than their southern counterparts. In many cases they enjoyed more freedom, learned to read and write, and had their marriages legally recognized. Some Native Americans captured during wartime also served as slaves.

The three main types of slave laborers were skilled workers, house servants, and field hands. Skilled slaves worked as carpenters, bricklayers, and blacksmiths (among other trades), and a few were even permitted to sell their services in their spare time. Female house slaves served as cooks, maids, and nurses; male house slaves served as butlers and coachmen. Field hands drained swamps, cleared and planted fields, and cultivated and harvested crops. The gang system, used on most tobacco plantations, involved groups of slaves working under the control of the master or an overseer from morning until evening. The task system, used on most rice, indigo, and Sea Island cotton plantations, gave each slave a specified assignment for the day. Once completed, the slave had some control over the rest of his time, and some areas developed a vibrant internal slave economy. The task system became increasingly common in the mid to late 18th century.

The majority of colonial Americans, even in the deep south, could not afford to own slaves. Large slaveholders were a minority. In many areas of the south, however, slaves began to outnumber whites, and the threat of slave rebellions became an omnipresent fear. Revolts such as the 1739 Stono Rebellion in South Carolina, and the promise of freedom to runaways who could make their way to the Spanish colony of Florida further fed these fears. Colonies began to pass slave codes severely regulating behavior and movement, starting with Virginia in 1682. South Carolina had the harshest slave codes and other colonies copied many of its features. Whites expected slaves to show deference and often abused, overworked, and

A 1667 illustration shows the drying and rolling of tobacco leaves. Identified are 1) stripping the tobacco leaf, 2) twisting it, 3) rolling it, and 4) hanging it to dry.

underfed them. Those slaves who did not run away or revolt found other more subtle ways to protest their enslavement, such as deliberately slowing their work pace, deliberately committing careless mistakes, injuring themselves or feigning illness, breaking tools, stealing, and drinking among other measures. Few people or groups outside the Quakers in Pennsylvania openly opposed the institution of slavery.

COLONIAL INDUSTRY AND ITS WORKERS

The mercantilist theory prevalent in the 17th century dictated that the colonies were meant to supply raw materials to Britain and serve as markets for imported British manufactured goods. Parliament passed laws forbidding or heavily regulating and taxing most types of colonial industry. Many colonists also lacked the capital to start businesses, and the scattered nature of the early colonial population did not provide ample markets for goods. Some colonial industry, however, did develop. In a few cases, such as the early glassmaking shop at Jamestown, Virginia, Britain actively encouraged certain industries that were not prevalent at home, and skilled workers were among colonial immigrants from the colonies' inception. Families developed domestic industries within the colonial home, including both production for family use and surplus production for the marketplace. Such products included such everyday household items as cloth, clothing, candles, and soap.

The manufacture of textiles and clothing became increasingly important as both a domestic and a commercial industry by the 18th century. In the early

Craftsmen made shoes, using shoemaking equipment like the forms pictured at right.

Candles (below), cloth, clothing, and soap were made for family use as well as to sell at the marketplace.

A modern reconstruction of Benjamin Franklin's print shop. Two ink balls are on the wall, hanging to the left of the hand-operated press.

colonial period most families relied on imported British cloth and clothing due to the necessity of concentrating their labor in the establishment of homes and farms in the New World. Once colonial society became more developed, the age of homespun cloth and clothing began in earnest. Households began to manufacture textiles not just for family use, but also for the burgeoning market. Merchants supplied wool, flax, or hides to farm families to be processed into cloth, leather, or clothing. At the same time early efforts at commercial textile and clothing production began, mostly in the New England region. In addition manufacturers began producing other articles of attire, such as shoes, belts, wigs, corset stays for women's dresses, and hats. Fashionable beaver hats were a profitable byproduct of the fur trade with Native Americans. The colonial production of cheap wool hats so alarmed British hat makers that Parliament passed the Hat Act of 1732, which banned the colonies from exporting hats, among other restrictions designed to halt colonial competition.

Many colonial Americans worked in the various maritime and related industries. Fisherman caught cod, salmon, mackerel, and other fish off the New England Atlantic Coast. New England farmers often supplemented their income by fishing during the winter period while their farms lay dormant. Smaller fishermen were paid for whatever they caught, while crews on larger vessels divided the remaining profits after the cost of supplies and payments

Barrels were instrumental for storing a wide variety of products, such as flour, corn meal, grain, molasses, maple syrup, cider, beer, salted meat, and fish.

to the ship owners were deducted. New Englanders also dominated the colonial whaling industry, at first capturing those whales that came close to shore, and later putting out to sea as the whale population began to decrease. Like the crews of large fishing vessels, whaling crews shared in a ship's profits, with those of higher ranks receiving a larger share. Whale byproducts contributed to a number of colonial industries, including the oil made from melted blubber, the whalebone used in women's corset stays, the ambergris used in perfume manufacturing, and the spermaceti used in candlemaking. Colonial seamen also sailed aboard merchant vessels transporting both goods and slaves in the international transatlantic trade.

The colonial maritime industry was interrelated with colonial industries based on forest products, as sawmills sprang up in the colonies to process cut logs. Shipbuilders utilized much colonial timber and the related naval stores industry used many of its byproducts, manufacturing the pitch, tar, hemp, turpentine, and resin needed to finish ships and make them watertight. The naval stores industry was especially large in the Chesapeake colonies and the Carolinas. Timber was also instrumental to the small paper making industry that developed in colonial America. Most of the colonial paper mills were located in the Philadelphia area and utilized skilled laborers who had emigrated from Germany. Colonial printer Benjamin Franklin supplied many of the linen rags that were used to make paper. Books and newspapers were printed on the paper. Other key wood-based industries included furniture making and coopering (barrel making). Barrels were instrumental for the storage of a wide variety of colonial products. Other related industries included the making of charcoal and potash, a substance used in the manufacture of soap, glass, and fertilizer.

Colonial Americans also worked as wheelwrights; brick, tile, and stonemasons; blacksmiths, saddle and harness makers, clockmakers, and funeral arrangers among a wide variety of occupations. A small colonial glassmaking industry began in colonial Jamestown, Virginia as early as 1608, although most colonial glass manufacturers did not last long against stiff British competition. Baron Stiegel in Pennsylvania and Caspar Wister and his son Richard ran two of the most successful colonial glass factories in the 18th century. A colonial iron mining industry led to the development of several large ironworks in Pennsylvania that produced finished items such as tools, pots, and stoves for the colonial marketplace. Pennsylvania was also known for its manufacture of the Kentucky rifle and the Conestoga wagon in the 18th century. The retail trade employed many colonial Americans as merchants, particularly after the 18th century commercial revolution led to increasing demand for both domestic and imported luxury goods, including fine furniture, silverware, wallpaper, and coaches.

Women performed a variety of work functions, both inside and outside the colonial home. Domestic manufacturing was increasingly common by the 18th century. Women produced surplus goods such as yarn, cloth, clothing, and farm products for the market or the community, in addition to their household chores for the family. Outside the home they worked in more traditional female occupations like dressmaking, hat making, hairdressing, and midwifery, as well as more traditional male occupations like shoe making and metalworking. Some even went to sea or to war by disguising themselves as men. Colonial women often aided their husbands whether on the farm or in the shop, with some widowed women taking control of their husband's businesses when they were wid-

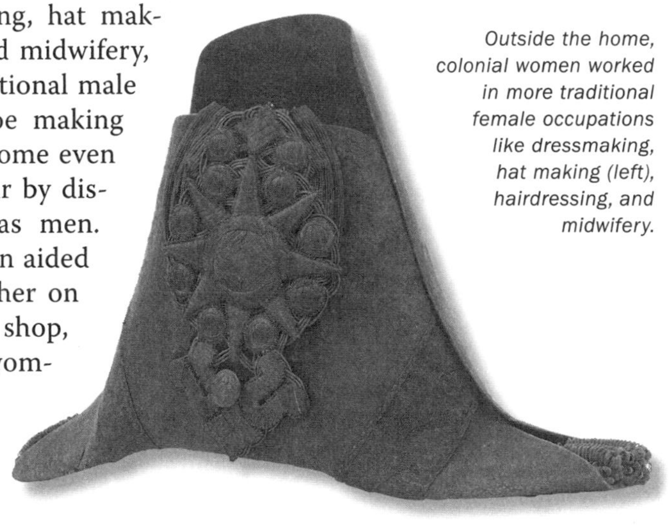

Outside the home, colonial women worked in more traditional female occupations like dressmaking, hat making (left), hairdressing, and midwifery.

Colonial Midwives

Midwifery was one of the colonial careers that was open to women and also paid good wages. Most colonial midwives were older women past the years of childbearing and honed their skills through practical experience. Those who were skilled were highly respected by their communities and in great demand, as there were few doctors in colonial America, and men did not attend births because most people considered it indecent. A few even received small salaries or a house from communities seeking to recruit their services. Many midwives also aided in the baptisms and deaths of infants, and some even aided in animal births. Historian Laurel Thatcher Ulrich's *A Midwife's Tale* provides insight into the roles of colonial midwives through the diary of Martha Ballard, a colonial housewife and midwife who lived and worked in late 18th-century Maine.

Martha Ballard was married with nine children, three of whom died in infancy. Ulrich's social history utilizes Ballard's experiences to explore gender and labor roles, medical beliefs and practices, and the social aspects of childbirth in colonial America. One of the many common beliefs surrounding pregnancy and childbirth was that working would result in an easier delivery, so many women worked right up until they went into labor. Childbirth was difficult and dangerous, and many women approached it with fear. Alcohol was the only painkiller that was commonly used during labor. Exhaustion, heavy bleeding, and infections were ever-present dangers that could result in severe illness or death. Most women gave birth at home with the aid of female family members and neighbors and a midwife was often present. By the late 18th century women midwives became less common as many upper-class families began to insist on the use of a physician.

owed, some even becoming master craftsmen. Poor parents often sent their female children out to other homes or businesses to learn domestic arts such as sewing, weaving, and cooking until they were married. Legally, married women's labors and profits were the property of their husbands.

A number of trained artisans had immigrated to the colonies, attracted by the high wages in comparison to those earned for comparable trades in Europe. Colonial craftsmen first learned their trade through the apprentice system brought over from Europe and modified in adaptation to the colonial economy. Apprenticeship was regulated on the local level in colonial America, so the institution was not as uniform as that of Europe, but the general pattern of exchanging labor for training in a particular craft remained the basis. Formal education was uncommon in the colonial period, and even professions such as medicine and law utilized an apprentice system to train new members. An apprentice worked for a predetermined period of service, generally from four to seven years. Apprentices were young, and regulations stipulated cutoff ages for service of 18 years old for women and 21 years old for men. Parents or legal guardians often signed the contracts binding out their children for apprenticeship. Orphans were also routinely bound out as apprentices. Master craftsmen in certain trades limited the number of apprentices, and thus potential competition, through fees charged to take on apprentices, while other master craftsmen paid small wages to their apprentices in rural areas where candidates were scarce.

Like indentured servants, apprentices were required to serve faithfully and not run away or marry. The master craftsmen would teach the trade and provide room and board. Sometimes they also provided basic education and a set of tools upon the end of the apprentice's service. After their terms of service were complete, apprentices became journeymen and hired themselves out to master craftsmen as supplemental labor. Those journeymen who had the required skills and money would eventually become master craftsmen with their own stores. The guilds that regulated the trades and apprentice system in Europe did not rise in the colonies, leaving local governments to

A recreated cabinetmaker's shop. Many artisans immigrated to the colonies, and craftsmen first learned their trade through the apprentice system brought over from Europe.

regulate the system. The few trade associations created in colonial America did not endure for any length of time. Apprentices and journeymen in colonial America usually served shorter terms of service and more readily rose to become master craftsmen than their European counterparts. In one of colonial America's most well known examples, Benjamin Franklin ran away from his apprenticeship in his brother's print shop and went on to open his own highly successful business running several newspapers.

Colonial craftsmen worked 12 or more hours on an average workday, but took frequent breaks. Some colonial workers protested against unsafe working conditions, poor pay, higher costs of living, or regulations of their leisure time and personal habits, but strikes were extremely rare in the colonial period. Labor associations were also uncommon, although a few did exist. The largest colonial labor association was the Carpenters' Company of Philadelphia, formed in 1724. Some towns formed local charitable societies that aided workers in times of sickness of financial distress. The most militant of colonial laboring groups were those aboard ships. A ship's crew would strike, whether in port or at sea, if they felt that they were being mistreated or if the ship was not in safe condition to put to sea. Sailors who stopped work while at sea would strike the ship's sails, hence lending the name "strike" to a work stoppage. Most industry workers, however, were not as militant, even as wage labor became increasingly common in the 18th century.

18TH-CENTURY DEVELOPMENTS IN LABOR AND EMPLOYMENT

Work patterns began to change in the 18th century, as colonial American society and economy stabilized and developed. Agriculture became more diversified and commercial as new crops were planted and European demand for colonial agriculture increased in times of war and famine. The consumer revolution led to the development of new industries and the expansion of older ones. Work roles became more diverse and impersonal. It became increasingly less common for master to work beside slave in the field, or for shop owners to work beside employees. As the colonial population increased, available land became more distant and scarce, resulting in increasing numbers of landless workers. These 18th-century transitions occurred gradually, rather than in a clearly defined period.

Wage earners had been only a minority, but increasingly came to dominate the colonial labor force by the end of the 18th century. The trend began in the coastal cities and slowly permeated the rest of the colonial economy. Wage earners could be found in both colonial agriculture and industry. Most colonists preferred to work the family farm or work their way into a trade through apprenticeship, options more widely available in 17th-century America than they had been in Europe. Wage earners were generally worse off economically, with temporary and day laborers earning the least. Steady employment was rare, and women and children often worked to

An engraving by Paul Revere is entitled: "The Bloody Massacre Perpetrated in King-Street Boston on March 5th 1770 by a Party of the 29th Regt., 1770."

The Role of Laborers in the Boston Massacre

The 1770 Boston Massacre was the most well known example of disputes involving the working class and British soldiers, and highlights the role of workingmen in the growing patriot movement. British soldiers had arrived in Boston in 1768 to maintain order in the city. Many Boston citizens resented the soldiers' presence and frequently insulted them with names like "lobster back" in response to the bright red uniform coats they wore. Fistfights were also common. When off-duty, many of the soldiers competed with colonial workers for jobs to supplement their small military pay, increasing tensions between the two groups. Workers were thus especially resentful of the presence of the British soldiers in their city.

On the afternoon of March 5, a group of rope makers insulted one such soldier looking for work, and the tensions of the past months erupted into angry confrontations. Later that same evening, an even larger and more heated confrontation developed outside the Boston Customs House between the 29th Regiment standing guard duty, led by Captain Thomas Preston, and an angry mob of civilians who gathered nearby. The crowd was yelling insults and some were throwing snowballs at the soldiers. During the resulting chaos, shots were fired into the mob, despite the fact that the soldiers had been ordered not to fire. Five of the mob were killed and an additional six were wounded. African-American sailor Crispus Attucks was the first to be shot and killed, becoming a well-known martyr to the revolutionary cause.

supplement the head of household's meager wages. Destitution was a constant worry, as families sought to avoid having to indenture themselves or submit to life in the poorhouses that sprang up in many colonial towns.

During the late 18th century workers and their interests played an important role in the patriot movement leading up to the American Revolution. Colonial workers made up a significant proportion of the protests against the British acts such as the Stamp Act, Townshend Duties, and Intolerable Acts in the years leading up to the Revolutionary War. Patriot groups such as the Sons of Liberty and the Committees of Correspondence, which organized boycotts, protests, and other forms of resistance, included representatives of all levels of the colonial workforce. The working class also played a significant role in the Revolutionary War. The majority of the soldiers who made up the Continental Army were common farmers and laborers. Women served as cooks, seamstresses, laundresses, and nurses, and some even disguised themselves as men in order to fight. Slaves also fought on both sides during the war, lured by their own for hopes for independence or the promise of freedom. The patriotic ideals of independence and egalitarianism would have an impact that would extend into the working world of the post-Revolutionary period and beyond.

MARCELLA TREVINO

Further Reading

Foner, Philip S. *History of the Labor Movement in the United States Volume I: From Colonial Times to the Founding of the American Federation of Labor*. New York: International Publishers, 1947.

Galenson, David. *White Servitude in Colonial America*. New York: Cambridge University Press, 1981.

Galenson, David. *Traders, Planters, and Slaves: Market Behavior in Early English America*. New York: Cambridge University Press, 1986.

Innes, Stephen. *Work and Labor in Early America*. Chapel Hill: University of North Carolina Press, 1988.

Kessler-Harris, Alice. *Out to Work: A History of Wage-Earning Women in the United States*. New York: Oxford University Press, 2003.

Kulikoff, Allan. *From British Peasants to Colonial American Farmers*. Chapel Hill: University of North Carolina Press, 2000.

Murolo, Priscilla and A.B. Chitty. *From the Folks Who Brought You the Weekend: A Short, Illustrated History of Labor in the United States*. New York: New Press, 2001.

Polk, William K. *The Birth of America: From Before Columbus to the Revolution*. New York: HarperCollins, 2006.

Quimby, Iam M.G., ed. *The Craftsman in Early America*. New York: W.W. Norton, 1984.

Reich, Jerome R. *Colonial America*. Upper Saddle River, NJ: Prentice Hall, 1998.

Ulrich, Laurel Thatcher. *A Midwife's Tale: The Life of Martha Ballard, Based on Her Diary, 1785–1812*. New York: Vintage, 1991.

Wertheimer, Barbara M. *We Were There: The Story of Working Women in America*. New York: Pantheon Books, 1977.

Wright, Donald R. *African-Americans in the Colonial Era: From African Origins Through the American Revolution*. Arlington Heights, IL: Harlan Davidson, 1990.

CHAPTER 13

Military and Wars

"Naked and starving as they are
We cannot enough admire
The incomparable Patience and Fidelity of the Soldiery."
— George Washington

WARFARE WAS NOT brought to North America by the Europeans, as there were violent rivalries between the native peoples. Unlike those parts of Central and South America where major empires conquered surrounding peoples, warfare in North America was usually short and limited, although no less deadly to its victims.

Spain was the first European power to establish an enduring colonial presence on the North American mainland. Following the fall of the Aztecs in Mexico, the Spanish gradually expanded their sphere of influence and control into what is now the southwestern United States. On the Atlantic Coast, they made five efforts between 1513 and 1527 to establish a base on the Florida peninsula. Each one ended in failure. In every case there was military conflict between the explorers and settlers, and the natives. A serious exploration of the American southeast landed on the Florida coast in 1539, led by Hernando de Soto, a veteran of Francisco Pizarro's conquest of the Inca Empire, with ambitions of carving a similar domain for himself. The expedition ended in1542 after the Spanish inflicted a great deal of violence on the region.

Meanwhile Spain's major rivals, France and England, launched a number of explorations between 1524 and 1536 which led to, among other things, the French territorial claim for what is now Canada. In 1562 and 1564 the French made efforts to establish a colony in Florida. Both of these efforts were undertaken by French Huguenots, eager to serve their nation while escaping from the religious persecution that they faced back home. If successful the colony would provide a base for privateer ships to prey on the Spanish treasure fleet. In response the Spanish sent an expedition under Pedro Menendez de Aviles, which forced the French to surrender; almost all of them were executed.

Menendez established a number of posts along the Atlantic Coast as far north as Chesapeake Bay, beginning in Florida with *San Agustin,* modern-day St. Augustine, the oldest permanent European-founded settlement in the United States. Menendez sought to use the posts to bring the region under permanent Spanish control. All but St. Augustine failed because of pressure from rival European powers or conflicts with the natives. It was not until the initiation of a strong missionary program among the natives in the 17th century that Florida came firmly under Spanish influence, and even then, the presence of white settlers and soldiers outside of St. Augustine was limited.

Military concerns also played a part in the Roanoke ventures of the English between 1584 and 1587. In addition to the typical European colonial goal of extracting the largely imaginary riches expected to be found in the interior, the English also hoped that the Roanoke Island colony might serve as base for privateer operations in the Spanish Main. As in the case of other European colonies, mutual misunderstandings and aggressiveness on the part of the settlers sparked conflict with the local natives. Whether or not these conflicts had anything to do with the disappearance of the famous Lost Colony, or the surviving settlers merging with the neighboring peoples, as is usually considered more likely, is unknown.

THE FRENCH, THE ENGLISH, AND THE NATIVES

As the 17th century began both the French and English made renewed efforts to establish colonies in North America. The French in Canada won friends among such native peoples as the Algonquin and the Huron, but relations took a fateful turn when explorer Samuel de Champlain sided with them against the powerful Iroquois Confederacy. The first clash between the Iroquois and the French and their allies occurred at Lake Champlain on July 29, 1609. It set the stage for later conflict, as the British, French, and Spanish sought to exploit the rivalries between various Native-American peoples in their own wars, while the natives sought to exploit the rivalries among the Europeans.

The two earliest successful English colonies survived their initial crises largely due to the actions of military figures who accompanied them. In Virginia, John Smith, a soldier with prior military experience fighting for the Hungarians against the Turks, became the de facto leader of the colony as the governing councilors died off. Smith imposed his will ruthlessly on the survivors, instilling tight discipline. He also put up a bold front against the Powhatan Indians, leading the settlers in clashes against them. At Plymouth Plantation, the Separatist Pilgrims were

Defensive Measures in the English Colonies

The English colonists relied on organization, firepower, and fortification to protect their frontier settlements from native attacks. Given that the English government would not commit large numbers of troops to the colonies, the settlers and their descendants would have to defend themselves. For this reason, the colonists imported the militia system from home. Unpopular in both England and America for its compulsory nature, the militia required every able-bodied male settler to serve. Members were required to convene at certain times of the year to drill.

The basic unit of the militia was the company, ideal in size for a community, but as the colonies grew, a regimental system was adopted. Getting companies together for regimental drills or large-scale field operations was often difficult, and colonial governments found it increasingly difficult to completely impose their will on the militia over time. Discipline and drill varied widely, from units led by individuals with some professional military background, to those led by well-placed opportunists. The growing use of the election of officers often contributed to the influence of the latter. Such problems persisted within the militia systems after the founding of the United States and well into the 19th century.

Firepower was another important component of colonial defense. The flintlock musket was a portable weapon that was quite effective at close range, particularly when fired in a mass volley. Artillery was also available for use. The battle formations used on European battlefields, however, proved of limited use in America, especially as the natives would not conveniently oblige the militiamen by fighting out in the open. Native peoples changed their tactics to compensate for colonial firepower, including adopting the use of muskets as well.

The colonists also relied upon defensive works. These ranged from protective palisades around settlements, to blockhouses and other forms of fortified dwellings, which families or groups of families could use for protection. As time went on more elaborate fortifications were devised to guard major port harbors and other key points. Devising defenses to protect crops and livestock was more difficult.

In general, the limited scope of military practice among the colonists was sufficient to provide both effective defensive and offensive operations against natives, although even the largest towns and units were not safe from a truly large or determined native attack. Nor could militia units function effectively in major operations against the colonies of rival European powers. For the latter, semiprofessional troops recruited from the militia were created for brief periods of service.

assisted by another professional soldier, Miles Standish, who had been brought along to provide military advice. Standish played a role in establishing a rudimentary militia system, and led the Pilgrims in combat. Similar militia systems were organized in other English colonies as time went on.

PRECARIOUS SITUATION

Despite the advantage given the English by their firearms, the situation remained precarious. Twice the Virginia colony came close to being wiped out by the Powhatan Indians, once in 1622 and again in 1644, as a the natives felt increasingly pressured by the continued expansion of European settlement. In the aftermath of both attacks the settlers ruthlessly retaliated, reducing the natives to submission. In 1675 violent friction with the Doeg Indians led to a rebellion among disgruntled settlers, angry over the slow reaction of the royally-appointed governor. The revolt fell apart with the death of its leader, Nathaniel Bacon, but

Daily Life of a Soldier

Two of the most common complaints of soldiers in the Revolutionary War were of monotony and a lack of decent food. In the colonial era, each colony provisioned its troops according to its own rules; the Continental Army formed by Congress was given a daily ration of one pound of meat, one pound of bread or flour, three pints of beans or the equivalent of some other vegetable, one half pint of rice (or a pint of "Indian meal"), one pint of milk, and one quart of cider or spruce beer—but these amounts were rarely met, and often a soldier would simply go without rather than be given a substitution. Many soldiers foraged for their own food as much as they were able, and bought from local farmers when possible—selling off the metal buttons from their uniforms, and trading their flour ration for a bite to eat. A soldier might even continue to work, making shoes or lending out his services as a carpenter, in addition to performing his military duties.

The inclusion of alcoholic beverages in military rations was common in an age when potable drinking water was more difficult to obtain (alcohol is antibacterial). The cider and beer was often weak, and when strong liquor like rum was provided, it might be mixed into a canteen full of water in order to prevent soldiers from hoarding it to get drunk.

In the camps, when not actively engaged in battle, life consisted of a good deal of waiting and marching. When not foraging, collecting firewood and water, or marching in drills, the men wrote letters home, read what few books they could carry, and played games. Checkers and chess were even more popular then than now, and card games were easy to carry and teach. Gambling, though outlawed among soldiers at war, was rampant—and arguably harmless, given how little they had to gamble with.

"The First Muster," Salem, Massachusetts, 1637. The history of the National Guard began when the General Court of the Massachusetts Bay Colony ordered the organization of the colony's militia.

not before the rebels had not only killed many natives not related to the initial conflict, but burned Jamestown as well.

In New England the settlers were more proactively aggressive. In 1636 tensions in Connecticut between Puritan settlers, local natives, and the Pequots, a tribe that had recently migrated into the area, led to tragedy. An English trader was killed by a local Native American who sought refuge with the Pequots. The Puritans, seeking an excuse to intimidate the natives, attacked and massacred a group on Block Island before going after the Pequots, killing many when the latter would not surrender the fugitive. In the ensuing months the Pequots harassed the settlers for revenge. The Puritans struck back in 1637 when a small force from Massachusetts Bay Colony and Connecticut, accompanied by allied native groups, destroyed one of the two principal Pequot villages and massacred its inhabitants.

Concerns about potential native violence led to the formation of a defensive league of all of the Puritan colonies, with the exception of Rhode Island. This organization, the United Colonies of New England, lasted until 1684. It faced its major test with King Philip's War (1675–78). Violent friction between the Wampanoag Indians and colonists was unfairly blamed on Philip, the Wampanoag sachem and son of the Pilgrims's ally Massasoit. He quickly withdrew with his followers to avoid attack. In the ensuing guerilla war, the Wampanoag and Narragansett Indians stymied the efforts of the United Colonies and their

Mohegan and Pequot allies to defeat them. In 1676 however, resistance faltered as the Native Americans suffered setbacks; following Philip's death, the survivors were nearly wiped out by the colonists.

As the 17th century came to a close, the English government became increasingly interested in colonial administration and the smooth enforcement of the Navigation Laws that regulated the nation's mercantilist policies. Former soldiers, usually close associates of the king, were often appointed as royal governors. Further, in order to centralize colonial administration, the Dominion of New England was created by James II in 1686, temporarily consolidating New Hampshire, Massachusetts, Plymouth, Rhode Island, Connecticut, New York, and New Jersey into one colony.

The Glorious Revolution of 1688 in England, in which Catholic James II was deposed in favor of his Protestant son-in-law, William of Orange, ruler of the Netherlands, led to revolts in the Dominion, not as a challenge to the monarchy or to English rule, but as expressions of discontent against the governor, his officials, and the various local elements and interests in league with them. In New York this resulted in violence between the rebels and English troops and the trial and execution of the leader of the English.

THE EXPANDING IMPACT OF EUROPEAN CONFLICT

Throughout the 17th century the European colonies were caught up in the imperial ambitions and rivalries of their founding nations. In 1628 a war between England and France led to a naval expedition against Quebec, which was captured in the following year. A peace treaty led to the return of that important

Quebec was captured under British commanders in September 1759, although the rest of New France did not surrender until the following year.

The Colonists and the British Army

As conflict between the major European powers increased in the late 17th century, the fighting spilled over into the colonies. Initially the battles largely involved the colonists themselves and their native allies, but eventually the use of regular troops was introduced for specific campaigns. During Queen Anne's War, King George's War, and the French and Indian War, the British sent support for operations against such key sites as Quebec and St. Augustine. These expeditions often included the use of colonial troops as a supplement to the European contingent.

While this idea seemed sound on paper, in practice it seldom worked. Much of the problem was due to tensions between colonial troops and British officers, soldiers, and sailors. Members of the British military often looked upon colonial troops with contempt for their lack of professional training, and that contempt was very much noticed. Further, the colonists had preconceived prejudices against the British military establishment, based on imported political rhetoric dating back to the military dictatorship of Oliver Cromwell.

The military operation that may have caused the most long-lasting damage between the colonists and Britain occurred during the War of Jenkins's Ear. An expedition against Spanish interests in the Caribbean was organized under Brigadier General Thomas Wentworth and Vice Admiral Edward Vernon, consisting of British warships and both British regular and colonial troops. The latter were commanded by William Gooch, lieutenant governor of Virginia. The American troops were to be paid and trained as British regulars, with regimental officers appointed by the king and the majority of the company officers appointed by the colonial governors. These moves seemed to presage a prominent combat role for the Americans, who would receive the same discipline, training, and treatment as their British counterparts. Once they arrived in Jamaica, however, they were treated as laborers or impressed by the navy for shipboard service. Many died of illness, and they were not paid as promised. In March 1740 the fleet reached Cartagena, the intended target. Wentworth and Vernon did not work well together, and the expedition fell apart by mid-April. American soldiers were again forced into service on the fleet as it departed. The Cartagena expedition provoked much long-lasting bitterness in the colonies against the British armed services, and it proved to be only one of many incidents.

As hostilities grew between the colonists and the British government after 1763, one factor was the presence of regular troops in the colonies. The quartering of British troops, the occupation of Boston by British forces, and the tragic events of the Boston Massacre only deepened the feeling of hostility which had begun during the colonial wars. These resentments played no small role in the rift that led to war and eventual separation between the colonies and Britain.

post to France. In 1654 while England was at war with the Dutch, the English sent a squadron to attack the New Netherlands colony. When peace was declared, the commander decided instead to attack Canada, capturing St. John, Port Royal, and Penobscot. These acquisitions were traded back to France in 1667 in exchange for previously disputed Caribbean possessions. In 1655 the Dutch seized New Sweden and incorporated it into New Netherlands; in 1664, it was the turn of the Dutch, as the English captured New Netherlands.

In 1689 the War of the League of Augsburg broke out in Europe between the France of Louis XIV on the one side; and Austria, Spain, the Netherlands, and assorted allies on the other. England became involved with the accession of William of Orange to the throne. As a result, the English and French colonies were drawn into the conflict, known in America as King Williams' War (1689–97). Both sides launched raids against their rivals on the frontier supported by various native allies. The fighting was vicious, with the English colonists bearing the worst of it. An expedition against Quebec in 1690 involving the cooperation of several colonies failed miserably.

Some New England Puritans felt that God was punishing the colonists for their sins; it is believed that the intense self-examination for these supposed faults contributed to the environment that produced the Salem witch hysteria in 1692. Peace was declared in 1697 with the Treaty of Ryswick. However peace was not a reality in all of the colonies. Violence between colonists and Native Americans continued, including a major ongoing war between the French Canadians and the Iroquois Confederacy.

WAR AGAIN IN 1702

The death of the king of Spain, Charles II, led to a new crisis as he named the grandson of the French king Louis XIV as his successor, arousing fears of an unbeatable French-Spanish empire. Thus war broke out again in 1702. The conflict was known as the War of the Spanish Succession in Europe, and Queen Anne's War in the English colonies. In America raids flared across the frontier border, particularly in the north. An attempt by South Carolina volunteers and Yamasee Native Americans to capture St. Augustine by siege in 1702 ended in failure, as did an expedition against Quebec in 1710 involving British ships and regular forces, supplemented by colonial troops. Although the war continued until 1714, England and France signed a peace treaty in 1713 that secured English gains in Nova Scotia and Newfoundland.

For the next several decades military conflict in America was primarily limited to conflicts between colonists and natives, with the exception of a brief Anglo-French war against Spain (1718–21) and another between England and Spain (1727–29). In both wars there was campaigning in Florida. Even while Queen Anne's War was in progress, there was a major outbreak of violence on the Carolina frontier, where the Tuscarora were hard pressed by the continual westward expansion of settlements. From 1711–13 South Carolina forces and their native allies attempted to crush the Tuscarora, killing or enslaving many and driving the rest northwards, where they joined the Iroquois Confederacy. This was succeeded by a conflict with the Yamasee (1715–18), who had been allies of the British during Queen Anne's War and of South Carolina against the Tuscarora. Although casualties were heavy on both sides, the chief result was to make the Yamasee allies of the Spanish in Florida. Other conflicts occurred in New England with the Abenaki (1722–27), while the French moved against various tribes in the north and in the Mississippi Valley.

KING GEORGE'S WAR

A new phase of warfare began when a series of originally unrelated conflicts merged into one great world-wide war. In 1739 Britain and Spain went to war in the oddly-titled War of Jenkins's Ear, the result of the Spanish search of English vessels believed to be involved in an illegal trade with Spanish ports in the Caribbean. A truce was declared in 1743. In the meantime, in 1740 the War of the Austrian Succession began between Austria and Prussia, the latter eventually allied with several lesser Germanic powers and France. France and Britain then went to war in 1745, with Britain allying itself with Austria. Spain resumed hostilities against Britain as France's ally. Fighting continued until 1748. The major American phase of the conflict (1745–48) was referred to in the colonies as King George's War, after George II of Britain.

In 1740 James Oglethorpe, the founder of the colony of Georgia, led a mixed expedition of South Carolina and Georgia forces and Native Americans, in cooperation with a Royal Navy squadron, against St. Augustine. Friction between Oglethorpe and the South Carolina troops and a lack of cooperation from the naval commander led to the lifting of the siege. A major British expedition against Cartagena in the Caribbean in the same year, which included the presence of colonial troops, was also unsuccessful. Once war resumed with France, several northern colonies mounted a successful expedition in conjunction with a British naval squadron against the important fortress of Louisbourg on Cape Breton Island, which guarded the approach to the St. Lawrence River. It fell after a siege in 1745 and proved to be a defining moment for the colonists in their growing sense of importance. However it went back to France with the Treaty of Aix-la-Chapelle in 1748.

The next conflict began in North America. British efforts to expand in the Ohio Valley, supported by Virginia and neighboring colonies whose wealthy land speculators with powerful political ties were eager to carve up the region, ran up against French territorial claims. In 1754 an expedition sent by the governor of Virginia and under the command of George Washington was defeated by French and native forces. Both nations began sending small bodies of troops and ships to America. In the following year a mixed British and colonial column, including Washington under the command of Major General Edward Braddock, was sent to capture Fort Duquesne, near the juncture of the Ohio

Marquis Montcalm trying to stop natives from attacking British soldiers and civilians as they leave Fort William McHenry, built during the French and Indian War (1754–63).

and Monongahela Rivers. Braddock's advance column was ambushed near the fort on July 9 by the French and their native allies and routed, with Braddock himself among those killed. Other British expeditions mounted at the same time fell short of their goals. The French in turn launched a series of raids. Such activities continued into the following year.

REALIGNED ALLIANCE

Meanwhile a series of diplomatic maneuvers resulted in the realignment of the alliance system in Europe. Prussia allied with Britain, while Austria allied with France. Hostilities formally broke out in 1756. The conflict, known in Europe as the Seven Years' War, was primarily fought on the continent by Prussia; subsidized by Britain; against France, Austria, and Russia. In the meantime, other fighting took place on the high seas and in such zones of colonial competition as India. In America two expeditions of French regulars, Canadian militiamen, and allied natives entered into New York, capturing Fort Oswego in August, 1756, and Fort William Henry in August 1757. After the surrender of both forts the allied natives killed some of the prisoners, the most serious of these incidents occurring at Fort William Henry. The bitter feelings engendered by these events continued throughout the war.

During this time William Pitt became prime minister of Britain. Pitt developed a serious strategy for victory which, unlike the earlier colonial wars, placed America at the center of British strategy. The capture of New France was the goal. A series of efforts under able commanders led to the capture of Quebec in September 1759, although the rest of New France did not surrender until the following year. Meanwhile Spain and France forged a new alliance, leading to a British declaration of war against the former. This led to the Spanish losses in the Philippines and in Cuba. In the Treaty of Paris (1763), Spain gave up Florida in exchange for the return of its territorial losses; France ceded control of Canada and its lands in the Ohio and Mississippi Valleys (with the exception of New Orleans) to Britain; and New Orleans went to Spain in compensation for Florida.

COUNTDOWN TO REVOLUTION

Although Great Britain emerged from the Seven Years' War as the largest colonial power in America, the outcome was anything but peaceful. The native peoples quickly were alarmed by the threat that increased British power posed, and were annoyed by many broken promises and abuses. Even while the Seven Years' War raged, conflict erupted with Britain's Cherokee allies in 1759, the result of pressures from Virginia and South Carolina. The struggle ended inconclusively in 1761.

From 1763 until 1765 another struggle was waged in the Ohio Valley. Often identified with the Ottawa chieftain Pontiac, its most prominent early leader, the native resistance in the Ohio region was prompted by a number of issues, especially the growth of unauthorized white settlement on tribal lands. The natives first surprised several isolated posts before moving to besiege some of the larger forts in the region. As in the case of other conflicts, tribes that were not even involved in the resistance were attacked by colonists in retaliation. The situation bogged down into a military stalemate, and a peace was negotiated in 1765, which acknowledged the continuing British military presence.

Before word of the fighting in the Ohio region reached London, in 1763 the government issued a proclamation establishing the Appalachian Mountains as a line between the colonial settlements and the native territories. Although intended as a basis for future peace, the move was widely resented by the colonists, especially among would-be settlers and land speculators, who often chose to defy the law. As British forces in America were widely spread out, it was impossible to enforce the edict, ensuring that tensions remained on the frontier.

The presence of British troops to both protect the settlers and enforce the law was a cause for fear among many colonists, playing upon decades of political rhetoric imported from England about the dangers posed to liberty by standing armies. In addition the British government ended a series of large subsidies paid to the colonies for support during the French and Indian War and began enforcing more rigidly the Navigation Acts, both to insure imperial efficiency and pay off the nation's tremendous war debt. New laws were instituted to raise more taxes, beginning with the Stamp Act of 1765. These measures were met with growing concern, anger, and ultimately pressure and violence in the colonies, and exposed

A scene from a 1903 postcard titled "Burning of Stamp Act, Boston."

long-standing differences of opinion and perception between Britain and the colonies.

The former saw the colonies in an inferior position, obligated to Britain for having sustained and protected them during the colonial wars, and duty-bound to pay for the costs of war and the upkeep of the empire. The colonists felt that they should be viewed as equal partners with Britain in the empire and should not be taxed without direct representation in Parliament. Colonists also nursed long-held resentments regarding the abuse and waste of colonial troops during many campaigns and of the haughty arrogance of British generals, admirals, troops, and sailors in encounters over several decades. These feelings were exacerbated by the Quartering Acts of 1765 and 1774, the first of which authorized the billeting of British soldiers in public or vacant buildings, the second in private homes.

Throughout the 1760s and early 1770s intransigence hardened on both sides as British merchants pressured the government to not back down. Parliament, even in repealing the Stamp Act, affirmed its prerogatives to tax the colonies. Groups such as the Sons of Liberty sprang up to coordinate anti-British activities. Unrest was particularly strong in the larger colonial towns, where altercations between urban laborers and British troops were not uncommon. One such incident led to fatalities when hard-pressed soldiers fired upon members of an urban mob in Boston in March, 1770. The Boston Massacre became a rallying cry among anti-British propagandists.

By 1775 the situation reached a crisis point. The port of Boston had been closed in 1774 in retaliation for the mass dumping of tea in the harbor the previous year in protest against a law imposing a duty on imported tea. Militia companies drilled with increasing frequency and arms were stockpiled. Reports of the latter led to the dispatch of British troops from Boston to gather up weapons and arrest prominent leaders of the resistance movement. The results were the clashes at Lexington and Concord on April 19, 1775.

The British were driven back into town, and a siege of the city by the militia began. In mid-June the Second Continental Congress created a Continental Army, with George Washington appointed commander-in-chief of all forces. Before the end of the year a Continental Navy was created when a few ships

The Continental Army

When fighting began between the British and Americans in 1775, the Continental Congress created an army. Originally it was comprised of the already extant militia companies, with the largest group concentrated at Boston. Although eager, the militia lacked the military edge of British soldiers, who, like members of other European armies, were trained and disciplined in standard tactics and doctrines. George Washington sought to mold his new army into something at least resembling a contemporary army as much as the circumstances allowed. His task was a tough one: not only did the independent-minded militiamen lack the background themselves, but so did their officers.

It soon became obvious that the militia alone could not do the job, as its members tended to come and go as they pleased, and they usually did not match up well with the British in open battle. For these reasons Congress decided to create regular units for use in the war. Originally some militia companies were converted into regular units, but soon all-new companies were recruited. These troops were uniformed, equipped, and trained along European standards, and were expected to hold up against their British counterparts in a stand-up fight. The militias were still used in a secondary role, to take care of local threats, and to swell the ranks of the main American armies as they operated in a particular area.

The Continental soldiers never achieved the level of professionalism as their British, French, or German counterparts that served in America. However they grew better over time, through both training and experience. Initially enlistees were enthusiastic. The setbacks of 1776 and 1777, however, dampened that fervor, as did the harsh conditions of life in the field. Nevertheless Continental units performed with increasing confidence as the war continued, and played a crucial role in such victories as the Saratoga campaign, Monmouth, and the siege of Yorktown.

During the American Revolution, African Americans found themselves in a precarious position. In the northern colonies some free African Americans participated in militia units, and in the years following the Revolution, the states of the region abolished slavery within their boundaries, in apparent recognition of the fact that black Americans had fought alongside white American patriots. However in Virginia loyalist Governor Lord Dunsmore offered freedom to those slaves who would fight for the British. Several thousand slaves deserted their plantations and jumped at the chance for freedom. After the war, the British provided transportation for many of them, some to the Bahamas, but most to Nova Scotia, where they were given parcels of land.

Women participated in the war near the front lines, some as "camp followers," often the wives of officers and enlisted men, who maintained the camps and cared for the wounded. A few, like Molly Pitcher, attained fame for assisting at the battle front, becoming a legend in the lore of the Revolution.

Weapons and Drill

Muskets fitted with bayonets (knives that attached to the end of the barrel) were the most common military weapon of the period. Descended from the arquebus, the musket of the 18th century was primed with powder, loaded with a spherical lead bullet which was tamped down along with the powder by means of a ramrod stored below the barrel, and then held with the butt to the shoulder before firing. Until rifling was developed in 1800, the musket was an unreliable weapon, requiring considerable time and effort to reload in exchange for little accuracy. Unlike modern weaponry or bows, the skill of the marksman contributed little. Muskets were too unpredictable to be aimed with true precision—there was no way to control the spin of the shot as it exited the barrel, which in turn affected the direction the shot took.

Like archers before them, musketeers were usually deployed in formation—their inaccuracy made up for by the deadliness of their firepower. Volleys would be fired at the same general area by men standing shoulder to shoulder and some would inevitably hit. A trained unit could fire every 15 seconds for as long as four minutes before enough discharge had accumulated in the musket's barrel to require a more thorough cleaning.

The musket was essentially the portable version of a cannon, which was the primary weapon of artillery. A cannon—a large, heavy barrel on wheels—was loaded with a single solid ball, small shot (ranging from buckshot to muzzle shots), or hollow iron balls filled with gunpowder. From a range of several hundred yards, the cannon had a good chance of doing real damage if launched into a dense crowd of targets. The addition of cannon support to a regiment was nearly always sufficient advantage to defeat unsupported infantry, regardless of other advantages. This in turn sometimes led to the use of "Quaker guns"—fake cannons made of painted wood, used (successfully, in many cases) to intimidate the other side into surrender.

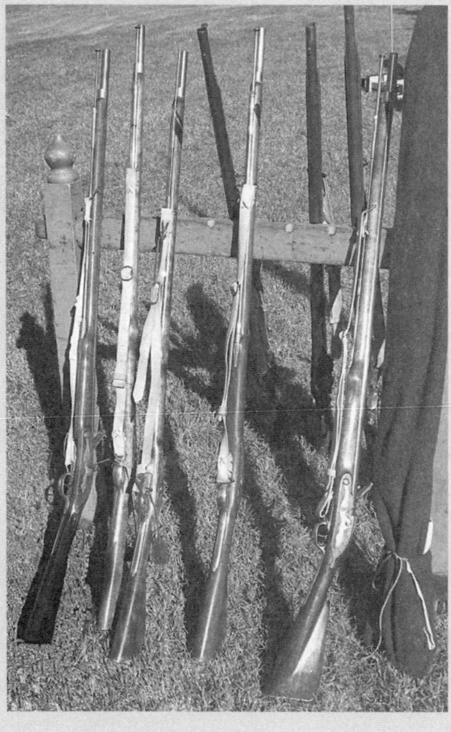

18th-century muskets were the primary weapon of artillery.

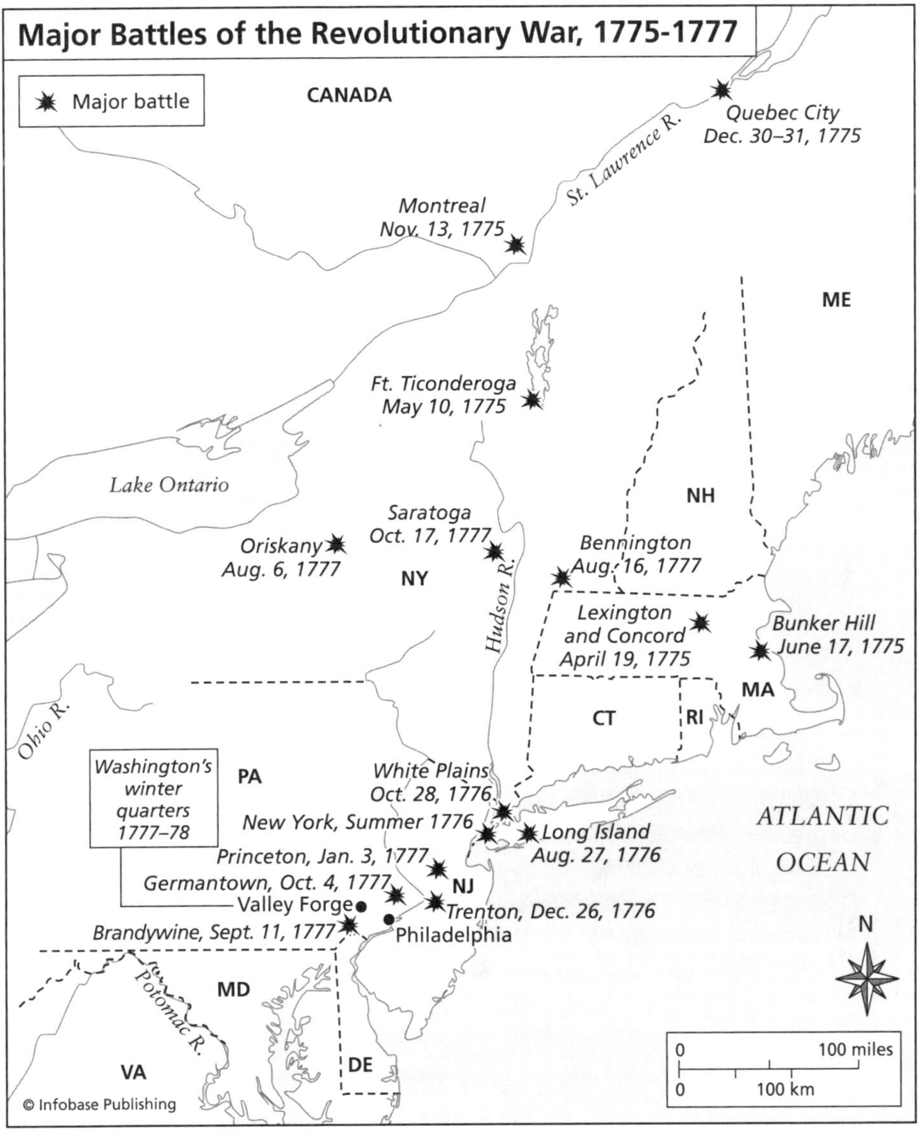

were assigned to act as privateers. In the meantime British efforts to improve their defensive position at Boston led to a bloody but indecisive clash at Bunker Hill on June 17. Washington arrived to take charge at Boston in early July. While he directly supervised the siege, a two-pronged offensive was launched against Quebec; it was repulsed at the end of the year. The British meanwhile withdrew from Boston in March 1776, when the American seizure of Dorchester Heights made the defense untenable. With the signing of the Declaration of Independence in July, the crisis had reached the point of no return.

THE ROAD TO INDEPENDENCE

New York City was the target for the first British offensive. Once that important city was seized, they would drive up the Hudson River and link up with another force advancing southward from Canada. If successful New England would be severed from the remaining colonies, leading to the collapse of the rebellion. The New York part of the plan was successful, as the British landed in July. Washington's army was badly beaten in late August, and the city was occupied. He at first withdrew northward, suffering more setbacks, before crossing the Hudson in November and

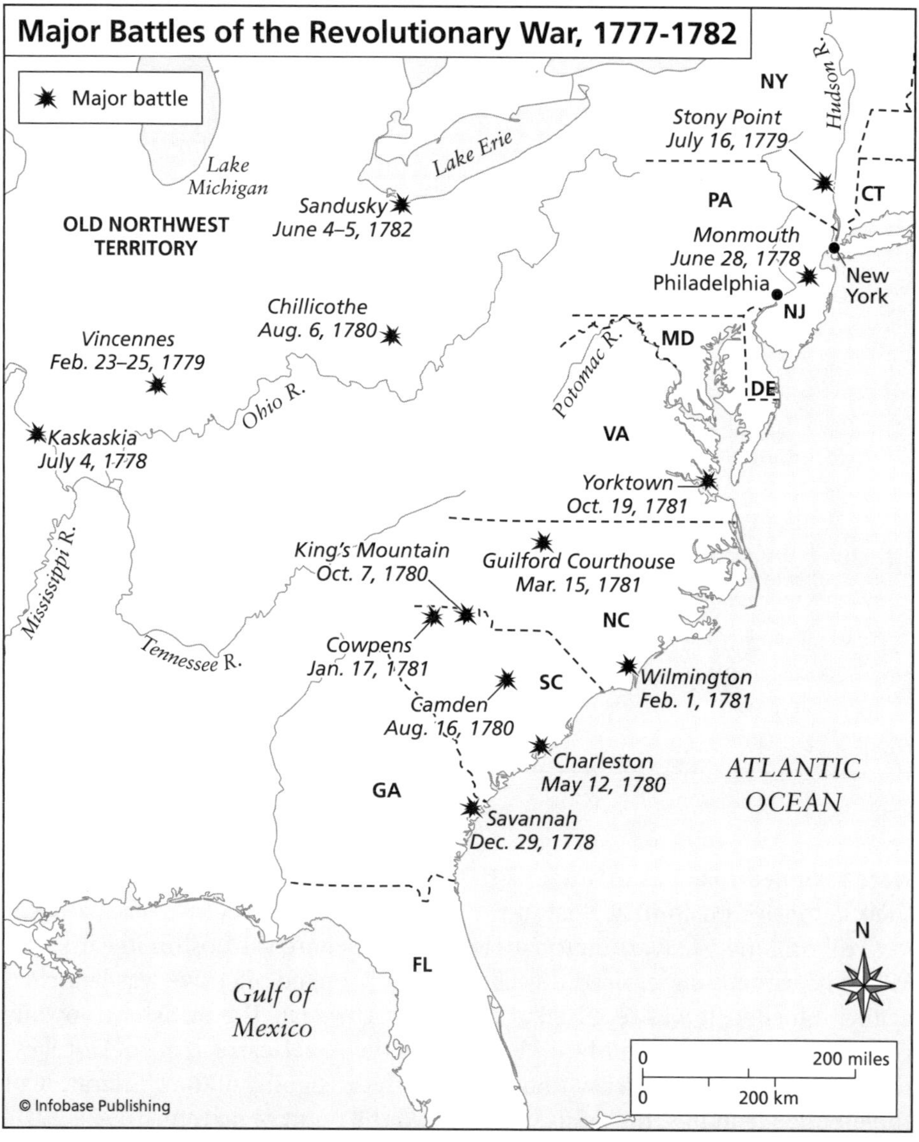

An engraving titled "First Blow for Liberty" depicts the scene at the Battle of Lexington in 1775. The Battle of Concord was fought on the same day.

moving southward into New Jersey. In late December he crossed the Delaware River with his dwindling force and inflicted a sharp defeat on German units in British service at Trenton and another against the British at Princeton in January 1777.

While Washington held his ground in New Jersey, the British prepared for a new round of operations. As one army moved on Philadelphia, another from Canada would move southward. The latter force encountered disaster, however, suffering a series of defeats at the hands of American forces commanded by Horatio Gates, Benedict Arnold, and John Stark. The climactic battles at Freeman's Farm led to the surrender of the British at Saratoga in October. The expedition against Philadelphia was all too successful, as not only was the city taken, but once again Washington suffered a series of defeats. He managed to save his army from destruction, however, and it survived the difficult winter camp at Valley Forge. In June of the following year Washington won a convincing victory against the British at Monmouth Court House in New Jersey, as the latter withdrew from Philadelphia.

While the campaigns of 1777 had mixed results in a strictly military sense, the American victory at Saratoga was of major political significance, as it was enough for the new nation to win diplomatic recognition from France and its entry in the war on the American side in the following year.

The Dutch and the Spanish would also go to war against Britain. The conflict now took on an international dimension as had the earlier colonial wars, with

A print shows General George Washington consulting with other Revolutionary War generals. In 1775 Washington was appointed commander-in-chief of the American Revolutionary forces.

the Spanish and French attempting to take Gibralter from the British, and naval action around the world.

In addition to the battles between the major armies, there was much fighting on a smaller scale on the frontier and in the backcountry. Those who supported the revolutionary cause fought against others who backed Britain, known as Loyalists or Tories. The native peoples also participated, as different tribes sided either with the British or the colonists. Rangers and other irregular forces clashed in the Ohio Valley, with the Americans emerging victorious. The clashing visions of what American freedom might mean also played a role in the conflict. Both free blacks and slaves fought in the Continental Army, many of the latter in exchange for their freedom. Other slaves backed the British side as a chance to win their freedom by aiding in the overthrow of their masters. This was especially true in 1775 when the loyalist governor of Virginia called for a slave uprising and formed units made of runaway slaves.

On the seas fighting was scattered before the intervention of England's rivals brought their fleets into the action. Most American war vessels acted as privateers. There were several ship-to-ship engagements, however, perhaps the most famous being the American victory of John Paul Jones's *Bonhomme Richard* over the British *Serapis* off of the coast of England in September 1779.

As the war dragged on the British shifted their active operations southward, where they counted on Loyalist support to help defeat the rebels. A small expedition took Savannah in December 1778, granting the British control of Georgia. A much larger expedition was sent in December 1779, which besieged Charleston, South Carolina. The city surrendered in May 1780. Gates was sent to take command of the battered American forces in the south, and in August marched towards Charleston. Lord Charles Cornwallis, the British commander, routed him at Camden, South Carolina. He followed up his victory with a move into North Carolina. A Loyalist force attempting to secure the backcountry was defeated by backwoodsmen at King's Mountain in October. In addition guerilla activity plagued Cornwallis's line of supply and communications, forcing him to pull back to South Carolina.

Nathaniel Greene was appointed by Congress to command the revolutionary forces in the south in October. He reorganized the army and sent part of it south under Daniel Morgan. Morgan clashed with a force under Lieutenant Colonel Banastre Tarleton at Cowpens, South Carolina in January 1781, and defeated it. Morgan and Greene then reunited in time to face Cornwallis at Guilford Court House (modern Greensboro), North Carolina, in March. Cornwallis won a pyrrhic victory that forced Greene's withdrawal. While Cornwallis moved to the port of Wilmington

An N. Currier lithograph of the "Surrender of Cornwallis." The British commander Charles Cornwallis was besieged at Yorktown, Virginia, and surrendered on October 19, 1781.

George Washington: Address to the Officers of the Army

At the end of the Revolutionary War the finances of the new nation were so strained that soldiers were being sent home without pay. Major John Armstrong in what is now known as the Newburgh Address urged the dissatisfied soldiers to override the civilian authority unable to meet its obligations. In an address to his officers on March 15, 1783 (partially reprinted below) George Washington forcibly challenged the assertions made in the Newburgh Address and strenuously defended the idea of civilian authority of the military.

Gentlemen:

By an anonymous summons, an attempt has been made to convene you together. How inconsistent with the rules of propriety! How unmilitary! And how subversive of all order and discipline let the good sense of the Army decide.

In the moment of this summons, another anonymous production was sent into circulation, addressed more to the feelings and passions than to the reason and judgment of the Army. The author of the piece is entitled to much credit for the goodness of his pen, and I could wish he had as much credit for the rectitude of his heart; for, as men see through different optics and are induced by the reflecting faculties of the mind to see different means to attain the same end, the author of the address should have more charity than to mark for suspicion the man who should recommend moderation and longer forbearance—or, in other words, who should not think as he thinks and acts as he advises. But he had another plan in view, in which candor and liberality of sentiment, regard to justice, and love of country have no part; and he was right to insinuate the darkest suspicion to effect the blackest design.

That the address is drawn with great art and is designed to answer the most insidious purposes; that it is calculated to impress the mind with an idea of premeditated injustice in the sovereign power of the United States, and rouse all those resentments which must unavoidably flow from such a belief; that the secret mover of this scheme (whoever he may be) intended to take advantage of the passions while they were warmed by the recollection of past distresses. . . .

While I give you these assurances and pledge myself in the most unequivocal manner to exert whatever ability I am possessed of, in your favor, let me entreat you, gentlemen, on your part, not to take any measures which, viewed in the calm light of reason, will lessen the dignity and sully the glory you have hitherto maintained. Let me request you to rely on the plighted faith of your country, and place a full confidence in the purity of the intentions of Congress; that, previous to your dissolution as an Army they will cause all your accounts to be fairly liquidated, as directed in their resolutions, which were published to you two days ago, and that they will adopt the most effectual measures in their power to render ample justice to you for your faithful and meritorious services.

and then north to Virginia, Greene marched into South Carolina to mop up the various British detachments scattered there.

Washington now saw an opportunity to trap Cornwallis on the York-James Peninsula. He moved south with his army and a French army under the Comte de Rochambeau, while two French fleets blocked any hope of withdrawal by sea. By mid-September Cornwallis was besieged at Yorktown, surrendering on October 19, 1781. This ended major military operations in North America. Worn out by its reversals and its resources stretched, Britain sought terms. The Treaty of Paris was signed in September, 1783, recognizing the independence of the United States, insuring the collection of debts on both sides, and urging compensation for the Loyalists. The latter two provisions would prove hard to enforce in the postwar era. The British were to evacuate the Northwest Territory (the area bounded by the Ohio River, the Great Lakes, the Mississippi, and the Appalachians), although it would be years before all British posts were evacuated. Other arrangements were made, including the return of Florida to Spain. The Americans would face new decisions about the role that its armed forces would play in the future.

MICHAEL W. COFFEY

Further Readings

Anderson, Fred. *The War That Made America: A Short History of the French and Indian War.* New York: Viking, 2005.

Higginbotham, Don. *War and Society in Revolutionary America: The Wider Dimensions of Conflict*. American Military History Series. Columbia: University of South Carolina Press, 1988.

Leech, Douglas Edward. *Arms For Empire: A Military History of the Colonies in North America, 1607–1763.* New York: The Macmillan Company, 1973.

Leech, Douglas Edward Leech. *Roots of Conflict: British Armed Forces and Colonial Americans, 1677–1763.* Chapel Hill: University of North Carolina Press, 1986.

Middlekauff, Robert. *The Glorious Cause: The American Revolution, 1763–1789. Vol. 3 The Oxford History of the United States*. New York: Oxford University Press, 1982.

Royster, Charles. *A Revolutionary People at War: The Continental Army and American Character, 1775–1783.* Williamsburg/Chapel Hill: Omohundro Institute of Early American History and Culture/University of North Carolina Press, 1979.

CHAPTER 14

Population Trends and Migration

"America was indebted to immigration for her settlement and prosperity."
— James Madison

WHEN COLONISTS FIRST caught sight of the American wilderness, they approached with a certain amount of trepidation. The virgin forests and dense undergrowth held any number of unknown terrors, from hostile natives and strange animals, to deadly diseases. Pilgrim settler William Bradford deemed the American wilderness "a hideous and desolate wilderness, full of wild beasts and wild men." Not surprisingly early settlers clustered together around the safety of small forts cut out of the forests. The conquest of the American continent was first measured in feet, not acres.

A cautious approach to the conquest of the American wilderness made sense, given the small number of settlers alone in a very large landscape. In 1610 there were only about 300 Englishmen in America, compared to a native population estimated at 30,000 in the surrounding Chesapeake Bay region. By 1630 the English population had climbed to around 4,600. With the so-called Great Migration of Puritans into New England in the 1630s, by 1640 the population had jumped to 26,600, and almost doubled over the next decade to 50,400 in 1650. Sixty years after the first English colonists arrived, the colonial population had crossed the 100,000 threshold, and by 1700, exceeded 250,000. Fifty years later in 1750, there were 1.7 million residents. In 1780, in the midst of the Revolution, there were an estimated 2,780,400 American citizens.

Populations grow in two ways: by natural increase, and by immigration. Natural increase relies on several factors, among them a healthy population, a good balance of females to males, and a subsequent birthrate that is higher than the death rate.

In New England, where the colonists tended to come in family groups and which had a healthy (if chilly) environment, natural increase was possible from the very beginning. A saying at the time held that "a sip of New England's air is better than a whole draft of Old England's ale." Life expectancy was about 10 years higher than in England, and perhaps 20 years higher than along the Chesapeake. It was not uncommon for New Englanders to live into their late 60s and 70s. Women generally gave birth to 10 children during her lifetime; an average of seven or eight of these children would survive, and most would go on to have children of their own.

In the south this trend was reversed. The southerner's life expectancy was 10 years lower than in England; living into their 40s or 50s was something of an accomplishment. Most emigrants were young males, with only one female migrant for every three males in the 17th century.

No matter what gender, all new settlers had to endure what they called the "seasoning," as they came in contact with diseases for which they had no natural immunity. Malaria, typhoid, and dysentery took a huge toll, with mortality rates of between 40–70 percent annually. By 1650 the gender imbalance was huge, with six males for every one female. This meant that most males were unmarried, and few women remained single for long. The average marriage lasted just seven years before one of the partners died. A woman's widowhood was generally short, but gaps between marriages led to a slightly lower birthrate for southern women. Mortality rates for children in the south were very high, with 25 percent dying before age one, and 50 percent dying before their 21st birthday.

These trends began to reverse between 1670 and 1700, as immigration increased, standards of living improved, and immunity to some endemic diseases developed. By 1690 Virginia was home to 59,000 people and was the most populous colony in America.

IMMIGRATION

The American experiment never would have survived without a constant influx of immigrants from England and beyond. As long as the settlers numbered in the hundreds, they were vulnerable to any number of catastrophic threats, including attacks by natives—the indigenous population east of the Alleghenies in 1607 has been estimated at about 500,000—and environmental disasters like starvation or epidemic. Immigrants filled the void left by high mortality. They brought their energy, capital, cultures, technologies, and

Old World Ethnic and Racial Groups in the British Mainland Colonies, 1700 and 1775

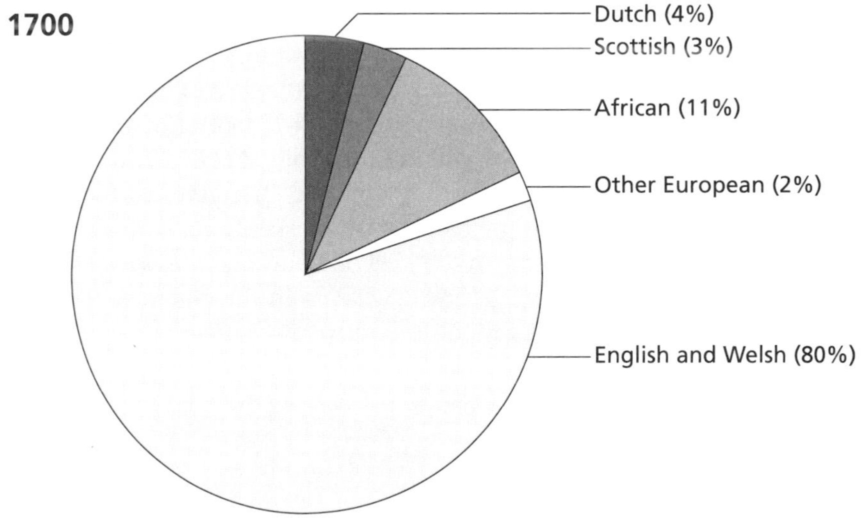

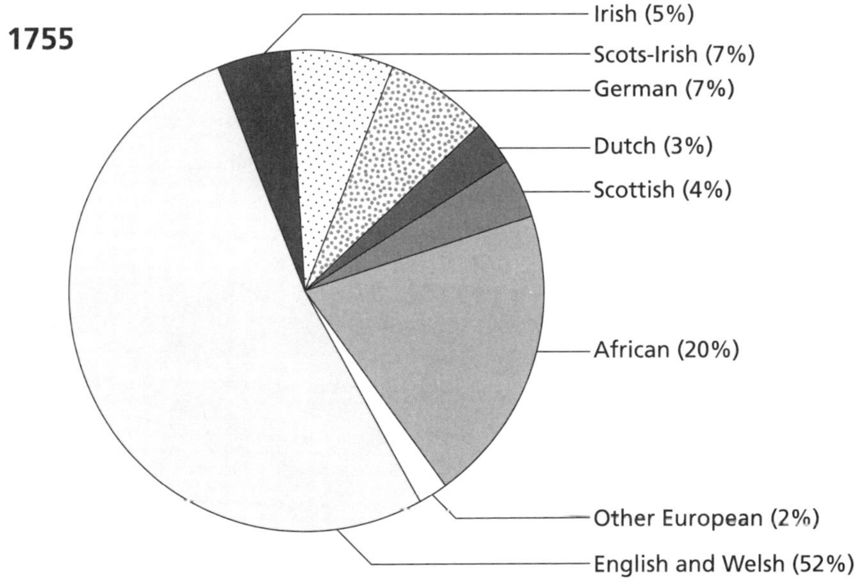

Source: Thomas L. Purvis. "The European Ancestry of the United States Population," *William & Mary Quarterly* 61 (1984): 85–101.

ideas. In their sheer numbers they pushed the frontier boundaries beyond the coastal settlements, moving the American colonies 1,000 miles to the north and south, and almost as far to the west.

Conditions in Europe during the 17th and 18th centuries strongly favored trans-Atlantic migration. Historians generally categorize these conditions into three groups: religious, political, and economic, although in truth there was usually a considerable amount of overlap between the three. Conflicts between Catholics and Protestants, and between competing Protestant groups were a major contributing factor. The first stirrings of a capitalist economy were widening the gap between the rich and the poor, and strengthened the grasp of the rich on political and economic control. The discontented, oppressed, and persecuted all began to find hope in the idea of a new life in America.

If immigrants could survive the first few years in the colonies, they had a good chance of making at least a modest living and practicing their chosen re-

Pilgrims arriving in the New World in a painting by Bernard Gribble. Pilgrim settler William Bradford called America "a hideous and desolate wilderness, full of wild beasts and wild men."

ligion without fear. And unlike Europe there was a greater possibility of social advancement, so within a generation or two, a family could climb from the lowest ranks of society to its powerful heights. Colonial immigration came from all over northern Europe and beyond. Although North America would remain in British control, a variety of groups, including Germans, Scots-Irish, and Africans, would have a huge impact on the development of the American spirit.

THE BRITISH AND GERMANS

British migration set colonization in motion, but it peaked relatively early. The exact number of British immigrants during the colonial period has been surprisingly difficult to calculate. Many historical demographers have attempted to estimate a figure based on calculation of natural increase, attributing any figure over what would be reasonable through the natural cycles of birth and death to immigration. One leading historian has stated that about 400,000 British-born people set out for North America in the 17th century, with about 200,000 landing in the Caribbean. Others point out that the total known immigration out of England during the century was 500,000, with at least 200,000 going to Ireland—leaving 300,000 for North America and the Caribbean.

Most of the emigrants were far from wealthy. Indenture was the mechanism by which most British settlers made their way across the ocean. The system of indentured servitude allowed men (and a few women) to come to America and sell their labor to a willing buyer for a period of four to seven years in exchange for room and board. At the end of the contract period the servant would generally receive a small parcel of land to begin their own farm, sometimes along with tools or a small gift of money.

Before slavery became the dominant form of labor in the south, indentured labor was the motor of the region's agricultural economy. Of the 2,675 documented immigrants who landed at Virginia between 1623 and 1637, almost 2,100 were indentured servants. By 1670 about 75 percent of all immigrants were servants. Indenture was practiced throughout the colonies, but was most critical in Virginia and Maryland, due to the dependence on the labor-intensive tobacco crop. Wherever practiced, the system was ripe for abuse. While indentured servants were not technically slaves, neither were they entirely free. Laws provided little protection from abusive masters. If a female servant became pregnant during her term of service, two years were immediately tacked on to her contract. Servants ran the same risk of disease faced by all settlers of the time, and died in the same numbers. When their service was complete, they didn't always get the best piece of land; some towns in Massachusetts prohibited the granting of land to former servants, pushing them to marginal lands on the fringes of the settlements.

The first German immigrants arrived in Pennsylvania in 1683 under the leadership of a Pietist named Franz Daniel Pastorious. Pastorious and his followers established a settlement called Germantown, now a part of greater Philadelphia.

Immigration increased dramatically after 1690, when the political, religious, and economic situation in southern Germany made the idea of resettlement in American much more appealing. Most colonial Germans hailed from the Palatinate region, an area along the Rhine near the contested border with France. The War of the Grand Alliance (1689–97) and the War of Spanish Secession (1701–13) brought destruction and suffering to the people, especially Protestants, who lost their churches when Catholics established control over the region. Immigration was often curtailed during periods of open warfare, but whenever possible, families and individuals made their way up the Rhine to the port at Rotterdam, where they boarded ships for America.

Three-quarters of German immigrants entered through the port of Philadelphia, and from there moved north, west, and south, forming communities in Pennsylvania, New York, Maryland, and the Shenandoah Valley of Virginia. As with the British, the precise number of German immigrants is unclear, but it exceeded 100,000 before the Revolution. German colonists tended to form into communities with other German-speakers. As farmers, they were drawn to inexpensive land on the frontiers, and soon established themselves in fertile river valleys from New York to Georgia.

The exclusivity of German settlers did not curry them any favor with their English-speaking neighbors. They did not participate heavily in colonial politics, at least until the late 18th century. They worshiped in their own churches, drank ale in their own taverns, celebrated their own holidays, and wore their own plain clothing. No less a figure than Benjamin Franklin once questioned, "Why should the Palatine boors be suffered to swarm into our settlement, and by herding together, establish their language and manners, to the exclusion of ours?" This was, perhaps, the first statement of nativism, a form of racism that would plague immigrants throughout American history. Most colonial Germans would likely not have described themselves as isolationists. They enjoyed "the famous English liberty" that was allowing them the freedom to live and worship the way they chose—a right denied them in their homeland. Some were happy to assimilate when and where they could, as long as assimilation did not require them to give up their principles.

The Germans were in many ways the perfect colonial settlers: sober, honest, industrious, thrifty, literate folk who believed in the concept of owning their own land and stewarding it well. They generally prospered wherever they went, and as a result, colonies with high concentrations of German settlers had a higher per capita income than those without.

THE SCOTS-IRISH

If the Germans represented the best of colonial immigration, the Scots-Irish in many ways represented the worst—or at least many colonial observers would have argued. In reality the Scots-Irish brought a unique culture to the American landscape, one that can still be seen today all along the spine of the Appala-

Colonial California, New Mexico, and Florida

As the English colonies grew along the Atlantic Coast in the 17th and 18th centuries, 2,000 miles to the west and south, the Spanish were consolidating their grip on local populations in the future U.S. states of California, New Mexico, and Florida. Beginning in the Caribbean in 1492, the Spanish had conquered most of South and Central America. Florida's colonial period began in 1565, New Mexico's in 1568, and California's in 1769.

While wholesale killing and enslavement of native populations had marked the first generation of the Spanish conquest, by the 16th century, assimilation had proven a more effective method of settlement. The Spanish gained control by first Christianizing and Hispanizing indigenous peoples with the establishment of religious missions, bringing natives into the Catholic Church and encouraging them to take on Hispanic dress, language, and cultural norms. *Presidios* (forts), created military and administrative centers, and *pueblos* (towns), kept populations together in manageable areas, with surplus food production going to the presidios and and missions.

The Spanish presence in North America was a thorn in the side of the early U.S. government, and had it continued, would likely have lead to war. However, in the early 19th century, the Spanish Empire began to destabilize, and one by one their colonies declared independence. By 1821 the Spanish had pulled out of the American south and southwest, leaving behind a cultural legacy that remains to this day.

A modern-day reconstruction of Mission San Juan Bautista in California. Originally built by the Spanish in the late 18th century, it was destroyed by the earthquake of 1906.

The 13 Colonies: A Brief Timeline of Settlement

1607	Virginia
1620	Massachusetts
1623	New Hampshire
1624	New York
1632	New Jersey
1633	Maryland
1636	Rhode Island
1636	Connecticut
1638	Delaware
1653	North Carolina
1663	South Carolina
1682	Pennsylvania
1732	Georgia

chian Mountains. The Scots-Irish were Scots who had been sent by the Protestant King James I to settle in Catholic Ireland. As Presbyterians they had been persecuted by both Catholics and Anglicans. They were shut out of trade and prohibited from owning the land on which they farmed.

The year 1717 was a watershed for the Scots-Irish. The leases on many of their tenant farms were due to expire, raising the likelihood of higher rents. Between 1717 and 1760 an estimated 100,000 made their way across the Atlantic to what one immigrant called "the best country for working folk and tradesmen of any in the world."

The Scots-Irish became America's first backwoodsmen, although not entirely by choice. Prejudice pushed them out of many settled areas, including New England. Most ended up trying to carve out a life on the fringes, consigned to the isolated mountains of Pennsylvania, Virginia, and the Carolinas. Having survived life in some of the harshest, least productive parts of Scotland and Ireland, they adapted to life in America with few problems. Like the Germans their culture remained virtually intact and their settlement homogenous. They developed a reputation—not entirely undeserved—as a hard-drinking, hard-fighting people, quick to brawl, and suspicious of outsiders. "The settlement of five families (from Ireland) gives me more trouble than 50 of any other people," a Pennsylvania official once said.

At the same time they were loyal, generous, and brave, plunging into wildernesses where others had not dared to go. Their fighting spirit was instrumental in the small wars leading up to the Revolution, and no fewer than 25 revolutionary officers had Scots-Irish roots. While they did not prosper in the same way the Germans did, they nevertheless found a place for themselves relatively free from the oppression they had faced in the British Isles.

THE AFRICANS

Not all who landed on America's shores in the colonial era were there voluntarily. It is impossible to calculate just how many Africans were transported across the Atlantic during those years, but their numbers were substantial—

perhaps 50,000 between 1700 and 1740 alone. The first Africans arrived by chance in August 1619 in the hold of a Dutch man-of-war. Colonist John Rolfe noted in a letter that Captain Jope was in need of "victualls" for his ship, but had nothing to trade except "20 and odd Negroes." The governor gave the captain supplies, and the Africans were brought ashore.

They were not slaves. At that time the English had no law on the books that allowed for permanent slave status. The Africans became indentured servants, freed after they had completed their term of service. Those that survived went on to build their own farms; some may have even married into the English community.

The increasing need for workers on southern plantations and the growing profitability of tobacco in the 18th century drove business-minded owners to move away from indentured servitude and toward slavery. Because Europeans of the time saw Africans as something less than human, it was easy to start looking on them as another commodity, like farm animals—a self-reproducing resource that could be used for work in the good times, and sold for profit in the lean times.

The trans-Atlantic slave trade built rapidly in the final quarter of the 17th century. African and Arab slave traders fanned out across West Africa, kidnapping tens of thousands of innocent people and transporting them to the coast, where they were sold to Portuguese, Spanish, Dutch, English, and French trad-

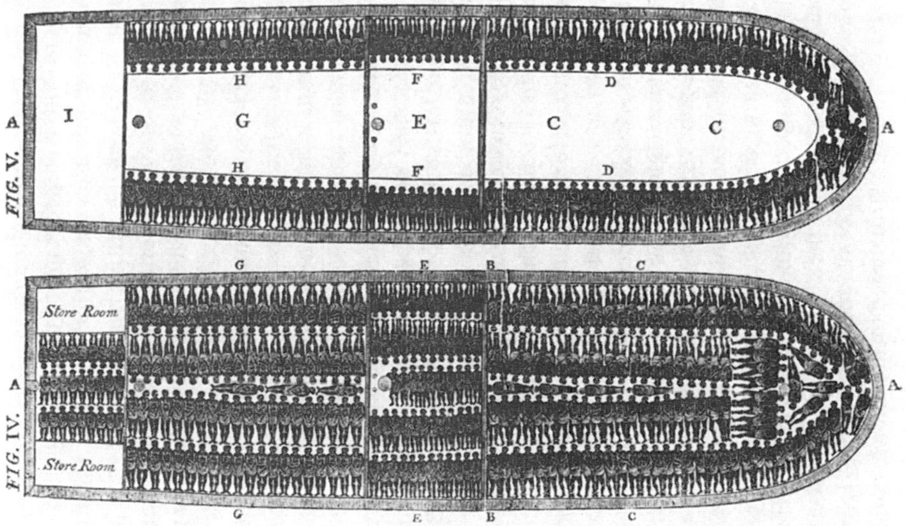

A diagram of a slave ship from the Atlantic slave trade from an abstract of evidence delivered to a select committee of the English House of Commons in the late 18th century.

ers who shoved the unfortunates into horribly overcrowded ships bound for world markets. Historians estimate that between 12 and 18 percent of captives died during the voyages of the "middle passage." Those who survived ended up in the slave auction of America and the West Indies.

Owners relied on the trans-Atlantic trade for a generation. Male slaves were in high demand, as they were able to do more of the heavy work. First-generation female slaves were often infertile as a result of disease, malnutrition, or simple trauma. Africans faced the same risks of disease as their white masters, with many dying during the "seasoning." It was not until the early 18th century that there was a large enough number of African-Americans to form a naturally-reproducing population.

A SLAVE'S DAY

Once on the plantation unceasing work was the focus of a slave's life. Different regions favored different methods of organizing their slave workforce. The majority of slaves worked as common field hands. The staple crops of the colonial south—tobacco, rice, and indigo—were labor-intensive, requiring endless hoeing, weeding, and irrigation. Soil depletion meant there was always more land to be cleared. Since plantations were large self-sustaining farms, there was constant work needed, just to keep the community running smoothly. Slaves worked dawn to dusk, six days a week, with Sundays and some holidays free. Women served in the fields as hard as the men. Most worked through their pregnancies and returned within a couple of days of birth. Children were cared for until they were six or seven years of age by older slaves who could no longer work the crops. Then they were given light work, and by the time they were aged 10 or 11, they were working full time, just like their elders.

Perpetual slave status based on race was codified in colonial law beginning in the mid-17th century. Maryland formally acknowledged slavery in 1638. In 1662 Virginia passed an act stating that the child of an English man and a slave woman retained the slave status of the mother. Maryland passed similar legislation in 1664. In the early 18th century colonial governments began to pass stiff punishments for slaves alleged to be involved in insurrections or revolts. The harshest slave control laws were passed in the south. New England took a comparatively benign approach to slavery, because it was never as large a part of its economy or culture. In 1760 there were only about 5,000 slaves in all of New England.

While African Americans would inject their cultural richness into American life, they could not hold on to that culture for long. Slaves were seized from hundreds of tribes across West Africa; they did not share a common language or culture the way the British, Germans, or Scots did. To survive they had to learn to conform to the language and culture of their owners, and within a generation or two they lost many of their native traditions, practices, stories, and songs as

Small numbers of Dutch, French, Swedes, and Spaniards were also scattered throughout the colonies. Above, Dutch leave their homeland seeking a new life in colonial America.

they struggled to adapt to life in this harsh new world. An exception to this rule was the continued persistence of African cultural and linguistic traces among the African Americans of the Sea Island and coastal region of South Carolina and northern Georgia.

OTHER GROUPS AND EXPANSION

British Islanders, Germans, and Africans were the largest immigrant communities in colonial America, but they were not the only ones. Small numbers of Dutch, French, Swedes, and Spaniards were also scattered throughout the colonies. Further west, Spanish missionaries and settlers moved into New Mexico and California.

With such a burgeoning population, expansion was inevitable. From the first permanent settlements at Jamestown and Plymouth, colonial settlers began pushing outward. Over 150 years they founded colonies between the eastern slope of the Appalachian Mountains and the Atlantic Coast, and in the decade before the Revolution, breached the mountain range itself.

Colonial migration was dangerous and difficult work. When stretching into new areas, there were no roads. Pioneers had to cut and hack their way through virgin forest, mile by mile. Travel to a new area could take months of hard work. Movement into new areas inevitably brought tension with native tribes, which often turned into a cycle of attacks and reprisals that could go on for years. Once they had found their new home and set up housekeeping, settlers had to cope with the terrible loneliness of life on the frontier, so many miles from the nearest civilization.

Susanna Johnson wrote of her life on the New Hampshire frontier in 1754: "A detail of the miseries of a 'frontier man' must excite pity in every child of humanity. The gloominess of the rude forest, the distance from friends and competent defense and the daily inroads and nocturnal yells of hostile Indians awaken the keen apprehensions and anxieties which conception can only picture." Whenever she left her cabin to go to the well or tend the animals, she never went around a corner "without first looking with a tremulous caution, to see if a tomahawk was not raised for my destruction." Mrs. Johnson and her family were captured by Indians in August 1754 and marched to Canada, where she spent the next four years, before she was released and made her way home.

BEYOND THE PEAKS

For decades lines of colonization moved north and south, with Massachusetts Bay colony spawning Connecticut, Rhode Island, New Hampshire, and eventually, Maine and Vermont. Settlers flowed into New York, Pennsylvania, and New Jersey. Virginia was soon bracketed by Maryland, Delaware, and North Carolina. South Carolina and Georgia followed to the south. Generally, people moved inland only about as far as they could sail or row up navigable rivers. Penetration into the interior was less than a thousand miles, even after a century or more of migration.

By the early 18th century people were fascinated by the prospect of what lay beyond the peaks of the Appalachians. A few intrepid souls had hiked over the mountains and were stunned by what they saw: "I had gained the summit of a commanding ridge," Daniel Boone said in his autobiography, "and, looking around with astonishing delight, beheld the ample plains, the beauteous tracts below: on the other hand had I surveyed the famous Ohio river, that rolled in silent dignity, marking the western boundary of Kentucky with inconceivable grandeur. At a vast distance, I beheld the mountains lift their veritable brows, and penetrate the clouds."

Descriptions such as these inspired people to move out of the increasingly crowded colonies in search of new lands in the west, but without a trail or road, the kind of wagon travel needed by potential settlers was out of the question. Travel down the Ohio River was, in theory, the easiest route into Kentucky, but most deemed it too dangerous, and preferred a land route. Cumberland Gap, a narrow passage through the mountains at the corners of present-day Virginia, Kentucky, and Tennessee, was the most feasible land route. Boone and the Transylvania Company marked out what came to be called "The Wilderness Road" along the path of an old buffalo trail in 1775. This steep, rutted path through the forests became the main artery of migration west of Virginia for the next 50 years.

The colonial period marked the mere beginning of the movement westward. In 1775 no American knew exactly how far west their country stretched. Thirty years after the Declaration of Independence was signed in Philadelphia, Meriwether Lewis and William Clark completed their epic journey across the North American continent and first caught sight of "the great Pacific Ocean."

HEATHER K. MICHON

Further Readings

Bridenbaugh, Carl. *Vexed and Troubled Englishmen, 1590–1642.* New York: Oxford University Press, 1968.

Griffin, Patrick. *The People with No Name: Ireland's Ulster Scots, America's Scots Irish, and the Creation of a British Atlantic World, 1689–1764.* Princeton, NJ: Princeton University Press, 2001.

Hinderaker, Eric and Peter C. Mancall. *At the Edge of Empire: The Backcountry in British North America*. Baltimore, MD: Johns Hopkins University Press, 2003.

Hofstra, Warren R. *The Planting of New Virginia : Settlement and Landscape in the Shenandoah Valley*. Baltimore, MD: Johns Hopkins University Press, 2004.

Kulikoff, Allan. *From British Peasants to Colonial American Farmers*. Chapel Hill: University of North Carolina Press, 2000.

Lehmann, Hartmut, Renate Wilson, and Herman Wellenreuther, eds. *In Search of Peace and Prosperity: New German Settlements in 18th-Century Europe and America*. University Park, PA: Pennsylvania State University Press, 2000.

Leyburn, James G. *The Scotch-Irish: A Social History*. Chapel Hill: University of North Carolina Press, 1962.

Robisheaux, Thomas Willard. *Rural Society and the Search for Order in Early Modern Germany*. Cambridge, UK: Cambridge University Press, 1989.

Roeber, A.G. *Palatines, Liberty, and Property: German Lutherans in Colonial British America*. Baltimore, MD: Johns Hopkins University Press, 1993.

Webb, James H. *Born Fighting: How the Scots-Irish Shaped America*. New York: Broadway, 2005.

Volo, Dorothy and James Volo. *Daily Life on the Old Colonial Frontier*. New York: Greenwood Press, 2002.

Wokeck, Marianne S. *Trade in Strangers*. University Park: Pennsylvania State University Press, 1999.

CHAPTER 15

Transportation

"... to be and continue forever."
— General Assembly of New York on approving the construction and maintenance of public highways, 1703

MANY AMERICAN ROADS and railroads of today are built upon trails that natives had carved through the wilderness, centuries before Europeans set foot upon the land that is now the United States. Even after the Spanish, English, and other Europeans arrived, decades, and even centuries, would pass before these routes would be improved to the extent that travel would be comfortable.

The first of the Europeans to traverse the native trails were the Spanish, who in the early 16th century followed trails from Florida to Texas, to New Mexico, and into California. As years and decades passed, they carved out a system of trails through Mexico and into what is now the southern and southwestern United States.

The network of trails became known as *Los Caminos Reales* (The Royal Highways), with each individual road given the name *El Camino Real*. The trails were used for exploration and trade, and for proselytizing the natives. The Spanish gradually established missions, presidios, and settlements along *los caminos reales*. Along *El Camino Real* in California, for example, the Spanish established 21 missions between 1769 and 1823. Extending from San Diego northward to Sonoma, these missions were established approximately 40 miles apart, about the distance that could be traveled in one day.

To the north the French had settled in Canada in the early 17th century, and had quickly found the advantages of easily accessible river systems for

The original Kalmar Nyckel *sailed from Sweden to the New World in 1638. Its 24 passengers of Swedish, Finnish, German, and Dutch descent established the first permanent European settlement.*

travel and trade. By 1680 there were hundreds of French fur traders in the region of what is now Ohio, Wisconsin, Iowa, and Minnesota. They made use of native trails, including the footpaths that connected rivers and those allowing for easy portage of canoes, furs, and other trade goods and supplies from river to river. Like the Spanish with their missions, French Jesuit missionaries traveled paths into the wilderness for the purpose of converting the natives. The French did not have the great number of colonists and settlements that the English had in North America, though they did have settlements along the St. Lawrence River, which they controlled, and also settlements up the Mississippi to the Illinois River. They did not control the Ohio River and its tributaries, which was a situation that they hoped to remedy.

The Ohio River, as a tributary of the Mississippi, was considered by both the French and the English to be of primary importance as a corridor into the interior. By the middle of the 18th century individual American colonies had grown to the extent that several of them had aspirations of acquiring land and trade in the west. Traders from Pennsylvania, Maryland, and Virginia began to explore the Ohio Valley, threatening French plans for the region. When in 1753 the French constructed Fort Presque Isle on Lake Erie near present-day Erie, Pennsylvania, and Fort Le Boeuf at the headwaters of French Creek, a major tributary to the Allegheny River, and made plans to establish another fort at the forks of the Ohio, the British became alarmed. In 1754 the French drove a small party of English from their stockade at the three rivers and built Fort Duquesne. Two failed attempts by the British to capture Fort Duquesne, one under the leadership of George Washington in 1754 and the other under Major General Edward Braddock in 1755, sparked the French and Indian War.

This war became part of a world-wide conflict involving the major European powers and would ultimately lead to France's withdrawal from the North American continent. But until the French were defeated in 1763, the English colonists relied largely upon road building to take them westward. By the time the British finally succeeded in taking Fort Duquesne in 1758, General John Forbes had a choice of two roads to the fort. He chose an all-Pennsylvania route, which would become known as the Forbes Road. Some historians believe that if General Braddock had taken this shorter Pennsylvania route to Fort Duquesne in 1755, the French would not have been able to adequately prepare the fort for defense, allowing Braddock and the British to take the fort. They believe that if Braddock had not taken the time to widen the native trail, known as Nemacolin's Trail, to 12 feet so his guns and wagons could pass, the French and Native American War might have proceeded quite differently.

TRAVELING THE WATERWAYS

Throughout the colonial period the most efficient means of travel was by water, resulting in wide settlement of the regions along the coastline and near navigable bays and rivers. Studies of early North American settlement have shown that until about 1775 immigrant populations settled along the bays and river valleys as far as the fall line, the point above which rivers were no longer navigable; although there were a few settlements in the mountains and other outlying regions.

Watercraft used in these waterways varied. The canoe, another contribution of the natives, was soon adopted by European immigrants. There were two types of canoe. One was heavy, made from a large log that was shaped and hollowed by fire and cutting implements. This type of canoe was known as a dug-out canoe or a "pirogue." The second type of canoe, the bark canoe, was much lighter in weight. Strips of wood from trees such as cedar or spruce formed the frame, and was then covered with birch bark, which was attached by long, tough, and slender fibrous roots. Seams and cracks were covered with hot pitch, making the canoe watertight.

As the settlements grew, there became greater need for moving goods and people up and down American rivers. Some of the earliest boats to follow the canoe were pole-boats. They were known as pole-boats because they relied upon poles to propel them upstream. The smaller pole-boats were built from pine planks, were 20 to 30 feet long, and three to five feet wide. They were usually two to three feet deep, flat-bottomed, and pointed at both ends. Downstream travel was easy, but upstream travel was a different story. Depending upon the size of the boat, in addition to steersmen the crew consisted of four to eight men who manned the poles that propelled the craft upstream. The larger pole-boats were similar to the smaller version, but were about twice the size, and were equipped with a mast and sails.

Other colonial-era watercraft included small sailing vessels. The first such vessel launched in New England was the *Blessing of the Bay*, launched at Mystic in 1631. Within four years five more ships were built there, and by 1640 the boat-building industry was underway in Boston, Gloucester, Plymouth, Salem, New Haven, Newport, and other New England settlements. By 1676 colonists of Massachusetts alone had built at least 730 sailing vessels, and other New England colonists were busy doing the same. At least one seaport served each of the original 13 colonies, and while some of the shipping of trade goods was overseas or to other colonies, most of the trade was conducted up and down the seacoast and rivers of the home colony.

One of the greatest obstacles to early western settlement was the Appalachian mountain system, which reached from the Green Mountains of Vermont to the hills of Alabama, a region approximately 1,300 miles long and 300

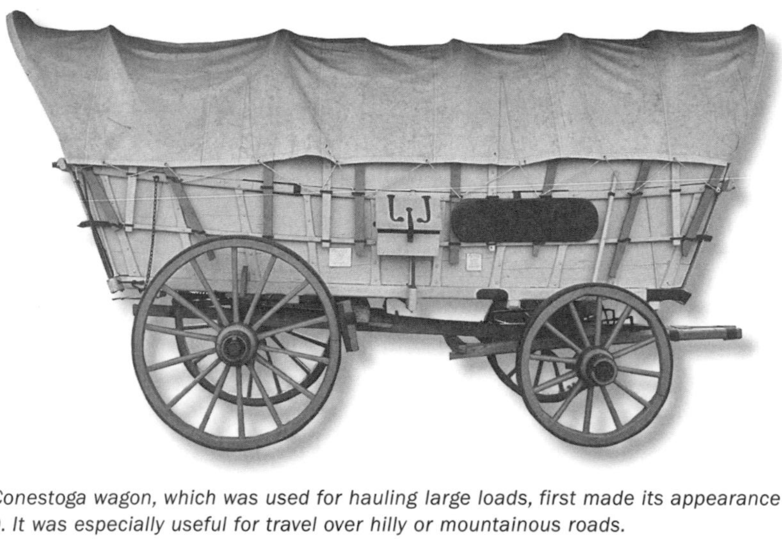

The Conestoga wagon, which was used for hauling large loads, first made its appearance around 1760. It was especially useful for travel over hilly or mountainous roads.

miles wide. Early traders and settlers made their way through the American wilderness by following old native trails, usually traveling on foot since many trails were too narrow for horses. As time passed and settlements grew, the paths through the forests were widened to make way for wheeled vehicles. In 1639 Massachusetts leaders passed an act to create wide roadways, and work on a road between Boston and Plymouth soon began. This was the beginning of the Boston Post Road, one of the earliest roads in America, which decades later would be approximately 250 miles of hardened roadway, stretching from Boston to New York City. By the 1660s other colonies had established laws aimed at building and maintaining local roads.

What constituted "road making" varied, but usually meant outlining a course for travel, clearing away fallen timber, cutting trees down to their stumps, and laying logs over marshy and swampy ground. Conditions of colonial roadways varied from place to place, sometimes depending upon the expenditure on roads designated by local governments, but often upon the general terrain over

The Great Wagon Road

When English colonists began to venture westward into the Shenandoah and Cumberland Valleys in the mid-17th century, they came upon a system of trails, known as the Warrior's Path, extending from New York to Georgia. Realizing the potential value of the western lands, in the early 18th century whites made treaties with the tribes of the Iroquois Nation, giving the colonists the right to use the Warrior's Path.

As the years passed travel along the trail increased as Germans, French, Scots-Irish, and others moved to the west and south from Pennsylvania in search of land upon which to build farms and create new lives. By mid-century English settlers were also making use of the trail, as were religious revival leaders of the Great Awakening. In the Lancaster Treaty of 1744 whites gained exclusive use of the trail, which was slowly becoming an important road, the Great Wagon Road.

Following the French and Indian War, in 1763 King George III of England issued the Proclamation of 1763, declaring that all land west of the Appalachians was native tribe territory and forbidding whites from settling there. White colonists, who had fought alongside the British to defeat the French, were angered by the proclamation. The remoteness of the Great Wagon Road afforded the settlers an opportunity to cross the mountains without interference from the British military. As the traffic increased ferries and taverns were constructed along the way. The Great Wagon Road eventually stretched about 735 miles, from Philadelphia to Augusta, Georgia, and served to populate much of Georgia and the Carolinas. During the American Revolution the Continental Army used the road to move men and supplies.

which the roads were built, and the season of the year. Often no official decree was needed to facilitate the building of a road since, as a result of frequent use, trails were gradually widening into roadways.

An example of community cooperation in road building occurred in mid-18th-century Pennsylvania when York County farmers realized that the distance to Baltimore, Maryland, was about 40 miles shorter than the closest Pennsylvania port at Philadelphia. To save shipping costs, they decided to build a road to Baltimore. When Baltimore merchants realized that the road would also be to their benefit, they joined in the effort to build the new road. Yet road building was slow and difficult because from Maine to Georgia, and from the Atlantic to the Mississippi, the land was largely covered by dense forests. There was some open country in what is now Illinois, Kentucky, and Indiana, but these areas were rarely visited by colonial-era colonists. New Englanders, concentrated in a smaller area than colonists of the middle and southern colonies, paid greater attention to their roadways, giving them a larger number of roads than found elsewhere.

When streams created an obstacle for road construction, sometimes just laying a log over the water would suffice. Bridges were often narrow, built to

The Wilderness Road

While exploring in the Blue Ridge Mountains in 1671, a group of Virginians discovered a Native-American trail, the "Warrior Path," that extended from the lands of the Cherokee in Tennessee northward to the Iroquois Nations in New York. A 50-mile portion of this trail would later become a part of the Wilderness Road, a road that would carry thousands of settlers through the Cumberland Gap and across Kentucky to the Falls of the Ohio. Daniel Boone became a frontier hero when in 1775 and 1776 he and his party built an approximate 200 mile pathway through the Cumberland Gap and beyond, creating a way to the west. Despite recognition that the route was of great value to western settlement, and that the Virginia legislature passed an act in 1779 to cause further study of the road as a practical route for wagonloads, clearing of the road for wagon travel did not take place until the 1790s.

While some travelers found their journeys along the Wilderness Road difficult, particularly through the mountains and the Cumberland Gap, William Brown traveled the road in 1782 and found his journey mostly uneventful. Traveling 555 miles from Hanover, Maryland, to Harrodsburg, Kentucky, Brown reported the road to be quite good from Hanover through the Allegheny Mountains. The trek through the Cumberland Gap was also described as "not very difficult," but he felt exposed to attack by Native Americans in some areas of the gap. He encountered some difficult terrain, a few high hills, and some streams to ford, but the journey, lasting from May 27 to July 18, was virtually without hardship.

The Pennypack Bridge over Pennypack Creek in Philadelphia, along what was known as the King's Highway to New York, was the first stone-arched bridge known to have been built in the United States.

carry only a horse and rider. As their use became more frequent and by the mid-18th century when horse-drawn carts became increasingly prevalent, bridges were often rebuilt to support the heavier and wider load. Decades might pass before bridges were widened. A horse bridge that was constructed over the Chebacco River near Gloucester, Massachusetts, in 1666 was repaired after a storm in 1672, but it was not replaced by a cart bridge until 1730.

The first major bridge in colonial America was probably the Great Bridge, which was built in 1662 to span the Charles River at Boston. The Great Bridge was constructed of wooden piles, covered with rough planks of wood. As time passed, sturdier and more elaborate bridges were constructed in the more populous areas of the colonies, along widely used roads. The Frankford Avenue Bridge, also known as the Pennypack Bridge, in Philadelphia was built in 1697 over Pennypack Creek in Philadelphia, along what was then known as the King's Highway to New York. This stone-arched bridge was the first of its type known to have been built in the United States.

While bridges might be built across streams, if the waters were shallow they could be forded. Eventually ferries became widely used, especially in the broader, deeper rivers where fording was not possible. Ferries and bridges could be found in colonial America by the mid-17th century. Once a road or a path of any importance encountered a stream that could not be forded or easily bridged, a ferry was usually established. Since bridge building was normally a more involved undertaking, bridges usually came after ferries. For example, a ferry established as early as 1636 in Beverly, Massachusetts, was not replaced

Colonial Ferries

Recognition of the need for transport by ferry came early in Massachusetts, where in November 1630, only two months after the founding of Massachusetts Bay, the colony's Court of Assistants made provisions for the establishment of a ferry between Charlestown and Boston. By the end of 1631 there were two ferries in the region, the second between Winnetsemet and Charlestown.

New York, like Boston, had numerous settlements along waterways surrounding the larger town, and made frequent use of ferries. As in the Massachusetts Bay region, many of the ferries in business around New York were built like barges and were equipped with sails. Ferrying around the New York area was often hazardous due to swift currents and frequent strong winds, and a large number of people and animals are said to have drowned when their ferries capsized.

Not all colonies were as well equipped with ferries as New York and Massachusetts. North Carolina, with its scattered population and poor roads, had few ferries before 1700, despite having more miles of inland waterways than the other colonies. It was not until 1727 that North Carolina provided the ferries needed to complete the King's Highway from Virginia to South Carolina, and even then the ferries could not always be relied upon. Problems with winds, high waters, insufficient vessels, and missing ferrymen frequently delayed travel along the way, at least until the 1760s.

By the end of the colonial era there were hundreds of ferries on American rivers. The sizes of ferries varied according to need and location, ranging from small canoes that could carry only one or two passengers, to rafts that were poled or pulled along cables across the stream or river, to barges with sails that could transport passengers, animals, and trade goods. Piraguas were used as ferries in some areas. These boats were made similarly to the log canoes, but were made broader by slicing the log down the middle, adding one or more planks, and then closing up the ends to keep out the water.

The Rocky Hill-Glastonbury Ferry, put into service on the Connecticut River in 1655, is the oldest continuously operating ferry in the United States. It began its existence as a small raft that was pushed across the river through the use of poles, but grew in size and efficiency as the need arose and as ferry designs improved. As was the case with many ferries of the era, the Rocky Hill-Glastonbury Ferry was operated by local entrepreneurs under a government charter.

Ferries were considered public carriers, and proprietors were held responsible for the safety of their passengers. It was not unusual for a ferryman to also own and operate a nearby ordinary or tavern, where travelers could stop for food and drink. In 1766 the North Carolina assembly passed legislation requiring that ferrymen who received more than four pence for transporting a rider and his horse keep an ordinary adjacent to their ferries.

by a bridge until 1788, and a ferry established in 1657 over the Chebacco River at Ipswich was not replaced by a bridge until 1700.

MODES OF OVERLAND TRANSPORT

During the early colonial era few people traveled beyond their neighborhoods, largely because most people lived in rural areas and traded only locally. In the larger towns along the eastern seaboard travel and trade was easier than in the interior, but still there were few well-traveled roads beyond the town limits. Among the exceptions were routes linking the major towns of Boston, New York, and Philadelphia, where by 1700 travel between these growing towns was quite common. But it would take years before long distance roadways could accommodate more than those who traveled by foot or horseback, and most people traveling between the three towns went by boat or ship.

Private coaches and horses began to make an appearance in the large towns at the end of the 17th century, but their use was usually confined to town since outlying roads were still little more than paths. Thus until the mid-18th century carriages were rarely found in America. A more common though less stylish wheeled vehicle of the colonial era was called a "chair," a two-wheeled vehicle with a seat for two that was pulled by a horse. Another was the "chaise," which was similar to the chair, but had a covered top made of leather. None of these early vehicles had springs. Most people traveled on foot, horseback, in horse litters, or, if they had servants to carry them, in sedan chairs. Benjamin Franklin

A print titled "The Concord Stage" shows a stagecoach in front of an inn with a British soldier on horseback. Private coaches began to make an appearance at the end of the 17th century.

Postal Routes

Sending letters by mail was expensive during the colonial era. Therefore the mail served businesses and wealthy people, but rarely served ordinary folks. The mail was carried by post riders who traveled roads when they could, but journeyed along trails and bridle paths to reach the more remote settlements. Early post riders would not begin their journeys until they had enough mail to meet their expenses for the trip, so the mail was not delivered regularly. Gradually roadways improved and mail delivery quickened, but in the early years it could take several weeks for a letter to reach a destination 100 or more miles away. The first delivery by a post rider between New York and Boston in 1673 took two weeks along the Boston Post Road. Postal service along that road ran continuously throughout the colonial era, except for a few years, as when there were disputes with the Dutch over New York or war with the Native Americans in New England.

By 1685 service was restored and continued uninterrupted. As late as 1717 it could take eight weeks for mail sent from Boston to reach Williamsburg, Virginia, during the winter months, and half that time the rest of the year. By the 1720s there was some regularly scheduled mail delivery in the larger cities, such as New York, Boston, and Philadelphia. In 1729 mail delivery between New York and Philadelphia occurred once a week during the summer, and once every two weeks in the winter.

In 1753 Benjamin Franklin became joint postmaster general of the colonial postal service. During the two decades that he was in charge, the postal system in the colonies saw great improvement. In 1763 he began an extensive survey of the post roads. He traveled 1,600 miles with an odometer on the axle of his carriage, measuring distances between post offices. Soon after Franklin took office mail between New York and Philadelphia was on a regular schedule, requiring delivery at least three times per week, with delivery expected to occur within 24 hours of the time the post rider departed the originating city.

In 1775 the Continental Congress appointed Franklin postmaster general of the new United States Postal Service. When the census was taken in 1790, seven years after the American Revolution ended, there were only about 1,875 miles of postal roads in the United States and only 27 post offices, and mail delivery between New York City and Philadelphia usually took two days.

An illustration of a man blowing a posthorn as he delivers the mail.

Benjamin Franklin, about to be conveyed in a sedan chair, generally carried by servants. Most people traveled on foot, horseback, or in horse litters.

was fortunate enough to be carried in a sedan chair, at least during his later years. In some of the colonies travel by vehicle, or for any distance beyond the church or meeting house by any other means, was prohibited on Sundays. A law passed in mid-17th century Connecticut, for example, proclaimed "that if any person shall profane the Sabbath by unnecessary travel . . . in the time of public worship, or before or after . . . shall pay five shillings for every such offense, or sit in the stocks one hour."

The coming of winter in the northern colonies required adjustments to means of transport. Horse-drawn sleighs, which varied in style from crude to elaborate, carried people and possessions across snow and ice. Frozen lakes and streams offered smooth rides for travelers. When the snow was too soft or too deep for horses, or if people were traveling short distances, they traveled by foot on snowshoes. For added support the traveler would carry a pole with a wide, flat piece of wood at the bottom that was usually of oval or round shape. Another means of winter travel was by dogsled, another method of transport learned from Native Americans. Dogsleds were small, carrying only one person, and were pulled by a team of two to six dogs. Historians have noted that in some regions sleds were used for transport throughout the year.

Shipping goods overland to a distant market proved expensive in the colonial era. Estimates place the average cost of shipping goods overland a distance of 30 miles as being equivalent to shipping them 3,000 miles over water. Produce from outlying farms was taken to town in oxcarts or horse barrows, a type of two-wheeled cart. Some of the early carts are reported to have been

This tavern on King's Highway in Haddonfield, New Jersey, was built in 1750. By the winter of 1777 columns of British soldiers tramped up and down the King's Highway.

quite crude, constructed with very little iron, and having wheels made of logs that were sawed off at the ends. Historians have found that Pennsylvania's colonists were more likely to own carts and wagons than colonists in most other regions. The large German population in the colony's interior needed wagons for shipping surplus produce, which gave impetus to the invention of the Conestoga wagon, a broad-wheeled covered wagon that was named for the Conestoga Valley in Lancaster County, Pennsylvania. The Conestoga wagon, which was used for hauling large loads, first made its appearance around 1760. It was especially useful for travel over hilly or mountainous roads.

As the colonies grew in size and population, travel gradually improved. In 1766 there was a regular line of stagecoaches running between New York and Philadelphia. The journey lasted three days when service began, but 10 years later had been shortened by a new coach, "the flying machine," to two days during the summer. A stagecoach journey from Boston to New York usually lasted five or six days.

None of the coaches and carriages traveling about the colonies had springs, making every journey a jolting and wearying experience. If a coach became stuck in the mud, the passengers were obliged to help lift or push it out. Travel expenses for a single person could also mount up, as tolls for travel aboard ferries, combined with stops for food, drink, and lodging in taverns and inns along the way could add up to a substantial sum.

THE AMERICAN REVOLUTION

Transportation played a major role during the American Revolution, as both the Americans and the British, along with their allies, sought to move troops and supplies as rapidly as possible. With their large and powerful navy, the British had virtual control of the shipping lanes along the North American coast. However they had the disadvantage of having to transport men and supplies across the Atlantic, while the American militias and Continental Army could draw their supplies and men from within the colonies. General William Howe and other British military leaders concluded that if they could gain control of the Hudson River, then they could isolate New England from the colonies to the south. Cutting off communication and transportation of men and goods between two important regions of the country would, they believed, bring them a quick victory in the war. The Americans were cognizant of this strategy, and they made every effort possible to retain control of the Hudson River.

In the process of implementing the British strategy, General John Burgoyne encountered the hazards of the American wilderness as he attempted to move more than 7,000 men south from Fort Ticonderoga to Albany, New York, where he planned to meet up with General Howe. Also with Burgoyne and his troops were 2,000 wives and other camp followers, and numerous supply wagons, including 30 that carried his personal belongings. The campaign was a disaster, largely due to his lack of adequate supply lines and his underestimation of the time it would take him to travel through the wilderness.

The Americans were able to make better use of North American roads and geography. With the British in control of the Atlantic Coast, General George Washington and his troops made use of their knowledge of trails, roads, and rivers to quickly reach their destinations. The Great Wagon Road was well-used during the Revolution to move men and supplies in the interior. At one point General James Clinton wanted to move 1,500 men southward to join General John Sullivan's forces at Tioga. Clinton built a dam at the source of the Susquehanna River on Otsego Lake at Cooperstown, New York. When the water was released, it sped the general and his men quickly down the river.

After the war was won, the American transportation system was set to grow along with the young nation.

June Melby Benowitz

Further Readings

Bannon, John Francis. *The Spanish Borderlands Frontier, 1531–1821*. New York: Holt, Rinehart and Winston, 1970.

U.S. Postal Serice. "Benjamin Franklin: Postmaster General July 26, 1775 to November 1776." Available online, URL: http://www.usps.com/postalhistory/_pdf/franklin.pdf. Accessed May 10, 2007.

Hart, Val. *The Story of American* Roads. New York: William Sloane Associates, Inc., 1950.

Holbrook, Stewart H. *The Old Post Road*. New York: McGraw-Hill, 1962.

Holmes, Oliver W. and Peter T. Rohrbach. *Stagecoach East: Stagecoach Days in the East from the Colonial Period to the Civil War*. Washington, D.C.: Smithsonian Institution Press, 1983.

Hulbert, Archer R. *The Paths of Inland Commerce: A Chronicle of Trail, Road, and Waterway*. New Haven, CT: Yale University Press, 1920.
Ketchum, Richard M. *Saratoga: Turning Point of America's Revolutionary War*. New York: Henry Holt and Company, 1997.
Meyer, Balthasar Henry, et al. *History of Transportation in the United States before 1860*. Washington, D.C.: Peter Smith, Carnegie Institution of Washington, 1948.
Richter, William L. *The ABC-CLIO Companion to Transportation in America*. Santa Barbara, CA: ABC-CLIO, 1995.
Rouse, Parke, Jr. *The Great Wagon Road*. New York: McGraw-Hill, 1973.
U.S. Department of Transportation. *A Nation in Motion: Historic American Transportation Sites*. Washington, D.C.: U.S. Government Printing Office, 1976.
Watson, Alan D. "The Ferry in Colonial North Carolina: A Vital Link in Transportation," *North Carolina Historical Review* (v.51, 1974).

CHAPTER 16

Public Health, Medicine, and Nutrition

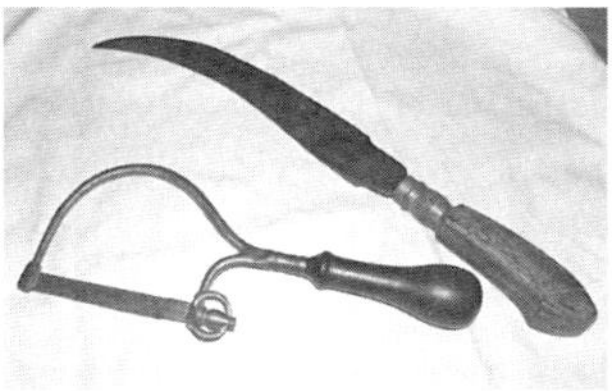

"Be sober and temperate, and you will be healthy. Be in general virtuous, and you will be happy."
— Benjamin Franklin

LIFE IN COLONIAL and revolutionary America was generally harsh, and the average life expectancy for the period ranged from 25 to 35 years. In the first American settlements in Jamestown, Virginia, and Plymouth, Massachusetts, starvation and disease wiped out large portions of the population. Both children and adults were fatally susceptible to smallpox, malaria, tuberculosis, pneumonia, influenza, rickets, and a host of other diseases. New immigrants often arrived in America after months at sea in precarious mental conditions and with immune systems depressed. Many were also suffering from scurvy, a vitamin C deficiency disease caused by a lack of fresh fruit. Immigrants who were ill with communicable disease often infected other settlers.

The medical profession was in its infancy in the new country, and no public health system existed. As a result,colonial waters and garbage piles were filled with fleas, rats, roaches, mosquitoes, lice, flies, and bacteria. Consequently diseases were rampant, and the understanding that germs and diet were connected to the spread of diseases was far in the future. Both birth and death rates were high. In 1789, the year that George Washington (1732–99) became the first president of the United States, life expectancy was 34.5 years for males and 36.5 for females. Despite these conditions Americans tended to be healthier than Europeans, in part because of the lack of overcrowding that plagued many European cities. As settlers adapted to the new land, food became more plentiful, and American diets became more nutritious.

The greatest threat to the lives of colonial Americans was from epidemic diseases such as smallpox, diphtheria, scarlet fever, and measles and from gastrointestinal and respiratory conditions. The climate of the south was particularly conducive to yellow fever, typhus, and hookworm, and northerners frequently suffered from exposure-related conditions. For several centuries tuberculosis, a respiratory disease, was a major cause of death in the United Sates, and over time it became the leading cause of death among the native population. By the end of the 17th century malaria had become a major threat throughout the colonies. All sections of the United States also experienced outbreaks of various childhood diseases, fevers, diabetes, parasites, cancers, and accidents. Children were particularly vulnerable to diphtheria, which arrived in the United States in the 1730s. For instance in Hampton Falls, New Hampshire, 210 deaths occurred among the population of 1,200. At least 95 percent of the victims were children. In 20 families, every member under the age of 21 died.

SMALLPOX EPIDEMIC

The most devastating of colonial epidemics involved smallpox. The Americas were free of smallpox before European explorers reached the North and South American continents. By 1519 the first cases had been reported in South America. The epidemic of 1524–28 was instrumental in devastating the Incan population of Peru, causing an estimated 200,000 deaths. It is also believed that a smallpox epidemic occurred in what is now the United States shortly before the Pilgrims landed on Plymouth Rock in 1620. Along the coast of Massachusetts, nine of every 10 in the native population were wiped out between 1617 and 1619. Many white settlers claimed that the hand of God was preparing the land for European settlement.

Ironically Christian zeal was partially responsible for the spread of smallpox among Native Americans. As part of the Jesuit baptismal ceremony, converted natives who were required to kiss crucifixes spread the disease to other converts. A number of incidences have been documented in which smallpox was intentionally introduced into native populations. One of these cases involved a trader who presented a wrapped peace pipe swathed in a flag on which smallpox postules had been smeared to native leaders as a token of "good faith." Smallpox was also spread among tribes by returning raiding parties and by tribes that fled from infected areas.

Native Americans were not the only people susceptible to smallpox. Philadelphia, Pennsylvania, the cultural and political center of colonial America, was considered a major repository for the disease. In 1721, after ships from the West Indies imported smallpox into Boston, Puritan minister Increase Mather (1639–1723) began advocating inoculation as a means of preventing the

Jamestown and Disease

In spring 1607, 105 adventurous Englishmen landed at what would become the settlement of Jamestown, Virginia, the first permanent European settlement in North America. The Jamestown settlers had no way of knowing that the nearby marsh was a perfect breeding ground for various diseases. As the cold weather set in, the colonists began suffering from a severe shortage of fresh drinking water and food. By January 1608 only 38 colonists were on hand to greet the ship that brought new settlers and much-needed supplies.

By the spring of the following year, the population of Jamestown, which had grown to around 500, experienced new outbreaks of typhoid and dysentery. In what became known as the "starving time," the severe shortage of food led the most desperate among the settlers to cannibalism. The majority of the survivors managed to get by on a daily intake of corn kernels that had been "enhanced" with ants or boot leather. Only 60 settlers survived to see the beginning of 1610. A major reason for the shortage of food was that many of the colonists had spent the time before the famine searching for nonexistent gold, rather than locating and storing supplies of food for the winter. It is tragically ironic that even as the Jamestown settlers were starving, 50-pound wild turkeys roamed the land, and the nearby waters contained foot-long oysters and gigantic clams.

After the famine the remaining residents of Jamestown chose new leaders, and the entire population settled inside the Jamestown fort to fend off attacks by hostile natives. New sanitation rules were established. Emptying water into the street was forbidden, and the practice of laundering clothes within 20 feet of the public well was banned. All areas within a quarter of a mile of the stockade were protected from use as latrines. The following decades continued to see the population of Jamestown rising and falling in response to famine, disease, native conflicts, and infighting. By 1625, 80 percent of 6,000 immigrants that had arrived in the colony had died before survival skills emerged and immunities to diseases developed.

The mortality rates among diseased Native American groups was even greater than those among the white settlers because the natives had little immunity to European diseases. The Jamestown colony was abandoned in 1699, and the capital of Virginia was relocated to nearby Williamsburg.

As the cold weather set in, the Jamestown settlers suffered from a shortage of fresh water and food.

Above, a print titled "Vaccinating the Baby" is a view of a colonial family protecting themselves against smallpox.

A Brief Rule to guide the CommonPeople of *New-England* how to Order themſelves and theirs in the *Small-Pox* and *Meaſels*.

THE *Small Pox* (whoſe nature and cure the *Meaſels* follow) is a diſeaſe in the blood, endeavouring to recover a new form and ſtate.

2. THIS nature attempts — 1. By Separation of the impure from the pure, thruſting it out from the Veins to the Fleſh. — 2. By driving out the impure from the Fleſh to the Skin.

3. THE firſt Separation is done in the firſt four Days by a Feveriſh boiling (Ebullition) of the Blood, laying down the impurities in the Fleſhy parts which kindly effected the Feveriſh tumult is calmed.

4. THE ſecond Separation from the Fleſh to the Skin, or *Superficies* is done through the reſt of the time of the diſeaſe.

5. THERE are ſeveral Errors in ordering theſe ſick ones in both theſe Opera-

A tions

At right, a guide to smallpox and malaria published by Reverend Thomas Thacher, in which he suggests "Let the sick abstein from Flesh and Wine."

spread of smallpox. On June 26 Increase Mather convinced Zabdiel Boylston of Boston to inoculate his six-year-old son and two slaves with pus gathered from a small pox patient. These three test cases developed only mild infections and were thereafter immune to the disease. Not a single death occurred among the 35 people who were eventually vaccinated in Boston. Despite this success, smallpox inoculations remained extremely controversial. Subsequently Cotton Mather's son Samuel arrived at the home of his father after his Harvard roommate died of smallpox. Mather inoculated Samuel, who became the only one of 16 Mather children to outlive his father.

In 1738 another severe smallpox outbreak occurred in Charleston, South Carolina. In 1751 Boston experienced a major epidemic in which one out of every five members of the population perished. In the face of continued controversy, interest in smallpox inoculations continued to spread. Founding Father Benjamin Franklin (1706–90) became a strong advocate of inoculations after losing his four-year-old son to the disease. By 1766 most Americans had accepted the viability of the smallpox vaccination. Nevertheless a smallpox epidemic occurred in Boston in 1776 as recruits from rural areas flocked to the city to enlist in the Continental Army. As commander of the American troops, George Washington inoculated his troops against smallpox.

OTHER DISEASES

Throughout the colonial and revolutionary periods, yellow fever was a leading cause of death in America. From the beginning of the 18th century until the beginning of the 19th century, outbreaks occurred regularly. The first cases appeared in the United States in 1648 among seaman who traveled to America from the Caribbean. Major port cities including Boston, New York City, Baltimore, Norfolk, and Charleston were ultimately affected. Yellow fever epidemics struck the population of Philadelphia in 1666, 1741, 1747, and 1762, and a tenth of Philadelphia's population was wiped out in 1793. Because Philadelphia was the capital of the United States at the time, a number of the most influential political figures of the time were living in the city, including the first three presidents, George Washington, John Adams, and Thomas Jefferson, as well as Alexander Hamilton, the first secretary of the treasury and the leading motivator behind the Constitutional Convention of 1787. In the south Georgia experienced devastating losses. Between 1817 and 1820 Savannah lost one-third of its population. Because of a unique combination of climate, geography, and other conditions, yellow fever was more epidemic in New Orleans, Louisiana, than in any other American city.

In the south, scrotula, also known as Negro or slave disease, was rampant among the slave population, although white southerners were rarely affected. It was believed that scrotula resulted from poor nutrition or from the common slave practice of sleeping with a blanket over the head. Many members of the slave population had come from African nations where milk was not included in the diet, and scientists later theorized that lactose-intolerance may have made slaves more susceptible than white southerners to the disease, which is a type of bovine tuberculosis. Those slaves who had come from sub-Saharan African nations with ties to Europe had built up some resistance to common diseases such as smallpox, measles, diphtheria, and the plague. However they were more susceptible to tuberculosis, because it was then unknown in sub-Saharan Africa.

Although measles occurred less frequently in the United States than in Europe, in America the disease tended to be more severe and was not limited to the young as it was in Europe. The first outbreak of measles in the Americas took place in Canada in 1635. Boston suffered severe outbreaks in 1657, 1687, 1713, 1729, 1739, and 1740. The most severe measles epidemic in the United States occurred in 1722 when 800 children died in Charlestown, Massachusetts. In 1747 outbreaks occurred in South Carolina, Pennsylvania, New York, and Connecticut.

EARLY MEDICAL PRACTITIONERS

In colonial and revolutionary America, most people who became ill were cared for in their own homes. Many early Americans learned to care for themselves and their families through knowledge gained by books and folklore. Remedies of the time ranged from the use of herbs, to superstitious practices brought to the colonies by other cultures. In the absence of trained physicians, ministers and magistrates frequently served as community medical advisors. Cotton Mather of Boston and John Witherspoon (1723–94) of Connecticut were

Benjamin Rush (1745–1813)

Dr. Benjamin Rush, a Presbyterian physician and signer of the Declaration of Independence, was one of the major reasons that Philadelphia was considered the healthiest of all colonial American cities. Rush, often called the first American psychiatrist, was accepted as the foremost medical mind of the period. Because medical instruction was generally unavailable in the United States during this time, Rush studied medicine in Edinburgh, Scotland. After graduating in 1768 Rush opened a medical practice and accepted the position of professor of chemistry at the College of Philadelphia. He later became a professor of medical theory and practice. When the college merged with the University of Pennsylvania in 1793, Rush introduced clinical instruction for medical students. He subsequently established the Pennsylvania Free Dispensary to provide medical care for the poor, and was a cofounder of the College of Physicians and a founder of Dickinson College in Carlisle, Pennsylvania. Rush published the first American textbook on chemistry.

A strong patriot, Benjamin Rush was a member of the Sons of Liberty during the revolutionary period and served in the Continental Congress. He is remembered in large part for his pioneering work with the mentally ill, because he was the first American physician to introduce humane and scientific treatment for patients suffering from mental disorders. Rush also waged battles against alcohol, nicotine, capital punishment, and slavery.

Despite his renown Rush was often a controversial figure. He clashed with other physicians over his continued use of bleeding as a treatment for a variety of diseases. Rush rejected the generally widespread American belief that yellow fever was a result of immigration, choosing to search for local causes of the disease. After being appointed as surgeon-general to the Middle Department of the Continental Congress, Rush came into direct conflict with Dr. William Shippen, the Director of Hospitals for the Continental Army. Rush subsequently resigned over what he insisted was gross mismanagement of American resources.

probably the best known of these ministers/healers. In the plantation culture of the south, owners and their wives often served as medical advisors for the family, slaves, and neighbors.

Midwives, often known as healers, were called upon to deliver babies, give advice during pregnancy, and offer general medical advice. Barbers bled patients and pulled teeth, and apothecaries dispensed medical advice along with medications and herbal remedies. Some medical providers were itinerants, offering their services and hawking medications that ranged from useless to dangerous. Surgeons, physicians, and apothecaries all engaged in setting fractures, lancing abscesses, pulling teeth, giving enemas, treating fevers, and dispensing advice. Internal injuries were virtually untreatable, and little was done to deal with pain that accompanied major illnesses, childbirth, and surgery. Since medical practitioners knew little about treating common diseases, the focus was on keeping down fevers and letting diseases run their course. Many colonial Americans believed that diseases were sent by God, sometimes as punishment for wrongdoing.

FORMALIZED MEDICINE

The term *doctor* was not used in America before 1769. It has been estimated that as many as four out of five medical practitioners in colonial and revolutionary America received no formal training. The exceptions were British physicians who immigrated to the colonies, greatly enhancing the practice of American medicine. Potential American physicians with the means to do so also trained at European schools. Others gained experience by apprenticing with older practitioners. The training period generally lasted from five to seven years, and apprentice physicians were expected to do everything from sweeping, to horse currying, to collecting medical fees. In Massachusetts Bay they were forbidden to marry, gamble, or visit taverns or theaters.

By the mid-18th century colonial presses were adding American volumes to medical libraries that had previously included only those by European authors. Founding Father Benjamin Franklin's *Poor Richard's Almanac* was a popular source of health information. Franklin also advanced the practice of colonial medicine by creating a flexible urinary catheter and bifocal glasses, and through experiments in mesmerism and the physiological effects of electricity. A number of physicians concentrated their research in specific areas. Scottish immigrants William Douglass (1691–1752) and John Lining (1708–60), for instance, focused on scarlet fever and yellow fever respectively. In 1775 New York surgeon John Jones (1729–91) concentrated on treating wounds and fractures. In the late 1760s a group of illustrious Philadelphians formed the American Philosophical Society to further the studies of science, medicine, and related fields. By 1770 the group boasted 228 members.

Some physicians in New York, Philadelphia, Newport, and New Brunswick began offering courses in subjects such as anatomy. During the colonial period Philadelphia was considered the medical center. The first general hospital was established there in 1751. The formalized study of medicine in America was considerably advanced when John Morgan (1735–89) returned to the United States after completing training in Europe. Morgan and fellow Philadelphia physician William Shippen (1712–1801) convinced the trustees of the College of Philadelphia that the school needed a medical department to train physicians who had completed apprenticeships. The medical school, the first in the country, opened in November 1765. Morgan and Shippen made up the entire staff, with Morgan teaching the theory and practice of medicine, and Shippen covering anatomy and surgery. The school graduated 10 physicians in June 1768.

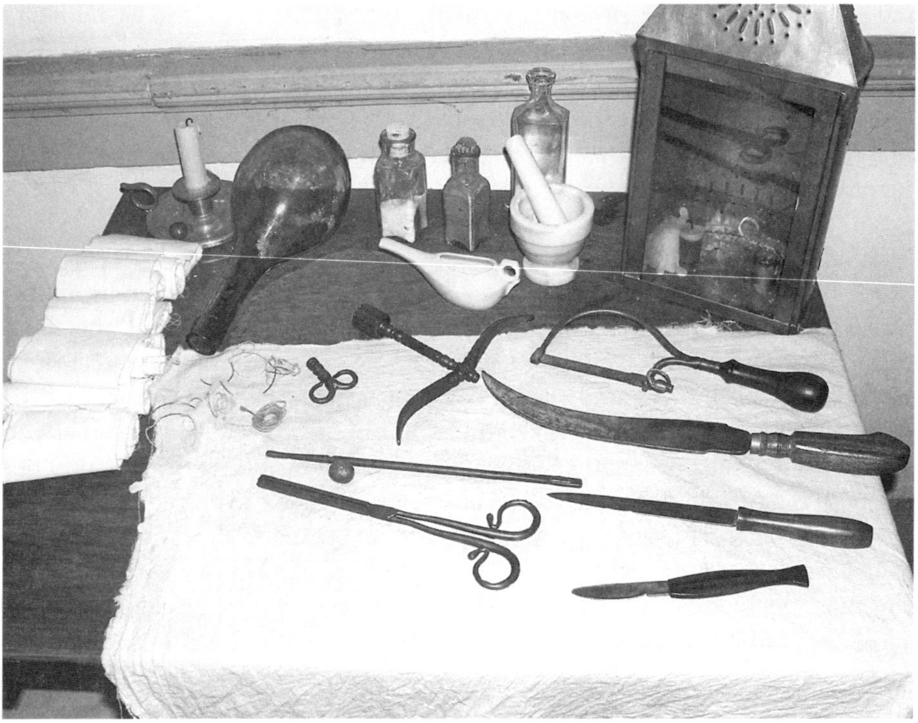

A colonial surgeon's tools included a mortar and pestle for mixing medications, forceps, scalpels, and a saw to perform amputations.

Over time, midwifery, chemistry, botany, pathology, and physiology were added to the curriculum.

A second medical school opened in New York at King's College (now Columbia University) in November 1767 with a faculty of six physicians offering classes in medical theory and practice, surgery, anatomy, botany, chemistry, study of medications, midwifery, and clinical medicine. By 1775 41 Bachelor of Medicine degrees (B.M.) and seven Medical Degrees (M.D.) had been awarded. After the Revolutionary War additional medical schools were opened at Harvard University in Boston and Dartmouth College in New Hampshire. In 1760 New York began licensing physicians, and New Jersey followed suit in 1772. As the number of trained physicians grew, practitioners began lobbying for licensing of all doctors. By the mid-18th century Massachusetts, New York, and New Jersey had enacted licensing laws, and state medical societies had been established.

WATER, ALCOHOL, AND SANITATION

In the early colonial era, more than 95 percent of all Americans lived in rural communities, often isolated from one another. Most farmers grew only those

Supplies for Immigrants Coming to America

When European immigrants set sail for the American colonies, they received specific instructions on the supplies that were necessary to survive onboard and to get them started once they arrived. Supplies for the voyage included wheat flour, claret wine, canary sacke, conserves, marmalades, dried Neat's tongue, legs of mutton that had been minced or stewed and packed in sewet or butter and placed in earthen pots, suckets (dried lemon peel), spices, salad oil, prunes for stewing, live poultry, gammons of bacon, lemon juice, rice, butter, Holland or Old Cheshire cheese, pork, and beef preserved with vinegar.

To set up housekeeping in America, each immigrant was instructed to bring eight bushels of meal, two bushels of oatmeal, one bushel of peas, one gallon of oil, two gallons of vinegar, one gallon of aqua vitae, one bushel of Bay salt, sugar, spices, and various fruits. Required utensils included an iron pot, an iron kettle, a large frying pan, a grid iron, two skillets, a spit, and various platters, dishes, and wooden spoons.

Other suggested household items included malt for beer, a hogshead of beef or pork, firkins of butter, from 100 to 200 pounds of cheese, a gallon of honey, and equipment for making cheese. Those who intended to farm were advised to bring wheat, rice, oat, and barley seeds, along with kernels of pears and apples and any stones and seeds of fruits, roots, and herbs that might prove useful. Immigrants were also expected to bring products such as wine, sugar, prunes, raisins, currents, honey, and spices to trade with natives for cattle, hogs, poultry, and corn.

Winters in America were harsh so immigrants were warned to bring sufficient supplies to sustain themselves, including wheat flour, marmalades, and preserved meats.

A conjectural sketch of colonial women brewing beer, by Sidney E. King, commissioned by the National Park Service.

products needed for survival. Since roads were poor and transportation difficult, there was little trading of farm products. However grain products were sometimes sold to distilleries. Few cities existed. Roads were poor, and travel among colonies was difficult and time-consuming.

For those who did not live close to water sources, transporting water was a complicated and expensive task. Rural families often had access to their own water supplies, but access was problematic in urban areas. Water supplies throughout the colonies were often polluted. Consequently many Americans made cider by squeezing hundred of apples into a device known as the Mobby tub. The juice was then placed in covered earthenware jugs for storage. Some colonial Americans brewed their own beer. Alcohol consumption was a major facet of life, and by the end of the 17th century taverns were found in many areas, particularly in port cities. Over time most Americans rejected tea and whiskey in favor of coffee and rum.

By the 1740s America had established regular trade routes, and food was transported from one area of the country to another. Bread and beer were exported from Philadelphia, beef from New England, okra and rice from the Carolinas, and ham from Virginia. Foreign trading routes also developed, such as the Triangle Trading Route in which molasses from New England was turned into rum in Boston, New York, and New Haven. Rum and iron were then shipped to Africa where they were traded for slaves.

When the government tried to profit from the American love of alcohol by imposing a tax in 1793, farmers revolted in what became known as the Whiskey Rebellion. The fact that distilled alcohol was a more compact product than the grains used to produce it meant that western farmers relied on whiskey production as a means of converting their crops into a readily transported project. Thus the Whiskey Rebellion represented another aspect of west-east conflict in the period.

No public health departments existed and the concept of public health was still more than a century in the future. As a consequence sanitation was primitive. Even in large cities such as Boston, Philadelphia, and Baltimore, cattle and poultry roamed the public streets at will. As a result both human and animal

Eating Habits Among Native Americans and Slaves

When the first European colonists arrived in America, eating patterns were already well established among native populations. Corn was the staple food because it was abundant and required little maintenance. Beans and squash, which could be planted among the trees of the forests, were also plentiful. Native Americans wrapped cakes, breads, and corn in leaves and placed them in the ashes to roast. Meats were cooked on sticks or platforms placed above the fire.

All day long stews simmered over open fires in stone or clay pots. In some tribes women cultivated crops, processed meat, and foraged for berries and nuts. Rising at dawn these Native American women began weeding, planting, foraging, and checking nets for fish and traps for game. Meals did not take place at specified times, but occurred at intervals throughout the day. The first meal of the day generally consisted of stewed vegetables left over from the previous evening's meal, eaten with bread made from Tuckahoe flour. Throughout the day as young braves returned, fish and meat were added to the stew. Foraging parties added fresh supplies of corn, beans, squash, berries, and roots.

In the south many house slaves ate the same food as their owners. Other slaves hunted and fished for food. Some slaves were allowed to keep their own gardens, and their quarters often had root cellars built near fireplaces. These cellars were used to store vegetables for winter to keep them from freezing. Common vegetables and fruits grown by slaves included potatoes, Indian peas, pumpkins, squash, collards, sweet potatoes, snap beans, peas, corn, cherries, peaches, and watermelons. West Indian foods such as yams, peanuts, rice, and dried beans were also popular. Slaves often created their own special dishes such as Hoppin' John, which was common in the Carolinas. In addition to the rice and beans, vegetables such as cowpeas, red peas, black peas, calavances, crowder peas, and whippoorwill peas could be added to give the dish varied flavor.

Field slaves were sometimes required to work three hours before they could eat breakfast. The noon meal was prepared in slave kitchens and carried to the field in large buckets. Most slaves prepared dinner in their own quarters. In the north some slaves ate meals with the family. Archaeologists have gathered extensive knowledge of the slave diet by examining food disposal areas that still survive on some plantations. For instance in the dry well at Monticello, President Thomas Jefferson's (1743–1826) Virginia plantation, diggers found that 30 percent of the food remains derived from domestic pigs and five percent from beef. It was assumed that Jefferson's slaves were probably better fed than the general slave population, because beef was rarely fed to slaves in colonial America at a time when pork was the meat of choice.

Sanitation laws were passed to control disposal of waste and construction of privies.

waste posed serious potential health threats for early Americans. Outdoor privies of wood or brick, sometimes containing multiple holes for large families, were built near homes and wells; and animal waste was ubiquitous. Massachusetts attempted to impose basic sanitation on its residents. Beginning in 1634 a series of sanitation laws were passed to control disposal of waste and the construction of privies. Other European-American communities eventually enacted basic sanitation laws.

EARLY AMERICAN DIETS

Colonial Americans often viewed food merely as a tool for survival, and diets were dependent on the availability of food sources. This availability varied according to geography, climate, and economic status. The first settlers were usually undernourished, and starvation was the norm during frequent famines. Conditions would have been even grimmer without the help of friendly natives. Once settlers learned how to take advantage of fish and game and plant crops that would grow in the New World, Americans became very well fed.

The first livestock was imported into the United States by Pilgrim settlers in 1624, and most farm families owned milk cows to produce dairy products and dry cows that were slaughtered for food. Because they were so important, the diets of milk cows were carefully controlled. In the winter milk cows were fed moistened hay, oats, cornstalks, rye grass, cabbage leaves, and softened roots such as carrots and cabbage. Some cows were also fed the waste from beer making. By the middle of the 17th century many Americans had built barns to shelter their livestock.

Corn and rye were the staple grain products in the colonies, and both were used in preparing a popular dish known as Injun bread. Because of wheat rust, consumption of other grains was generally limited to rye and oats. Yeast was difficult to obtain, and commercial yeast did not appear in America until the 1860s. The inability to preserve meat meant that it had to be consumed quickly, and salted pork was the most popular meat dish. Chicken consumption was low, partly because eggs were essential in many recipes.

Fresh vegetables and fruit were scarce in the early days of the country, and in British fashion, vegetables were generally used only in sauces and garnishes. Little milk was consumed. Because water supplies were often contaminated, alcoholic beverages were consumed, even by children, in large quantities. Overall the early American diet was high in fat, salt, and sugar and low in vitamins and minerals. Researchers believe that Americans of the colonial era were short in stature as a result of inadequate diet. By the time of the American Revolution, however, white males born in the United States reached an average height of 68.1 inches, a height comparable to American soldiers who fought in World War II in the 1940s.

English settlers soon reverted to established methods of cooking and preparing food with some variations learned from natives. Sugar was used to sweeten all kinds of food to cover blandness, and by the mid-1700s, America was second only to England in world sugar consumption. The use of spices varied according to region. In New England, sorrel, marjoram, sage, and thyme were popular, as they were in England. Seasonings in the deep south were influenced by African, Middle Eastern, and Caribbean cuisine, and stews and one-pot meals such as gumbo, jambalaya, and Brunswick stew were common. Cooks in the Chesapeake Bay area favored food seasoned with nutmeg, mace, and cloves. The middle-American diet was more varied than that in other areas because of the various cultures represented. The landed gentry that eventually emerged in colonial America ate well, drinking French champagnes and dining off such delicacies as potted swan and beef seasoned with spices from the Orient. The first free-standing American restaurants were

Sugar was used to sweeten all kinds of food to cover blandness, and by the mid-1700s America was second only to England in world sugar consumption.

oyster houses that sprang up along the coast. The first American cookbook was published in Williamsburg, Virginia, in 1742. Written by Eliza Smith, *The Compleat Housewife or Accomplish't Gentlewoman's Companion* proved popular, and a second edition was printed in New York in 1764.

By mid-17th century the colonists had learned how to feed themselves, and vegetables, meat, and fish were abundant in more settled areas. Colonial Americans generally ate three meals a day. Breakfast was either porridge, or leftovers from the previous night. Milk was generally reserved for babies and cooking. Southern cooks frequently added cheese, meat, pastries, fruit, and eggs to the breakfast gruel. In the middle colonies, a blend of cornmeal and head cheese (fresh pork sausage) known as scrapple was a popular morning meal. Other meals included various combinations of meat, bread, and, depending on the geographic area and time of the year, vegetables and fruit. The midday meal, usually referred to as "dinner," was often the heaviest meal of

Tin reflector ovens were used to cook food in the late 18th century and early 19th century, in conjunction with a home's fireplace. It was set on the hearth in front of the fire, and the heat that reflected off its polished back would bake, roast, or broil meat.

the day. Supper, which might be eaten as early as 3:00 P.M. on small farms, was likely to consist of leftovers from dinner. In more affluent families, supper was more elaborate and might be eaten as late as 9:00 P.M. In colonial Virginia, Georgia, and Maryland, meals were lavish affairs that often lasted for hours.

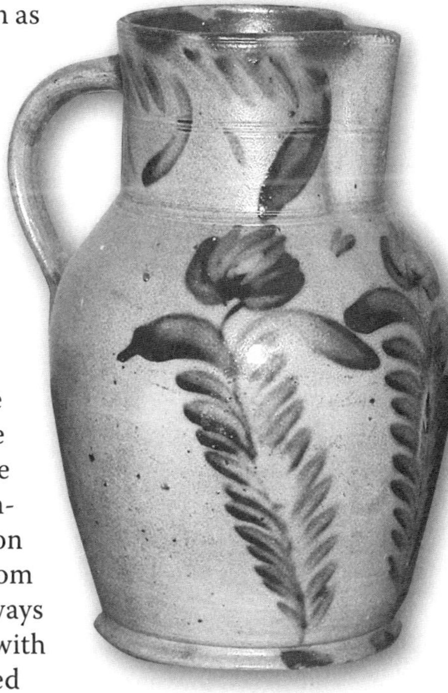
Pitchers were made of iron, pewter, earthenware, or stoneware.

COOKING AND EATING

Many colonial families did not have a dining table or chairs. If only one chair was available, it became the property of the male head of the family. Children often ate standing up or on stumps that had been brought in from outside. Eating utensils were not always available, so many foods were eaten with the hands. Greasy hands were wiped on clothing or whatever was handy. Cups were sometimes shared among family members. Meals in colonial homes were cooked over open fires or on hearths constructed from local stones. Later, more durable fireplaces were built of stone and mortar. Every home had a large iron kettle with three short legs that could be placed directly on the hearth or hung over the fire. These heavy kettles might weigh as much as 40 pounds when they were full, and they were difficult to handle. Burns were common.

Most American families used wooden mixing bowls, while cooking utensils were made of iron, pewter, earthenware, or stoneware. Meat was often prepared on spits over open fires, and meat drippings also caused fires. Eventually the makeshift spit was replaced with a crane that could be swung out for loading, and returned to the fire for cooking. These cranes usually had hooks attached to chains of differing links to allow cooks to control cooking time and intensity.

The choice of wood was also important. Oak and hickory were considered the best because they burned more evenly and gave off more heat. Temperatures were gauged by holding a hand over the fire. Since few homes boasted clocks, cooking time was estimated. Bread was cooked by the steam of the kettle or by lowering bread enclosed in tin directly into the kettle. Sweet puddings were often wrapped in cloth before being lowered into the kettle to cook along with the family stew.

On the Care of the Wounded

Dr. Benjamin Rush (surgeon general of the Continental Army) wrote a letter to George Washington on December 26, 1777 protesting the deplorable condition of the medical service and accusing Dr. William Shippen (director general of the medical service) of maladministration. The letter excerpt printed below outlines the condition of medical service and the causes as viewed by Dr. Rush. Washington would refer the matter to Congress, who cleared Shippen of the charges levied by Dr. Rush. In response Rush resigned the post of surgeon general.

I have delayed troubling Your Excellency with the state of our hospitals in hopes you would hear it from the director general, whose business it is to correspond with Your Excellency upon this subject. . . . I beg leave therefore at last to look up to you, and through you to the Congress, as the only powers that can redress our grievances or do us justice.

I need not inform Your Excellency that we have now upward of 5,000 sick in our hospitals. This number would cease to be alarming if our hospitals could afford such accommodations to the poor fellows as would ensure them a speedy recovery. But this is far from being the case. There cannot be a greater calamity for a sick man than to come into our hospital at this season of the year. Old disorders are prolonged, and new ones contracted among us. This last is so much the case that I am safe when I assert that a great majority of those who die under our hands perish with diseases caught in our hospitals. When I consider the present army under Your Excellency's command as the last hope of America, I am more alarmed and distressed at these facts than I have words to express. I can see nothing to prevent the same mortality this winter among our troops that prevailed last year. Every day deprives us of 4 or 5 patients out of 500 in the hospital under my care in this place. The same complaints are heard from every quarter. The surgeons have been blamed for these things, but without reason. I shall briefly point out to Your Excellency the real causes of them.

1. Too many sick are crowded together in one house. . . .

2. The hospitals are provided in the most scanty manner with the stores necessary for sick people, and these are too often withheld from them from the want of checks upon the officers of the hospital whose business it is to provide and administer them. Beef and bread are by no means suitable diet for men in fevers.

3. There is a want of hospital shirts, sheets, and blankets. . . .

4. There is a want of guards and an officer to command at every hospital.

5. The medical establishment is a bad one. It gives the director general the most incompatible offices. The offices held by him are held by no less than three physicians in the British hospitals, who are all independent of each other and who, by checking each other, perfectly secure to the sick all the good offices and medical stores that are intended for them by government.

In addition to the omnipresent kettle, most homes boasted a large frying pan that was known as a "spider" because of its three legs. Some cooks used a tripod to support pots when they were placed on fires. Bread tins were eventually replaced by Dutch ovens, portable metal boxes that were placed directly into fires with the open side facing the flames. The most sophisticated models had several shelves so that a number of items could be cooked at the same time. Stone masons of the 17th century produced movable ovens that gave cooks more control over the cooking process. Later on permanent brick ovens with several shelves were constructed in the walls of fireplaces. Fires could be lit directly in these ovens, and a week's worth of baking could be completed in a single day. Many baking ovens were constructed with hinged doors and dampers that could be regulated to control temperature.

FOOD PREPARATION

Because it was easy to grow, corn continued to be a staple of the American diet throughout the colonial and revolutionary period. In the absence of grist mills, many women ground their own corn. Six cups of meal were needed to feed a family of seven at a single meal. Many families slaughtered their own piglets and calves, scalding the meat in boiling water to remove bristles and skin. By-products were used in making sausage. To preserve pork, the meat was salted and hung on metal hooks. Beef was pickled by placing it in a solution of vinegar, salt, spices, and saltpeter that prevented it from decomposing. Since salt had to be imported from England, it was not always available. To compensate colonists adopted a native process known as "jerking" in which meat was dried by cutting it into thin slices, and placed it on sticks in the ground or on a rack above the fire.

The dairy was an essential element of food preparation. Originally a section of the kitchen was set aside for this function. By the 18th century more affluent Americans erected structures especially for dairying. In poorer families dairying was generally the responsibility of women and children. In middle and upper class families a dairy maid often performed this function. Milk was cooled in tubs and then strained into wooden bowls. After being placed in earthenware milk trays, it was covered with linen towels. The cream that settled at the top was skimmed with a slotted wooden paddle to make butter, which was salted, using an ounce of salt to a pound of butter, and placed in containers in layers. After it had set for several hours, the butter was kneaded to remove remaining moisture before being placed in firkins. The buttermilk that was formed during the churning process was fed to pigs to improve the taste of meat. Cheese was made as sugar in the extracted milk curdled. Colonial Americans learned from harsh experience that all dairy equipment had to be kept scrupulously clean because bacteria left in dried milk could cause illness, or even death.

Elizabeth R. Purdy

Further Readings

Booth, Sally Smith. *Hung, Strung, and Potted: A History of Eating in Colonial America*. New York: Clarkson N. Potter, 1971.

Bray, R.S. *Armies of Pestilence: The Effects of Pandemics on History*. Cambridge, UK: Lutterworth Press, 1988.

Bullough, Bonnie and George Rosen. *Preventive Medicine in the United States 1900–1990: Trends and Interpretations*. Canton, MA.: Science History Publications, 1992.

Cartwright, Frederick F. *Disease and History*. New York: Thomas Y. Crowell, 1972.

Cassedy, James H. *Medicine in America: A Short History*. Baltimore, MD: Johns Hopkins University Press, 1991.

Duffy, John. *Epidemics in Colonial America*. Baton Rouge: Louisiana State University Press, 1979.

Duffy, John. *The Sanitarians: A History of American Public Health*. Urbana and Chicago: University of Illinois Press, 1990.

Grob, Gerald N. *The Deadly Truth: A History of Disease in America*. Cambridge, MA: Harvard University Press, 2002.

Kalman, Bobbie. *Early Health and Medicine*. New York: Crabtree Publishing, 1991.

Levenstein, Harvey A. *Revolution at the Table: The Transformation of the American Diet*. New York: Oxford University Press, 1988.

McIntosh, Elaine N. *American Food Habits in Historical Perspective*. Westport, CT: Praeger, 1995.

Miller, Brandon Marie. *Just What the Doctor Ordered*. Minneapolis, MN: Lerner Publishing Group, 1997.

McWilliams, James E. *A Revolution in Eating: How the Quest for Food Shaped America*. New York: Columbia University, 2005.

Pillsbury, Richard. *No Foreign Food: The American Diet in Time and Place*. Boulder, CO: Westview, 1998.

Steckel, Richard "Nutritional Status in the Colonial American Economy." *The William and Mary Quarterly* (v.3/56, 1999).

Waverly, Root and Richard de Rochemont. *Eating in America: A History*. New York: William Morrow, 1976.

Wilkins, Robert. *The Fireside Book of Deadly Diseases*. London: Robert Hall, 1994.

Winslow, Charles Edward Amory. *The Conquest of Epidemic Disease: A Chapter in the History of Ideas*. New York and London: Hafner Publishing, 1967.

INDEX

Index note: page references in *italics* indicate an illustration, and references in **bold** indicate main discussion.

A

B

C

G

H

K

PHOTO CREDITS. Photos.com: vii, 99, 165, 191, 198, 205, 231; National Library of Medicine: 226; National Park Service: 158, 159, 225, 232; Library of Congress: 3, 6, 14, 20, 24, 35, 36, 40, 42, 43, 48, 49, 50, 52, 55, 59, 62 bottom, 63, 65, 67, 68, 77, 78, 80, 92, 97, 101, 109, 114, 123, 126, 128, 130, 131, 132, 139, 140, 143, 149, 150, 153, 154, 160, 161, 169, 177, 178, 182, 184, 189, 190, 201, 203, 217, 218, 219; Loretta Carlisle Photography: 1, 5, 8, 12, 13, 17, 18, 23, 27, 28, 30, 33, 37, 38, 39, 45, 46, 51, 57, 62 top, 64, 71, 81, 83, 84, 91, 94, 98, 102, 107, 112, 119, 135, 136, 145, 147, 157, 162, 163, 164, 167, 173, 186, 195, 209, 210, 212, 215, 220, 223, 230, 234, 235, 236, 237; iStockphoto: 111.

Produced by Golson Media

President and Editor	J. Geoffrey Golson
Layout Editor	Mary Jo Scibetta
Managing Editor	Susan Moskowitz
Copyeditor	Ben Johnson
Proofreader	Mary Le Rouge
Indexer	J S Editorial